The
Promise and
Pitfalls of
Revolution

Other Books by Sidney Lens

Poverty—Yesterday and Today
The Labor Wars
The Forging of the American Empire
The Military-Industrial Complex
Poverty: America's Enduring Paradox
Left, Right and Center
The Counterfeit Revolution
A World in Revolution
The Crisis of American Labor
Working Men
Africa—Awakening Giant
A Country Is Born
The Futile Crusade
Unions and What They Do
Radicalism in America

The Promise and Pitfalls of Revolution

SIDNEY LENS

A PILGRIM PRESS BOOK
from United Church Press Philadelphia

Library of Congress Cataloging in Publication Data

Lens, Sidney.
    The promise and pitfalls of revolution.

    "A Pilgrim Press book."
    Includes bibliographical references.
    1. Communism—History.   2. Capitalism—History.
3. Revolutions—History.   4. Economic history—
20th century.   5. Radicalism—United States.
I. Title.
HX40.L3872   330.9′04   73–19810
ISBN 0–8298–0254–1

Excerpts on pages 125 and 164 from *Coexistence and
Commerce* by Samuel Pisar, are copyright © 1970 by
Samuel Pisar. Used with permission of McGraw-Hill
Book Company.
    The quotation on pages 191–92 from *Economics* by
Paul Samuelson is copyright © 1955, 1958, 1961, 1967,
1970, 1973 by McGraw-Hill, Inc. All rights reserved.
Copyright 1948, 1951 by McGraw-Hill, Inc. All rights
reserved.

United Church Press, 1505 Race Street,
Philadelphia, Pennsylvania 19102

To my
alter-ego:
Shirley

Acknowledgments

I'd like to thank Arthur Okun, Sidney Peck, and Gil Green for having carefully read this manuscript and given me their critical views. Dr. Okun's differences with my thesis, I might state, were from the liberal focal point; and Dr. Peck's and Gil Green's from a radical estimate of history. None, however, agreed with my theme fully, so that whatever vices or virtues there are in the logic of my work are exclusively my own.

Contents

CHAPTER ONE

The Incomplete Ideology

I

Since the mid-1950s considerable numbers of youth have lost faith in "the system" and now consider themselves radicals or revolutionaries with a lower-case "r." This New Left has had a serious impact on our society. It has mobilized millions of people for protest on single issues, such as racism or the Vietnam war. It has modified the American culture to an extent, as witness the growing acceptance of common-law marriage, communes, the right of abortion, free sexual relationships, marijuana, rock music, long hair styles, and casual dress. It has changed popular attitudes toward blacks, Chicanos, and women, and it has sidetracked the anticommunism which contributed to national paranoia. It has made America a better place to live in, or at least prevented it from becoming much worse. But it has won few converts to the need of revolution per se. If it has raised important and disturbing questions about today's America, it has elaborated no cogent set of ideas on how that America should be restructured or told us what the "beautiful tomorrow" will look like and how to get there.

Radicalism in America is not credible. The unbelievability of radicalism is apparent from the disarray within its own ranks. Since the disintegration of the Student Nonviolent Coordinating

Committee (SNCC) and the Students for a Democratic Society (SDS) in the last years of the Johnson administration, there has been no polarizing agent in the radical movement. As Gil Green observes in his *The New Radicalism*, "Leaders come and leaders go in endless procession. New organizations and ad hoc committees proliferate, but they are here today and gone tomorrow. Few of the new organizations have displayed great staying power and none are free of internal dissension and crisis."[1] The new radicals have fragmented politically as well as organizationally. Some are now followers of Mao Tse-tung or Fidel Castro or Che Guevara or Kim Il-Sung of North Korea. Some have identified their radicalism with the counterculture and, like the pre-1972 Yippie, Jerry Rubin, seem to believe that if you poke enough fun at capitalism it will fall apart. Many others simply engage in day-to-day activity, such as electoral politics, consumerism, or antiwar work, without concern for ideology. "Spontaneity," laments Green, "could produce no more than it did—a hybrid type of eclectic thinking passed off by some as 'no ideology' and by others as 'new ideology.' " New or none, however, it has failed to proselytize any sizable segment of Americans to the necessity or inevitability of an American revolution.

The Old Left, which pivots around the Communist Party and the Socialist Workers Party, has enjoyed a modest resurgence in the last few years. But it is not really a viable force and is equally poor as a salesman for revolution. Indeed, it speaks infrequently these days of such ultimate objectives as the nationalization of industry or the dictatorship of the proletariat, and when it does it leaves the great mass of Americans cold and indifferent. It is more adept at criticizing that which is—capitalism, imperialism— than sanguine in describing how that-which-is can be cast aside. Its members, like those of the New Left, are as sensitive, intelligent, and devoted a force as one can find in this society. But *their* radicalism too lacks credibility.

Something obviously has gone awry; there is a leak in the tank that needs plugging. Marxian socialism differed from the teachings of the prophets and from the teachings of utopian socialists in that it professed to be a *science* of revolution, based on appraisal of fact, not the weaving of hopes. Admittedly, Marx himself, living in another epoch before the maturing of trade unions and before the full outlines of imperialism became apparent, could not have drawn a blueprint of the latter stages of capitalism—of Keynes-ianism, the military-industrial complex, and the present strug-gle between socialism and capitalism worldwide. But Marxism, in addition to being an analysis of nature and society, legated to future Marxists a *method* for applying this analysis to their own times. Quite obviously they have failed to do so with any degree of cogency. With that scientific method it should have been pos-sible to predict when, where, and how the socialist revolutions would take place, just as the science of physics predicted the explosive potential of nuclear fission. It should have been possible to spell out in advance some of the difficulties and dilemmas that socialism would face in its initial stages. It should have been possible to forecast the evolution from laissez-faire capitalism to controlled capitalism, and the temporary stabilization of the sys-tem through the application of Keynesian economic measures. Most of all, it should have been possible to explain the course of develop-ment in such a way as to make the need for revolution seem urgent and logical to a much larger constituency than the Left now commands.

In fact, that was what happened in the 1930s, when Marxian socialism impressed millions as a viable answer to the crisis of that period. The question "will there be a revolution," notes David Shannon,

> weighed heavily on many Americans' minds and hearts in 1931 and 1932. Most people hoped the desperation of Great Depres-sion victims would not trigger a revolution; a relative few hoped the whole social mess would end in revolt. But neither side would have been surprised had there been concerted and national vio-lence to achieve a revolutionary purpose. Fear of a revolution was very widespread during the last several months of President Hoover's administration."[2]

That fear—and hope—lingered on for some years during the Roosevelt administration. The gross national product of the United States had shrunk from $103 billion to $56 billion at its nadir; millions had not had a job for years; as far as the eye could see into the future there was barren desert. Thus revolution as an idea whose time had come seemed vividly real not only to esoteric layers of the population but to vast sectors in the core of society.

The Marxist movement of the 1930s may have been no larger than the radical constituency three decades later—it may have been smaller, it is difficult to say[3]—but the Marxist theory of revolution, whether interpreted along Communist, Trotskyist, or other left-wing lines, possessed credibility. Marxism could be put in simple terms so that even the least theoretical of people could see—better still, feel—its logic.

History, it was said, moves by a process of birth, growth, and decay from one system of social organization to another—from primitive communism to chattel slavery, to feudalism, capitalism, and finally socialism. Each system is progressive in its early stages, but there is an inherent contradiction between its mode of production and relations of production which—beginning with chattel slavery and moving through capitalism—polarizes wealth and power, exacerbates the struggle between the upper and lower classes, and finally leads to revolution.

Capitalism too was once a progressive vehicle for human development. But the contradiction between a social form of production and the private appropriation of its product has now made it regressive and reactionary. That evolution was inevitable, stemming as it did not from the malevolence of men but from the impersonal effects of something Marx called "surplus value." The price (wage) that an employer pays for labor power is less than the values the laborer adds to the materials he works on. This surplus accrues to the capitalist class in the form of profits, interest, and rent. There is thus the anomaly that the earnings of the producer (worker) are smaller than the values he produces; or, put differently, the worker produces more goods and services than he is able to buy back. Periodically these surpluses swell into a glut, so that while warehouses are full, workers are laid off and the economy staggers in unemployment and depression.

The other side of the same coin is an impulse toward imperialism and war. The capitalist, with surpluses on hand far beyond what he needs for his own use, seeks markets for goods and capital abroad. In order to assure those markets, he, his class brothers, and the government they control seize and dominate weaker countries. In due course the so-called "backward" areas are divided among the great powers as outright colonies or spheres of influence, and since there is now a shortage of colonies for the "have-not" powers, the struggle for domination eventually erupts into military conflict to *re*divide the world. It is a process that is as inexorable as day following night. Capitalism thus is a hopeless system which oppresses both its populace at home and its colonial people abroad, spewing forth with alarming regularity the poisons of depression and war. From this it follows that the oppressed class which stands at the center of the economy, the working class, has the historical obligation to overthrow capitalism; once it has gained the experience and leadership for that task, it will do so. Capitalism creates its own gravediggers.

Though Marx, Lenin, and other leftist leaders denied that this process was inevitable—since it required leadership and guidance by a "vanguard"—there was nonetheless a *flavor* of inevitability to their doctrine that the disenchanted and dispossessed could latch onto with enthusiasm. In the bitter 1930s, with one quarter of the working class unemployed and one quarter working part time, this thesis seemed unassailable. The scenario of *The Communist Manifesto* appeared to be unfolding exactly as outlined. Perhaps there were some flaws which disturbed the wary, but they were minor and could be explained.

Those who were distressed by the Soviet purge trials, which resulted in conviction and death for most of the Bolshevik leaders who made the 1917 revolution, found means of rationalizing their doubts. Soviet Russia, a socialist island in a capitalist sea, they said, was bound to be battered by counterrevolutionary tides. It was unfortunate but not surprising that some revolutionaries should be unable to stand the pace of a continuing revolution and should, in their alarm, turn to the enemy. But by eliminating these weak and traitorous men, so said the Stalinist zealots, Stalin had performed a major service for the future of socialism. Another rationale, by exiled Leon Trotsky, placed the shoe on the other foot: it was Stalin who betrayed the revolution, not Kamenev, Zinoviev, Bukharin, Radek, or himself. Stalin had converted the Soviet Union, said the former leader of the Red Army, into a "warped" workers' state. This, however, was a temporary lapse that would eventually be corrected by the Soviet people; it did not vitiate the Marxist doctrine per se.

When one looked deeper into the Marxist bag of ideas there were other flaws, such as the theory of immiseration—that the working class was destined to live at a progressively lower standard of living and become increasingly class- and revolutionary-conscious. Noting this weakness in doctrine, Lenin combined the theory of immiseration with his own theory of parasitism—namely, that capitalism was able to raise wages and bribe the proletariat at home from the superprofits it earned in the colonies. This addendum, however, also had its problems: American wages, for instance, were higher than those of Britain even though American profits in its sphere of influence were much smaller than those of John Bull.

Yet with all the gnawing doubts about this or that, Marxism in the 1930s remained a formidable edifice. The minions of the establishment sounded naïve against the predictions of Marxists about depression and decline. Just before the great depression that began in October 1929, President Herbert Hoover stolidly contended that "We in America today are nearer to the final triumph over poverty than ever before in the history of our land. The poorhouse is vanishing from among us."[4] Such gibberish on the eve of a shocking slump made Marxism all the more credible. Where the bourgeois economists had posited an unending and persevering expansion of the capitalist economy, the Marxists had described not only its limitations but its inexorable trend toward chaos. The system seemed to be neither patchable nor reformable; for hosts of sensitive young people, revolution was the only alternative and Marxism the only feasible insight into the process of revolution.

II

Since the 1930s three sets of experiences have intruded against the Marxist formulation of history.

The first was an outburst of five or six dozen revolutions in underdeveloped countries around the periphery of capitalism. This was not the sequence that Marx and Engels had postulated in their *Communist Manifesto* of 1848. The *Manifesto* had given history an alluring simplicity, almost like turning pages—from primitive communism to chattel slavery, from chattel slavery to feudalism, from feudalism to capitalism, from capitalism to socialism. From this schema one could rightly deduce that the expected revolution would come first to the most advanced nations, and in fact the *Manifesto* dealt almost exclusively with the conflict between bourgeoisie and proletariat. "What the bourgeoisie . . .

produces, above all," said the *Manifesto*, "are its own gravediggers. Its fall and the victory of the proletariat are equally inevitable."[5] Nothing was mentioned about who would be the gravediggers in the so-called backward areas, where feudalism or tribalism still prevailed. Indicative of Marx's preoccupation was his suggestion that the *Manifesto* "be published in the English, French, German, Italian, Flemish and Danish languages"—languages, in other words, of the highly developed capitalist states.[6] Nothing was said of the Chinese, Russian, Swahili, Spanish, Hindi, or Arab languages. The locus of revolution was to be in Europe and America, not Asia, Africa, Eastern Europe, or Latin America.

Had the scenario played itself out as Marx and Engels had projected, the transition to socialism would have been much less painful. Britain, America, France, et al. had the capital, the technological know-how, the educational standards, the infrastructure to shift from one system to another with a minimum of hardship. It was quite another matter for Russia, China, India, Cuba, Guinea, or Egypt, where all these factors were lacking and where the problems, therefore, were monumental. To meet them most of the revolutionary countries had to impose strict national discipline, and in doing so appeared to the world not only as impotent bunglers, unable to solve the material problems of their citizenry, but as totalitarian to boot.

Marx had never warned his followers of this possibility, for he believed that socialist revolutions occurred only after the "material conditions" for them had been well prepared. Writing in the *New York Tribune* in 1853 he hailed the building of railroads by Britain in India because "whatever may be the crimes of England" it was laying the material basis for a modern industry and therefore a bourgeois revolution.[7] As late as 1905 Lenin expected Russians to make a bourgeois revolution, not a socialist one. Radicals, by and large, were unprepared for Russia's proletarian revolution in 1917. Had the German revolution succeeded in 1918-19, the course of history might have proceeded more in accord with the original insights of Karl Marx. But it didn't; it was drowned in repression by the very Social Democrats who were alleged to be the foremost exponents of Marxism. Since then the center of social upheaval has been in the less-developed countries.

The Old Left, in the Soviet Union as well as in America, not only failed to anticipate this development but had few answers for the problems it was destined to bring in its wake. Having studied *Das Kapital*, the Leftists knew how capital was formed in capitalist countries, but not how it would be formed during the socialist transformation of countries that were overwhelmingly rural and where native capitalism was either infantile, immature, or nonexistent. This failure to predict the sequence of revolution proved to be a major miscalculation of Marxism, and it raised certain doubts—as we shall see in due course—about some of its theoretical assumptions.

The second set of experiences for which Marxism was unprepared was the resiliency of capitalism—the revitalization of its economy and the unprecedented high living standards it has brought to a considerable majority of its people. The post-World War II prediction by Eugene Dennis, general secretary of the Communist Party, that we were on the brink of "the next cyclical economic crisis" which would "enormously accentuate the dangers of fascism in the United States,"[8] has proven premature by a few decades at least. Neither fascism nor a full-scale depression has appeared on the horizon. On the contrary, the capitalist economy has been so buoyant, despite readjustments from war to peace and despite five recessions, that many people, including many former radicals, have concluded the magic of Keynesianism, with its compensatory spending and deficit financing, has worked its wonders and reduced the theories of Marx and Lenin to historical curiosities.

The third set of experiences which bedevils the Left, new and old, has been the evolution of the socialist system itself. In those countries where socialists have come to power, the goals of peace, prosperity, and humanism remain unfulfilled. It is too soon, admittedly, to expect "prosperity," but such occurrences as the Soviet interventions in Hungary and Czechoslovakia, the crimes of Stalinism—now admitted by the Soviet leadership itself—and the lingering authoritarian spirit, are depressing reminders that while there is a promise to revolution there are also pitfalls. The science of revolution was supposed to have helped radicals avoid these pitfalls; it hasn't.

Back in March 1919 the first congress of the Communist International stated that "The equality of citizens irrespective of sex, religion, race or nationality, which bourgeois democracy always promised but never carried out . . . is carried out by the Soviet government, or the dictatorship of the proletariat, immediately and to the full."[9] The assumption, a half century ago, was that the transfer of ownership of the means of production from private capitalists to the workers' state was enough to assure equality. But while there were many features of the Soviet experience to merit admiration—production advances, Sputnik, educational leaps—the nationalization of the means of production had not in itself produced the ideal society or anything approaching it. There is nothing in the Soviet evolution that can make young people, there or here, lyrical. And there is quite a bit that casts doubt, if not stigma.

The experience on both sides of the cold war, therefore, has befogged revolutionary ideology. It has dimmed the beacon and reinforced three oft-heard arguments against the need for revolution:

1. That it has not worked, or has worked poorly, as witness the results in the Soviet Union, China, Cuba, North Korea, and Eastern Europe. In every one of these countries and areas there is a lower standard of living than in the major capitalist states and, to make matters worse, less freedom.

2. That revolution is really unnecessary. With all its faults capitalism has provided its citizens with higher material benefits than socialism, and—equally or more important—with democratic rights beyond anything known in the Communist or Third World societies.

3. That even if revolution were necessary it would be futile. Human nature is so composed that equality, nonviolence, and the ultimate freedom of anarchy are unattainable by any community of mortals. There will always be wars. There will always be class struggles. There will always be inequality.

The Old Left in the 1930s did not have to contend with such arguments; it could brush them aside. How could anyone defend the virtues of capitalism at a time when its bounty was hunger and disintegration? And say what one would about Stalin's authoritarianism, there was no unemployment in Soviet Russia, and the statistics of economic progress under the first five-year plans were sensational—especially when compared to industrial decline in the West. The point about human nature being unreceptive to the goals of revolution could be dismissed as barren nit-picking—like talking about the danger of a blood transfusion while the patient was bleeding to death.

The arguments against revolution in the last two or three decades, however, seem more persuasive to the average citizen. In part this is due to the improved economic situation. But at least equally important is the fact that the Left has no answers to troubling questions. Capitalism was supposed to sink in the ebb tide of depression and war. Why then has it been able to stabilize itself, or at least give the appearance of stability? The Left doesn't really say. Nor does the Left tell us why a wholesale terror against millions of people was possible in a socialist country which claims to be the workers' fatherland. The transgressions of Stalin are attributed by Moscow to something called the "cult of the personality" and by Peking to the unfortunate failure of Stalin to recognize that even under socialism there exist contradictions among the people that are not *antagonistic* contradictions. Thus where Mao, learning from Stalin's errors, allegedly relies on persuasion to rehabilitate those who have gone astray, Stalin considered them class enemies and liquidated them. Perhaps Mao's thesis is valid, but his endorsement of Stalin as a great revolutionary, and the consequent downgrading of the vast terror as simply a tactical mistake, seems to rob socialism of its humanistic content. After all, what is the difference between the framing and execution of a Zinoviev in the Soviet Union and the framing and execution of the Rosenbergs in the United States—except that the number of Zinovievs was hundreds of times greater? The Old Left expired on these shoals; the New Left has not yet navigated them.

The failure to provide cogent answers to such questions has had three interesting results. The first was a sudden swing to the right on the part of many radicals and former radicals. In the wake of revelations after World War II about Stalin's crimes, and in the euphoria of a prosperity that seemed permanent, many an ex-Socialist or ex-Communist turned 180 degrees to the anti-Communist credo of the military-industrial complex. The Americans for Democratic Action, made up in considerable measure of former socialists, listed as their first postwar objective "effective American mobilization for the security of the free world against Communism." They stopped talking about the need for "state ownership of the means of production" and urged instead "free enterprise coupled with government responsibility for full employment and rising living standards."[10] The cover of Walter Reuther's pamphlet

A Total Peace Offensive described it as a plan "to stop communist aggression." Reuther, an ex-Socialist, was far from the most extreme. The woods were full of ex-radicals such as Jay Lovestone, former general secretary of the Communist Party, who were either working in or with the Central Intelligence Agency or writing books and tracts against "Communist treason." One need only mention Whitaker Chambers, Louis Budenz, Eugene Lyons, Max Eastman, Hede Massing, James Burnham, and perhaps half the editors of William F. Buckley's *National Review*. From advocates of communism they turned into advocates of capitalism—"warts and all." Eastman, one of the first American intellectuals to come to the defense of the Russian Revolution, concluded in his *Reflections on the Failure of Socialism* (1955) that the only choice is between "a system in which the amount and kind of goods produced is determined by the *impersonal* mechanism of the market . . . [and] a system in which this is determined by commands issuing from a *personal* authority backed by armed force."[11]

At the opposite pole was the emergence a decade after the war of the young middle-class radical, first as a beatnik, then as a political animal. The beatnik resigned from his parents' "degraded" and "hypocritical" world to do his own thing. Other new radicals, recoiling from the lack of humanism in American society, formed ad hoc groups to challenge the House Committee on Un-American Activities (HUAC), demonstrated for free speech at the universities, went south to join Martin Luther King's crusade for civil rights, adhered to the small antiwar movement then beginning to form around the Gandhian pacifist, A. J. Muste. They did not affiliate with the Old Left because they were equally repelled by the anticommunism of the Socialist Party and the Stalinism of the Communist Party, neither of which appeared to be a vehicle for humanistic radicalism. But in their day-to-day militancy they either had no time or no inclination to explain the very causes for their own birth as a New Left. It was not really necessary, they said. All the old arguments between Stalin and Trotsky, Earl Browder and William Z. Foster, John Gates and Foster were irrelevant. In the revulsion against old ideologies they turned their backs on ideology per se. Their central assumption, as Martin Oppenheimer points out, "is 'of a revolution which preceded ideology,' so that day-to-day practice creates the ideology, inductively."[12] It will come automatically, in due course, if you are active enough in the streets.

The third force affected by the confusion of the Left was the public at large. Despite burgeoning prosperity, there was in America a pervasive malaise, a malaise stimulated by the nuclear bomb, the "little" wars in Korea and Vietnam, the interventions in Lebanon and the Dominican Republic, the feeling of insignificance and alienation, unfulfilled dreams of equality, especially on the part of blacks, and mundane worries about taxes, law and order, and safety in the streets. But it was a malaise that was insufficiently cultivated; it never graduated beyond single-issue protest to recognition that something was wrong at the core of society. Most people thought (and still think) that Vietnam was a "mistake," not related to something more basic, imperialism. Most people saw no link between the big business they instinctively distrusted and America's domestic and foreign problems; they could identify the symptoms—e.g., "crime in the streets"— but not the cause. Thus the public at large, though unhappy, saw no answer to its travail in the nostrums of radicalism. If revolution were the answer, why was revolutionary Russia totalitarian? And if capitalism were "dying," why did it look so ruddy? In the absence of viable answers the malaise sought refuge in escapism. Perhaps the television tube, the automobile, the sailboat, and the snowmobile would have immersed America in escapism in any case, but the fact is that there was no vision from the Left to draw people away from it.

It was one thing to talk of revolution when the gross national product was shrinking from $103 billion a year to $56 billion, but quite another when it was growing steadily year to year, culminating in 1971 and 1972 in a GNP of a trillion dollars plus. It was one thing to talk of the working class sparking a revolution in the 1930s, when labor strikes took on the dimension of small wars, but quite another in the 1960s and 1970s, when strikes were humdrum waiting games and the unions by and large had grown fat and conservative. If revolution was still on the agenda for such countries as the United States, the radicals who sponsored such revolution would have to update both their analysis and strategy to take into account the experiences of the last three decades. The means and ends of revolution would have to be defined so as to make them *real and achievable*—and real and achievable to Americans, not Cubans, Chinese, or Brazilians.

III

What I propose to do in this book is to lay the groundwork for a reconstruction of radical ideology. It should begin, I feel, with a change in method, from microanalysis to macroanalysis. We tend to view each country and each of the two major social systems in isolation from the other. America is prosperous, it is said, because of certain things that have happened in America, and the Soviet Union is authoritarian because of certain things that have happened in the Soviet Union. Each gets credit or censure for its own successes or failures. In this microscopic image of history, capitalism and communism are growing from separate roots, developing in their own way, and if you compare them the former seems far more robust than the latter.

But if you change the focus from the micro to the macro—if, in other words, you study the interrelationship, the interplay between the various nations and between the two social systems —you see a world organism, with separate cells, involved in a multiplicity of minor and major conflicts, each of which constantly alters the character both of the cells and the organism. Capitalism thus not only has a life of its own but is drastically affected by its war against socialism; and socialism, though it too is fashioned by the follies and foibles of its own leaders and actions, is nonetheless decisively shaped by its relationship to capitalism. If we were to assume a situation—admittedly an impossible one—in which no capitalist nation used military force or policies of economic strangulation against a people in revolution, socialism would long ago have become the predominant world system. Given the actual state of affairs, however, and the ceaseless intervention by the old system against the new system, every national revolution was bound to be inhibited or warped.

Consider the narrow focus from which certain theorists make capitalism seem impregnable. Robert L. Heilbroner, a liberal economist who skirts the edges of socialism, concludes in one of his books that "for our lives and for those of our children, [capitalism] bids fair to confront us as the prevailing form of social organization in those nations where it is solidly entrenched,"[13] e.g., the United States. There is absolutely no chance, he says, that we can "replace the guiding principle of production for profit by that of production for use," or nationalize the big corporations and "end the concentration of private wealth. . . . One can debate whether all or any of these or similar changes are desirable, but there is little point in debating whether they are realizable. Barring only some disaster that would throw open the gates to a radical reconstruction of society, they are not."[14] Heilbroner assesses "the limits of capitalism" within the *framework* of capitalism, as if we were living in a vacuum and were confined to such tasks as producing ten million more automobiles this year to add to the hundred million already on the road, or to fattening unemployment compensation so that it runs for fifty-two weeks instead of twenty-six. The focus is on a compartmentalized United States—its institutional structure, its entrenched corporate system, its leaders, its resources, its politics, its apparent impregnability—all in isolation from the crucible of world developments.

This "Heilbroner fallacy" is similar, in my opinion, to what market researcher Daniel Yankelovich describes—in another context, Vietnam—as the "McNamara fallacy."

> The first step is to measure what can easily be measured. This is okay as far as it goes. The second step is to disregard that which can't be measured or give it an arbitrary quantitative value. This is artificial and misleading. The third step is to presume that what can't be measured easily really isn't very important. This is blindness. The fourth step is to say that what can't be easily measured doesn't exist. That is suicide.[15]

What can be measured in the capitalist saga is the gross national product, capital expenditures, money in circulation, wage rates, the number of automobiles and refrigerators. Based on these measurements it is possible to predict with a fair degree of accuracy that the GNP in the United States, for instance, will increase by so many billion dollars next year or that the rate of unemployment will decline by half a percent.

All this assumes, however, that other factors, not amenable to easy calculation, will remain the same—that Japan, for instance, will not revalue its currency by 10 percent, that the Common Market nations will not impose a heavy tax on U.S. investments or initiate a major trade war, that Israel and the Arab states will not resume hostilities or that if they do the hostilities will remain localized. It also assumes that there will be no social revolution in Brazil, Spain, Italy, South Africa, the Philippines, or Thailand. These are potentials that can't be run through a computer, yet it is evident they can drastically affect the future of America or Britain or Germany—or all of them collectively. One need only recall the impact of Vietnam on the United States—inflation, unemployment, further undermining of the dollar, balance of payments deficits, internal dissension, wage and price controls. And Vietnam is a small country, of little strategic significance, far away. Suppose there had been a Vietnam in Brazil, or a half-dozen Vietnams going on simultaneously? Or suppose there had been a Vietnam-type war in China back in 1948-49, in which Washington had similarly intervened with planes and troops. America would look very much different, economically, politically, and socially, than it does today. If capitalism looks formidable, then, judged by its domestic GNP, it appears more tenuous in the context of world revolution. In that context it may be like the man who drops dead of a heart attack one day after his doctor assures him he is in perfect health, or like the many societies Arnold Toynbee has written about which began to disintegrate at that moment when they seemed to be at the apex of their power.

If we turn from the static to the dynamic, from a national focus to one that emphasizes the international *interplay* of social systems, the durability of capitalism no longer seems so assured. The past century is notable for a long cycle of revolution and counterrevolution, in which counterrevolution was victorious until 1917. Beginning with the Russian Revolution, however, the conflict between revolution and counterrevolution became less one-sided, and after World War II the balance definitely tipped toward the former. After a half century we are still living in the midst of a vast *ongoing* conflict, which on the one side manifests itself as a permanent revolution against capitalism and its vassal systems, feudalism and tribalism, and on the other side as a permanent war against revolution. That conflict has its ups and downs, each swing affecting not only international relationships but the *internal* development of the various capitalist and socialist countries.

We propose to show in these pages how that ongoing contest contributed to the emergence of Stalinism in the Soviet Union—that

Stalinism, in other words, was not merely the outgrowth of Stalin's personality or conditions within Russia but of outside pressures applied by the advanced powers in the course of their permanent war against revolution. We propose to show as well that despite quantitative successes—those that can be measured by a computer —capitalism has been in retreat, on the defensive. Thrice in the last six decades its fate hung in the balance—after World War I, during the Great Depression, and after World War II. It escaped catastrophe by adopting a patchwork of Keynesian measures and by using the reserves of the one nation that still had a sufficient quantity, the United States, temporarily to stabilize a ship that was near capsizing. It was not the *inner* strength of the free enterprise system which saved it, but measures of an emergency and artificial nature. Without $1.3 trillion spent by the United States on militarism since World War II or the approximately $150 billion on foreign aid, not only would the counterrevolution have collapsed long ago but the advanced capitalist states themselves would have been immersed in revolution. Whether Uncle Sam can continue this artificial respiration indefinitely is a question we must look at more closely.

We propose to show finally that as the balance between capitalism and socialism is altered, the socialist world is destined to move more rapidly toward its original humanistic ideal—that, in fact, it has already taken quite a few steps in that direction. The Soviet Union, as the first socialist nation, experienced more hardship in resisting the capitalist powers than any other socialist state. But each new revolutionary nation (Vietnam is an exception) has an easier time of it. Some, such as Yugoslavia, have made considerable progress toward a *humanistic* socialism; all, including the Soviet Union, have liberalized internally far more than the West gives them credit for.

The myths that capitalism provides the better life and that socialism can only survive through totalitarianism can be sustained only if the problems of America or Germany or Italy are looked at in isolation. Once we move to macroanalysis and to a dynamic interpretation of history, those conventional wisdoms are less convincing. For we are in the middle rounds of a boxing match in which one fighter looks strong but is running out of wind, the other appears weak but is gaining strength.

In the course of our reinterpretation of recent history it should become evident where the science of revolution needs updating. Why did Marx fail to predict the locus of the present revolutionary upsurge? In my opinion, it was because his insights into the character of classes, the class struggle, the nature of the state, and the significance of *countervailing* power were inadequate. He misjudged the resiliency of capitalism and of course was unable to anticipate all the problems of socialism. It behooves the Left today to redefine its position on these subjects, just as it behooved Einstein to redefine the physics of Isaac Newton. This book is an effort to provide a modest part of that redefinition, so that we can proceed to an outline for a radical strategy—an American strategy —that *is* credible.

CHAPTER TWO

The
Double
Revolution

I

Out of the discord of history Karl Marx abstracted what he thought would be the salient features of this epoch. A cycle of birth, growth, and decay was unfolding, he said, in the following manner:

Birth: The middle class (burghers or bourgeoisie), aided by the peasantry, seizes power from the feudal class.

Growth: The bourgeoisie and the new working class confront each other in ever-intensifying class struggles, culminating in

Decay: A revolution by the majority, the proletariat, against the minority, the capitalist class, and the birth thereby of a new social order whose first phase would be the "dictatorship of the proletariat."

The cycle did not evolve, however, as outlined. Sometime during its second phase the class struggle between capitalists and workers in developed countries became less, not more, intense; and while the proletariat did spark revolutions in Russia, Bolivia, and perhaps one or two other places, no revolution has as yet succeeded in a country where the working class was a majority, or even a sizable minority.

A more accurate description of the cycle now in progress would be:

Birth: The middle class, aided by the peasantry as junior partner, promotes bourgeois revolutions in Holland, England, France, America (where a revolution that began in England is completed), and later in Scandinavia, Germany, Italy, and Japan.

Growth: The entrenched bourgeois nations occupy or otherwise dominate the weaker feudal and tribal nations and suppress every effort by these nations to make bourgeois revolutions of their own.

Decay: Beginning with Mexico in 1910, China in 1911, Russia in 1917, and especially after World War II, dozens of peoples rise up against the alliance of foreign imperialists and native reactionaries to liberate themselves and begin the arduous task of building a viable economy. They soon find that to do so they must proceed from the bourgeois revolution directly into a socialist revolution—condensing, so to speak, two revolutions in one.

Marx did not entirely foreclose such a possibility, but the thrust of his *Manifesto* and the total emphasis of *Das Kapital* on the contradictions of capitalism strengthened the thesis that there would be a *discontinuity* between the bourgeois and proletarian revolutions while history prepared the "material conditions" for the second uprising. The two social upheavals would not only be separated in time but each would confront and challenge a different set of institutions—in the one case feudalist, in the other capitalist. In the cycle as it actually occurred, however, the tasks of the two revolutions have been amalgamated into a single ongoing effort. The revolutionists of today are in large part contending against the same institutions as the revolutionists of the sixteenth, seventeenth, eighteenth, and nineteenth centuries. They too are fighting feudalism (or tribalism) but with two major differences: (1) that native feudalism and native tribalism have in the meantime been massively buttressed by international capitalism; and (2) that the amount of capital needed to forge a modern economy today is dozens of times greater than it was 100 or 150 years ago. Thus the revolutionists of this century have had to deal with both a more formidable enemy and a more formidable problem.

II

Without going into great detail, let us look at the enemy and the problem a little more graphically. The feudal system of Western Europe, against which the bourgeois revolution was first initiated, evolved from the chaos following the disintegration of the Roman Empire in the sixth, seventh, and eighth centuries. "It was a time," writes H. G. Wells,

> of confusion, of brigandage, of crimes unpunished and universal insecurity. . . . So men were forced to link themselves with others, preferably people stronger than themselves. The lonely man chose the most powerful and active person in his district and became *his* man. The freeman or the weak lordling of a petty territory linked himself to some more powerful lord. The protection of that lord (or the danger of his hostility) became more considerable with each such accession. . . . These natural associations and alliances grew very rapidly into a system, *the feudal system.*[1]

In its early stages, then, feudalism represented a necessary and progressive reaction to the tyranny of an older system, and it brought in its wake many improvements. One, of course, was the abolition of chattel slavery, but there were also technological advances which, though primitive by today's standards, were important innovations hundreds of years ago. They included, as Marion Gibbs points out, "wide-spread use of agricultural tools which made possible the cultivation of vast tracts of heavy forested land which hitherto had resisted all colonizing efforts," the use of mills for grinding corn, wheels driven by water and wind power, the exploitation of horses, the horseshoe, the fixed rudder which revolutionized shipping, the simple compass, the wheelbarrow, spinning wheel, gunpowder, printing, and many others.[2]

In due course, however, political and economic power crystallized so totally in the hands of knights, landlords, dukes, and kings—in that ascending order—that the system took on a static and reactionary character. It was a system bursting at the seams with implicit possibilities for great changes, but unable to make them because the institutions of feudalism squelched initiative and inhibited the formation of capital.

Government in the feudal society was based on the will of men in high places rather than on the stricture of law. Peasant, craft, and merchant enterprise were all controlled and un-free, subject to the whim of the ruling elites. The serf who tilled the land was usually assigned three parcels in various sections of the village, but he neither owned those parcels nor enjoyed tenure rights over them. In accordance with the principle of top-down rule, he could be dispossessed whenever it suited the lord to do so—and in fact this is what happened on a very large scale during the enclosures in England, when the lords decided to allocate more land for their own sheep-raising and reduced acreage for peasants' farms accordingly.

The lord—in this typical feudal village—determines unilaterally how the produce shall be divided between himself and the peasant, how much shall be charged for grinding corn or wheat, how many days each year the peasant shall work on the lord's own acreage, on roads, and on other jobs, and under what conditions the peasant can use the common grazing lands. Though the peasant may have worked the same strips all his life, he cannot pass that tenure to his children—except with the concurrence of the lord and the payment of a tax. The peasant owns no land yet is tied to it as if it were part of his body. He cannot move from it, except by permission of the man on high. He cannot change his occupation or escape to another village, unless the lord sanctions it. If he wants his parents to live with him he must seek dispensation. Admittedly, custom and paternalism moderated the harshness of this system, but in its juridical outline it was extremely repressive.

In such a society there is neither equality of opportunity nor equality before the law. Inequality is built into the structure so that, with few exceptions, a man's status at birth is his status at death. Under the circumstances there is little incentive for accumulating capital or making major technological changes. If the peasant has anything left over after paying rent and taxes, he is loath to invest it. Since he has no tenure rights, the improved land can be taken from him and assigned to someone else. And, of course, he cannot buy land, since ownership for the most part is vested in the upper classes. Though there is some commodity production, most production under feudalism is for use, not exchange, and is based on principles of self-sufficiency, not competition and technological advance.

The craftsman and merchant are similarly restricted. Normally they belong to closed guilds which set prices, determine wage scales for journeymen and apprentices, and establish standards of quality and rules of work—but all subject to approval by lords, dukes, and kings. It is a controlled enterprise, not a free one. The craftsman who produces shoes or furniture charges the same prices as other craftsmen who produce shoes or furniture. He does not compete with them; he engages instead in an imposed form of "cooperation." He may have the surpluses to invest in machinery or in a larger manufactory, but, as with the peasant, it would be risky because the lord can revoke his status in a nonce, and there is no court to which he can run to prevent it. Inequality is the accepted way of life.

No matter where you turn in the feudal system, there is no class that has an incentive to form capital, improve technology, or develop industry. The peasant doesn't have it. The craftsman and merchant don't have it. Nor, for that matter, does the lord. His power stems from heredity and control of the army, not from his talent as an entrepreneur. He loses his riches not when another lord undersells him on the market but when he is beaten on the battlefield or when his peasants rise up against him in rebellion. He has no need to expand through trade and manufacture; he need only impose another tax on his serfs or conquer the villages of another lord. The market, competition, capital formation—these mean nothing to him.

As the contradictions of this system led to confining restrictions and intensified misery, there was an inevitable stirring among the lower classes—by the peasants, bent on winning the right to tenure and ownership of land; by the middle class, the burghers or bourgeoisie, to gain freedom of enterprise and equality before the law. Time and again the peasants of Western Europe rose in violent revolt—in France in 1358, during the long war with England; in England in 1381, on the heels of the black death which reduced the population by at least a third; in Germany in 1522; and in Spain, Italy, Austria, and parts of Scandinavia at various other times. Each of these peasant revolts breached the feudal structure to an extent, so that by the time the bourgeois revolution came to a climax some land reform had taken place and some substantial rights had been won by the middle classes. Finally, beginning late in the seventeenth century, a relatively mature middle class led the common effort that toppled feudalism in Holland, England, France, and elsewhere. The institutional shackles of the past were broken, land reform extended, and a juridical system introduced that encouraged free enterprise and the accumulation of capital.

What is noteworthy in this first stage of the saga is that there was a certain coherence and logic to the revolutionary development. Land ownership gave the peasant an incentive to improve his agricultural techniques, to produce more, save more, and provide the surpluses which by a complex process could be turned into capital for trade and infant industry. And though the process was usually accelerated by brutal and repressive measures to "squeeze" the peasant, the amount of capital was usually small and within reach. In theory—though not in practice—the revolutionary transformation could proceed without undue turmoil.

One of the few places where the revolution did take place in an orderly fashion, without violent uprisings, was in Denmark. This revolution, proceeding in stages over the course of many decades, gives us an insight both into the goals of the bourgeois revolution and the relative painlessness by which they could be achieved under some circumstances.

Until the metamorphosis of Denmark got under way, eight hundred feudal estates owned three quarters of the land. In 1769 a decree was enacted offering freeholders a measure of protection, a reduction of taxes, and an opportunity to pass on their holdings to their children. From 1784 to 1790 nonfreeholders, the peasantry at large, won the right to land tenure for life. The peasant did not as yet *own* the soil he tilled, but he could not be uprooted from it either. Moreover, his attachment to the soil was abolished; he could move about at will. In 1786 the government opened a credit bank from which peasants could borrow money to buy the land they farmed. Nineteen years later a historical tragedy turned into a boon for the lower classes: the Danes went to war on Napoleon's side against the British. In the ensuing inflation of prices a large number of peasants were able to pay off their mortgages with cheap money and gain clear title to their acreage. They now enjoyed both tenure and ownership.

With economic power came political power. In 1814 the government passed an elementary education act. Seventeen years later the richer peasants secured the right to vote, and by 1841, when a rural local government act was passed, absolutism was finished in Denmark. A peasantry enjoying some education and economic power took the reins of local government into its hands. A few years later, in 1848—the year of revolution in Europe—a liberal constitution was drafted, and in 1849 a cottagers' law was enacted which gave the cottager the right to have friends or relatives live with him without permission of landlord or government. Labor service to the lord was abolished a few weeks later, and payment of rent and taxes in kind—grain or other crops—was changed to payment in cash. In the first constituent assembly, 50 percent of the delegates were from the peasant class. Thus step by step, under insistent pressures by the lower classes—not all of it effete, incidentally—the social structure of Denmark made the transition from feudalism toward capitalism.

Finally, two other historical "tragedies" stimulated Denmark to complete its peaceful revolution. One was competition from American wheat growers, who undersold the Danes on the world market. Another was the high tariff imposed by Germany on Danish cattle. Having lost most of its territory—Norway, given up to Sweden in 1814, and Schleswig-Holstein, yielded to Germany fifty years later—and now in the process of losing its main export markets as well, Denmark was forced to take stringent measures to keep afloat. It abandoned what remained of feudalism and changed to small-scale intensive farming, supported by cooperatives. With state help it introduced innumerable technological improvements and shifted from wheat and cattle to hogs, bacon, and butter. Before long it was one of the most efficient agrarian economies in the world.

Concurrent with the acquisition of freedom by the peasant was a stimulation of manufacture. The peasant needed consumer goods; factories sprang up to provide them. Large banks, newly established, converted savings into loans to finance a variety of businesses. Railroads meshed the country into a unified whole, further encouraging industry and trade. From 1860 to 1901 Copenhagen tripled its population; the percentage of people in the villages declined and that of urban areas rose dramatically. By giving the peasant the incentive of tenure, ownership, and freedom in decision-making, Denmark had spurred the process of capital formation and had established mechanized farming and a modern manufacturing industry.

Denmark, with only four to five million people, is of course a small country and was fortunate in that no foreign powers intervened to interrupt its social revolution—as was to be the case in Eastern Europe, Asia, Africa, and Latin America. Its conversion from feudalism to capitalism therefore was almost ideal, proceeding with little bloodshed and gaining for its citizens a great amount of social justice. Other nations were not so lucky.

III

Except for the tribal societies of sub-Saharan Africa and a few other areas, the whole world was ripe for a capitalist revolution during the nineteenth century. As a matter of fact there were eruptions in Asia, Africa, and Latin America, not a few of which achieved the first task of that revolution, national independence. Nineteen of the twenty Latin-American countries were able to break their bonds with Spain and Portugal; Greece, Egypt, and parts of North Africa severed ties with the Ottoman empire; the Hindus tumbled their Moghul rulers in India; the Poles rose repeatedly against their Russian masters. But except in Germany, Italy, Japan, and one or two other countries—toward the end of the century—the bourgeois revolution did not spread as it might have been expected to. The Concert of Europe, an alliance of reactionary monarchs guided by Prince Klemens von Metternich of Austria—Henry Kissinger's idol—effectively restrained the revolution for four decades after the Napoleonic wars. But Metternich's handiwork fell in disarray with the 1848 wave of rebellions, even though most were frustrated. Thereafter it was the very nations that had made their own bourgeois revolutions much earlier that became the main obstacles to similar revolutions elsewhere. Thus began the second phase of our cycle, the most important development—albeit of a negative nature—of the nineteenth century.

Imperialism—that is the name assigned to it by history—did not happen by philosophic intent or through subjective mischievousness but as a result of a seemingly inexorable law which proclaims that power seeks ever greater power.

The conflict between mercantile and nonmercantile countries was already long under way when the bourgeoisie became the ruling class of Holland, Britain, the United States, and France. The voyages of discovery by Spanish and Portuguese explorers which led Columbus to the Americas and Vasco da Gama around the Cape of Good Hope significantly enlarged international trade and set the great powers on the road to conquest. For a century Portugal held a monopoly of commerce with the Orient, until it was eventually challenged by others. Intoxicated by profits that ran as high as 5,000 to 6,000 percent per voyage, the English chartered the British East India Company in 1600; Holland, the Dutch East

India Company in 1602. The merchant companies, outfitted with arms and supplied with troops, then sought way stations from which to conduct their commerce—either by agreement with native rulers, by guile, by bribery, or by military force. Batavia became a Dutch settlement; Madras, Bombay, and Calcutta (after three little wars) English settlements; and so on. The poorly organized feudal regimes of Asia were forced to tolerate such incursions, though they were not happy with them, since most considered trade with the West either irrelevant or harmful. Indeed, China and Japan originally restricted international intercourse to one or two ports each. Inevitably, then, there were disputes, skirmishes, battles, invasions, small wars—especially where old empires, such as the Madjapahit empire in the East Indies or the Moghuls in India, were in the process of decline or where the existing forces were woefully weak, such as the American Indians or the sub-Saharan Africans.

The boom of capitalism intensified Western European efforts at penetration, especially in the wake of the industrial revolution, when the great powers found themselves in need of large amounts of cotton, coal, palm oil, jute, hemp, tin, rubber, and copper to stoke their new factories. It would be a gross simplification to say that they planned imperial conquest in advance, but it was an idea that grew with circumstance. At the beginning of the eighteenth century, for instance, the Moghul empire in India, following the death of Emperor Aurangzeb, began to fall apart. The Hindu opposition, however, was, in the words of Victor Harlow, a horde of freebooters who "carved out for themselves independent principalities and became a scourge on their suffering subjects. Everything was for sale, from the supreme control of a province to the private property of a wealthy neighbor." In this anarchy England faced the dilemma of rooting itself in India politically or losing its lucrative trade. "Gradually and reluctantly," writes Harlow, "it adopted the costly policy of political interference."[3] Hyderabad and Arcot were taken in wars against France. All of Bengal, on the east coast, was taken by Robert Clive in 1757 as a reprisal against the nineteen-year-old native nawab (governor) who attacked and temporarily seized Calcutta—where he imprisoned 146 men in the famous "black hole," eighteen feet long and fourteen feet wide. In due course, after innumerable wars against the Mahrattas from

1775 to 1843 and after the suppression of the Sepoy Mutiny of 1857, India was safely under British rule.

To maintain that rule—many thousands of miles from home and against a population many times larger than England itself—John Bull needed native allies. From what elements could they be recruited? Certainly not from the nationalists, who talked of a revolution which inevitably would expel foreigners. The only reliable friends the British could find here and elsewhere were the reactionary rajas, zamindars, pashas, sheikhs—landlords—who were willing to serve foreign powers if in the process they could save themselves from the wrath of their own subjects. Thus it was that a conjuncture of interests married capitalism to feudalism and tribalism. The foreign capitalist states gave arms and money to the ancient classes, to buttress them against their people; and though they encased the old order in a veneer of capitalism, they left its essentials inviolate.

Lord Canning, viceroy of India, observed in 1860 that if Britain "could keep up a number of Native States without political power, but as royal instruments, we should exist in India as long as our naval supremacy was maintained."[4] Some 562 princes were invested or reinvested with power, given arms, and permitted to live lavishly on taxes extorted from peasants and craftsmen. Some grew fabulously rich; the Nizam of Hyderabad, for example, amassed a fortune of four billion rupees. But they also became the instrument by which Britain enforced "law and order" and prevented revolt. "The situation of these feudatory states checkerboarding all India as they do," a British official said long afterward, is "a great safeguard. It is like establishing a vast network of friendly fortresses in a debatable territory. It would be difficult for a general rebellion against the British to sweep India because of this network of powerful loyal Native States."[5] By ruling part of the country themselves (also with the aid of princes and zamindars) and by relying on the old feudal class in the Native States, England forestalled and circumscribed nationalist rebellion.

The British, of course, fervidly endorsed free enterprise, nationalism, democracy—in the abstract—but there was just too much profit in aligning with native feudalism. Every year they drew from India many millions of pounds sterling from land taxes alone, which was then repatriated to England as capital for new industries. Even after such tragedies as the famine of 1770, in which

10 million of the 30 million people in Bengal perished, revenues continued to climb.

At the same time John Bull refitted the Indian economy to his own needs with the ruthless efficiency typical of rising empires. As were the thirteen American colonies, India was required to import finished goods from Britain only and was precluded from advancing its own manufacturing industries. From 1814 to 1844 Indian sale of cotton goods to England fell from 1,250,000 pieces to 63,000 pieces, whereas the English export of cotton goods *to* India zoomed from 1 million yards to 51 million. For centuries India had been an exporter of excellent quality fabrics; now she was importing one fourth of all British cotton exports. The native textile industry virtually collapsed, and what remained of it was forced to sell its wares at low prices dictated by Britain. The import of machinery was prohibited and the existing industries, such as shipbuilding, metalwork, glass, and paper, were either broken up or severely restricted. According to Jawaharlal Nehru, "the liquidation of the artisan class led to unemployment on a prodigious scale. . . . Their old occupations were no longer open to them, the way to new ones was barred. . . . India became progressively ruralized,"[6] so that the portion of its people in agriculture rose from half to three quarters and the portion in industry fell. Whatever its philosophical allegiance to democracy, Britain's prosperity at home depended on retaining feudal systems and tribal systems in its colonies. Understandably, then, wherever the occasion demanded it she suppressed incipient bourgeois revolutions with the utmost vigor.

It is this feature of imperialism, counterrevolution, which held back progress throughout the so-called backward areas for a century or more—and still does. We shall see the process at work in greater detail when we discuss China in the next chapter. Not only Britain but the other advanced states that had previously made their own national revolutions bent might and main to prevent national revolution from reaching fruition in Asia, Africa, and, in a unique way, Latin America. Occasionally, for short periods, they did support nationalists, solely to undermine *other empires*—the Ottoman, Manchu, Spanish; afterward they turned on their erstwhile allies and made common cause with feudalists and tribalists to establish their own dominance. In retrospect it was this aspect of the historical cycle—not the conflict of workers and capitalists

—that prepared the ground for the major social upheavals of the last six decades.

IV

In time the façade of the feudal and tribal world took on a capitalist appearance. Parliaments emerged almost everywhere, especially after World War II, but their members were either appointed by the ruling foreigners or chosen in hollow "elections" effectively controlled by the princes and pashas. The cities boasted modern sections, complete with skyscrapers, telephones, taxis, trolleys, banks, stock exchanges, and a few schools. There were oil wells, refineries, textile mills, all with the flavor of capitalism. Here and there, as with Turkey's statist economy, the state itself built factories, ran the railroads, and invested in new industry. But the whole thing was skin deep. Away from the big cities, the landlord, the moneylender, and the corrupt judge were still predominant. Half or more of the population was illiterate. Farm technology remained as primitive as it had been generations before. There were places in India, for instance, where the wooden stick was still used for plowing, and the peasant worked his land in strips without fertilizer or any other modern improvement. Instead of one peasant household producing enough surplus to feed one or two households in the city (or fifteen to twenty, as in the United States) it took three to five peasant households to provide enough surplus foodstuffs for one urban family. Whatever money income the peasant earned he used for salt, cloth, and similar rudimentary necessities. He did not save or invest, did not kindle the process of capital accumulation.

An early report of the United Nations emphasizes this central deficiency:

> Low national incomes in the Middle Eastern countries are aggravated by the marked inequalities which characterize their economic and social structures. The population consists largely of very small landholders or tenants whose income barely provides the necessities of life and *leaves little or no surplus for investment*. The same is generally true of the small but growing group of industrial workers. At the other end of the scale are large landowners, *who rarely invest in anything but*

land, and the important merchants, *who do not generally invest their capital in long-term projects.*[7]

The age-old problem of the feudal and tribal world remained: insufficient savings for conversion into capital, and an institutional structure, rooted in law and custom, that inhibited it in any case. To illustrate the point: A dozen years ago in the old section of Istanbul there used to be (perhaps there still is) a cobblestoned street where dozens of men operated primitive lathes to shape tree branches into furniture. Using a metal base the artisan placed the tree branch between two prongs, revolved it with a bow and string that he manipulated with his right hand, and cut into the wood with a chisel that he guided along the metal base with his naked left foot. The coordination of all these motions was a true art, and the finished table leg was as beautiful and symmetrical as one could wish for.

But why didn't this artisan buy a modern lathe? Why didn't he build a modern furniture factory or group together with eight or ten other artisans to form a capitalist corporation or a socialist cooperative? He certainly knew of power-driven lathe machines, for there were many of them in the state-owned factories. He also knew about corporate business structure. What held him back was the fact that there is no equality before the law in Turkey—or Iran or Thailand. To do business an entrepreneur needs permits, licenses, access to foreign exchange, and many other things for which he must secure the sanction of a government bureaucrat. But in the absence of democratic checks and balances, the only way he can get that sanction is through graft, bribery, or taking a government official in as a "partner."

The conventional explanation for backwardness in old feudal states such as Turkey or India was that they were too poor and their people too backward for modern economic development. Neither argument, however, is tenable. Many so-called backward nations had achieved a high degree of civilization when most of Europe was barbarian. They declined not because their people lacked talent but because of institutional weaknesses and wars. As for private wealth, there usually was plenty of it in the hands of merchants and feudal lords—plenty at least to begin the process of industrialization. Rajas in India owned scores, sometimes hundreds of *villages.* One raja I knew, by no means the richest one, earned $8 million a year before India became independent. When I asked him why he didn't invest his money in factories he said it was not compatible with his way of life and was too hazardous in any event. In his own villages he held the power; building a factory and marketing goods elsewhere depended on decisions made in Delhi where his influence was far weaker. It was too risky.

As for the men who traded at the bazaars or at the wharves, their profits too were astronomical, two to ten times what a Western capitalist would consider "fair." Thirty- to forty-percent profits were deemed "small," 100 percent "normal." When the daughter of an Asian merchant was married, the ceremony was as sumptuous as that of upper-class families in the West, often more so. The merchant held bank accounts in Zurich, Tangiers, Beirut—anywhere his money was safe. But he invested little if any of that money in industry at home. In a social climate where everything depended on family connections, bribery, and official corruption, it was far less hazardous to buy and sell goods, in quick turnover, than construct industrial plants where the turnover of money was slow and operations more complex. The merchant, with one eye cocked on authoritarian officials who might at whim demand a "partnership" or large bribe, preferred to keep his capital liquid and send his savings out of the country. Only a foreign capitalist who had the support of his home government's army, navy, and foreign office could risk such ventures.

V

The crime of imperialism was that it impeded orderly progress toward a bourgeois revolution in feudal and tribal countries, by stripping them of resources and potential investment capital and by binding them more firmly to old reactionary rulers. Thus in the third phase of our cycle, by the time old empires, such as the British and French, began to weaken and crumble, and the rebels of Asia, Africa, Eastern Europe, and Latin America were able to gain national liberation, they found that a capitalist way of life could no longer solve their problems.

If economically backward countries were to be modernized, they needed aggregates of capital many times greater than what the first capitalist states had required. The latter had been able to squeeze the necessary initial capital out of the hides of peasants through high taxes, foreclosures, and other means. But in our day, efficient agriculture calls for an input of capital so great that individual farming in underdeveloped countries is impractical. At the very least it must be bolstered by socialist institutions such as cooperatives for buying and selling, cooperative machine stations, cooperative credit banks. And in the opinion of many, agriculture in a backward economic milieu can flourish only under direct state operation of farms or through collectives or communes.

Consider the dimensions of the problem. In the United States, where land is plentiful but labor expensive, machinery substitutes for labor power. Of the 3.7 million farms in the United States in 1959, more than two thirds were 50 acres or larger, more than half were 100 acres or larger. The total investment in machinery and implements alone at that time was $18.4 billion. Each farmer, in other words, required $5,000 in capital for tractors, combines, trucks, balers, harvesters, corn pickers, milking machines. In other advanced countries, where there was an inadequate amount of land and the size of each holding was necessarily small, the emphasis was on *intensive* farming—farming that concentrated not so much on saving man-hours of labor but on assuring the greatest *yield per acre*. Japan has been the most successful practitioner of intensive farming and in recent years has increased yield 10 to 15 or more percent per year. But intensive farming requires large outlays of capital for irrigation, chemical fertilizers, seed, and various innovations, too.

The developing nations do not have the capital either for intensive or extensive farming of a modern nature. In 1952, five years after India became independent, its population was 363 million, its national income approximately $20 to $25 billion a year, and its per capita income, as recorded by the United Nations, $57. There were 424 million cultivable acres of land in the country, of which less than two thirds were actually cultivated. More than two thirds of the people lived on the land, but of these 35 percent were landless laborers, a similar percentage tenant farmers, and another 15 to 20 percent small farmers who owned only one to five acres per family. If the Nehru government had divided all the land it could seize from the rajas and zamindars it would hardly provide more than a couple of acres for each village family.

Assume, however, that Nehru had carried out such a land reform and 50 million families (250 million people) were endowed with small farms of their own. Where would the former tenant or landless laborer get the credit for seed, fertilizers, metal plows, animals? Under the old system the landlord and moneylender furnished credit. But if those two worthies were permitted to continue their depredations, all the land would soon be remortgaged to them. Moreover, there were billions needed for what the economists call infrastructure—dams, roads, wells, sewers, sanitation—not to mention schools and health clinics. India had no such sums at hand. Its total annual savings as a nation was perhaps $1 billion a year. Nehru decided to move slowly on land reform, therefore, until his factories could provide an adequate amount of bulldozers, rudimentary machinery, and fertilizers. China, on the other hand, faced with the same situation after 1949, decided on total land reform. It organized its villagers into collectives, later communes, and used muscle power, rather than bulldozers, to build dams and roads. In that way it was able to husband whatever meager capital resources it had at hand.

There is no question today which method was more apt. Whatever mistakes the Chinese may have committed, they have nonetheless made considerable progress. Indira Gandhi, before she became prime minister of India, told me that there was no question in her mind that the Chinese Revolution had done much more for its lower classes than the Indian Revolution—an estimate that was confirmed by American officials in Hong Kong, who were certainly no friends of China. From the Indian, Chinese, and other experiences, the conclusion is inescapable that no underdeveloped nation today can adopt a capitalist mode of farming, as in the United States or Japan, if it wants to erase centuries of backwardness. Socialist farming presents many difficulties, as we shall see, but it is the only feasible alternative to the past.

The same is true for the development of industry. A committee of United Nations experts estimated in the early 1950s that it would take $19 billion a year in new capital investments, for industry and agriculture, to raise the income of the underdeveloped world by 2 percent a year.[8] To increase the per-capita earnings of India, Pakistan, and Ceylon by one dollar a year would take almost $5.5 billion in new capital. In the early days of the industrial revolution in Britain or America a new job could be created with the investment of a few dollars or a few hundred at most. Today it takes a minimum of $2,500, in light industry such as textiles, and as much as $100,000 or more in heavy industry, such as steel or petroleum refining. Capital is in such short supply in the new nations that it must be used with the utmost judiciousness, if the unemployed are to be given jobs, if industry is to evolve in an orderly and coherent manner.

In the early days of capitalism the system could afford to wait for capital to find its way into the right places—say, the railroads, coal mines, or steel industries—on its own momentum, through the trial and error of competitive private enterprise. But in a nation as underdeveloped as China or Cuba or Tanzania or Bolivia, it would be suicide to permit this anarchistic process today. Such countries cannot allow capital to flow helter-skelter where it wishes to go—where the profit is highest or the private entrepreneur most aggressive. In a developing country only the state can effectively plan the formation and use of capital. Its resources are so small that it must make the choice, in each instance, whether to throw funds into a television plant or a fertilizer plant, an automobile factory or a farm implement factory, a luxury department store or a dam.

From whatever angle one looks at the problem, therefore, it is clear that the revolution in "backward" areas must proceed from feudalism and tribalism directly toward socialism, skipping the stage of capitalism—or, put differently, consolidating the tasks of the bourgeois revolution with those of the socialist revolution. It is this phenomenon, the twin burden, that accounts for the equivocal development of the revolutionary nations. Their problem, as we have already stated, is much more formidable than what the bourgeois states encountered when they were forging ahead. To expect them to move from the incredible poverty of the feudal and tribal orders to the affluence, say, of an America in one or two generations, is therefore either naïvely unrealistic or venal. Those countries must be judged not only by what they have already achieved but even more by the *direction* in which they are going, and they must be compared not to capitalist societies 200 or 300 years after the capitalist revolution but to capitalism at a comparable stage, say, in the seventeenth, eighteenth, and early nineteenth centuries. By such standards, they come out with remarkably good scorecards. The Chinese, for instance, are doing far better for their people than the British did for theirs during the seventeenth and early eighteenth centuries.

In any event, it is not possible to compare oranges with bananas, and even if it were, it would still leave out of account the most serious impediment to revolutionary development—namely, the role of the capitalist nations in trying to stifle it. China or India or Peru or Kenya have enough problems trying to condense two historical stages into one—without outside interference. But with foreign pressure insistently applied against them, the problems become multiplied many times over. The promise of revolution, already obscured by the fact that it must make a far bigger leap than expected, is obscured to the point of invisibility as a result of outside intervention.

Perhaps the best way to illustrate this fact is by reference to the long struggle of the Chinese people and the obstacles put in their way before, during, and after their 1949 victory.

CHAPTER THREE

The Syndrome of Intervention

I

The Chinese experience is not entirely typical of the great power intervention during the second part of the cycle discussed in the preceding chapter, in the sense that China was occupied not by a single nation but by many nations. It *is* typical, however, in revealing the syndrome that we call "inhibit-smash-warp"—*inhibit* the development of social revolution by joining with native reaction, *smash* the revolutionary uprisings when they do occur, and finally *warp* the revolution when it succeeds. China illustrates the persistence with which capitalist nations have tried to hold back revolutions similar to the ones they themselves made previously. It reveals as well not only how necessary revolution has been to the fulfillment of nations but how costly to them has been foreign intervention and counterrevolution.

At the start of the seventeenth century Britain, Japan, and China were all in various stages of feudalism, with China perhaps the most affluent of the three. In the middle of the century, around the time that Oliver Cromwell in England was leading Puritans against Cavaliers, the Manchus of northeast China overthrew the Ming dynasty that had ruled for 300 years and began their expansion from Manchuria and China proper into Mongolia, Tibet, Turkestan, Burma, Cochin-China, and Korea. By the end of the eighteenth century, they ruled the largest empire in Chinese history. It was certainly as imposing as that of the British, and vastly more so than that of the insular Japanese.

China, however, remained rigidly feudal, whereas Britain in 1642 and 1688 completed its bourgeois revolution and—at the end of the eighteenth century—was in the midst of industrial revolution. Social transformation opened the door to wealth and territory for the British; social stagnation caused the Chinese empire to rot away and become prone to intervention and division, as a dead body is prone to the nibbling of vultures. Indeed, postrevolutionary Britain was for a long time the leading vulture.

It is interesting how Britain played a Dr. Jekyll game at home, seeking to deepen bourgeois democracy, and a Mr. Hyde game overseas, seeking to subvert it. At first it wanted nothing more from China than the right to trade with it. Unfortunately, the Chinese monarchy was not interested. When an emissary of George III—the same King George against whom the American Revolution was fought—appeared before Emperor Ch'ien-lung in 1792 he was sternly advised that "The Celestial Empire possesses all things in prolific abundance; there is therefore no need to import the manufactures of outside barbarians."[1] Nonetheless the "outside barbarians" persevered and with the support of merchants in South China prevailed on the emperor finally to open one port, Canton, for British and other foreign trade. It was a decision the Manchus would soon regret. The British East India Company bought tea, silks, and cotton fineries from China, which it paid for initially with gold and silver and later with opium, brought in mostly from India.

The import into China of opium was illegal, but no one paid much attention to that technicality until 1839, when Peking dispatched a commissioner to enforce the law. This in itself might not have provoked the war that followed, but there were innumerable other grievances flowing from the fact that the emperor did not care to encourage foreign trade while the British did. In any case the Opium War of 1839-42 was a fiasco for China. Under the humiliating Treaty of Nanking the Manchus were forced to cede Hong Kong, open five ports for British commerce and residence, agree to low tariffs, and grant certain extraterritorial rights, such as the right of British citizens involved in crimes to be tried by their own consuls under British law, not by the Chinese under Chinese law. In the ensuing years the United States and France exacted similar concessions.

Military defeat, as happens so often in history, spurred internal revolution. In the backwash of the Opium War the Manchus were exposed to what the *Times* of London, a hundred years later, called "The World's Greatest Civil War,"[2] the Taiping Rebellion. From 1848 to 1864 the Taipings, led by a schoolteacher, Hung Hsiu-ch'uan, attacked in sixteen of the eighteen provinces of China proper and held Nanking for more than a decade. Influenced by Christian missionaries, they called Hung "the Heavenly Prince, younger brother of Jesus Christ," and in the spirit of "peace" promised land to the landless and made bonfires of the title deeds of landlords and the promissory notes of moneylenders. The effect on history, had the Taipings succeeded, would have been as significant for the East as the French Revolution had been for the West. But the British, Americans, and French, revolutionaries themselves not too long before, recognized the danger of a modern China to their imperial ambitions. In a wily game of divide-and-rule, the Westerners, led by Britain, at first aided the rebels. In 1856, with the dynasty severely weakened, a minor incident—the arrest of a Chinese crew on a British-registered ship—was used as the pretext for a new war against the Manchus; by 1858 the Manchus had again been subdued and forced to widen Western prerogatives as well as pay a hefty indemnity. Having exacted its pound of flesh, however, Britain now made a volte-face and assigned Major Charles George Gordon (abetted by American and French advisers) to suppress the Taipings. Major Gordon was equal to his task. A hundred thousand people were killed during three July days in 1864 when Nanking was recaptured for the dynasty. Hundreds of thousands more fled, as the city of 500,000 was literally reduced to 500. All told, the sixteen-year revolution cost millions of lives; by some estimates as much as 15 to 20 million.

Britain and its allies thus achieved a somewhat contradictory purpose; they suppressed a revolution against a feudal regime while simultaneously reducing the feudal regime to subservience. China was now headed for rapid and painful evisceration. Decade after decade thereafter, it lost control of its ports, its resources, its land, its judicial sovereignty. Russia annexed the area north of the Amur; France seized Indochina; Britain took Burma; Japan detached Korea and Formosa. In the heartland of China each of the great powers established spheres of influence, secured ninety-nine-year leases over strategic strips and land, and undermined the Chinese government until it could no longer call either its economy or its political system its own. The foreigners ensconced themselves in the big cities—with their own armies—and enjoyed extraterritorial rights that made them immune to the laws of the country in which they were living. Foreign manufactures, which came in at the ridiculously low tariff of 5 percent, effectively demolished the native handicraft industries. Foreign entrepreneurs, who were granted concessions for railroads, mines, and other businesses, gained a stranglehold over the economy. By 1900 Britain controlled 60 percent of China's external trade. The railroads, the major banks, the shipping companies, the mines, and the tobacco and cotton industries were for the most part in foreign hands; native capitalists generally played the role of compradors.

Thus, while feudalism made China an impotent giant, the Western powers kept it impotent. In 1900 there was another rebellion and another suppression. Militia bands of peasants—called Boxers by the Westerners—began killing outsiders and Christians under the slogan "protect the country, destroy the foreigner." The great powers intervened to quell these rebel forces; after a quick victory they imposed harsh conditions on China, as well as a $325 million indemnity. In the next decade foreign-controlled commerce doubled, and foreign products penetrated every hamlet.

By contrast with China, Japan during the same period was able to short-circuit outside intervention, with remarkable and beneficial results. Like China, feudal Japan had closed its doors to the West: only one port was open for foreign commerce, Nagasaki, and only Holland was permitted a restricted concession there. Then on July 8, 1853, Commodore Matthew C. Perry of the United States landed in Tokyo Bay with four ships, impressive-looking cannon, and 560 men. Lacking a navy or an industry capable of producing modern weapons, the Tokugawa shogunate could do little else in the next few years but sign treaties with the Americans, British, and others, granting them trade and additional privileges. For the land of Nippon it was a traumatic shock, so much so that it sparked a move to revamp the government. Japan was then under a dual form of rule, with an emperor who had little power and a shogun who was the actual administrative head. As the cry went up to "expel the barbarians," a young shogun named Keiki turned power back to the emperor in hopes of uniting the nation to prevent what happened in China. This event has become known in history as the Meiji Restoration (Meiji meaning "enlightened government"). Whether it was a revolution or not, in the accepted sense, it had immense revolutionary consequences.

The Meiji supporters, rallying around the slogan "honor the emperor, expel the barbarians," found that they had to adopt the barbarians' social system if they wanted to expel them. To produce cannon comparable to Commodore Perry's they needed an elaborate industrial machine which could not be developed under feudalism. Thus the young samurai around the emperor, whose own origins had been feudal, were forced to slash away at the feudal institutions until they had reconstructed their whole social order. They introduced land reform, mass education, a bicameral parliament, a civil service, a modern police, and a modern army. The government provided funds for railroads, telegraph, public utilities; constructed paper mills, cotton mills, and other factories which were then turned over to private enterprise; encouraged the silk industry; created a merchant marine; and gave loans to businessmen for almost every type of economic endeavor.

Unimpeded by foreign domination, the results were impressive. The Japanese economy did not rival that of America, Britain, or Germany until after World War II, but from 1895 to 1938 the Japanese rate of economic development was more rapid than that of other great nations in comparable periods. In those forty-four years its gross national product increased by an annual average of 6.5 percent, as against 2.5 percent for Britain (from 1812 to 1924), 1.8 percent for France (from 1812 to 1911), and 4.8 percent for the United States (1849 to 1929). Since World War II Japan's economic progress—despite defeat on the battlefield—has been even more spectacular. With a GNP exceeded only by that of the United States and the Soviet Union, its per-capita income in 1970 ($1,300) was ten times that of China. This achievement cannot be attributed to superiority of the Japanese character over the Chinese, but solely to the good fortune that Japan was able to transform its social system before the foreign capitalist states could slice it up and render it impotent—whereas China was unable to ward off the foreigners until 1949.

II

Every challenge, the sociologists tell us, evokes a response. In the last third of the nineteenth century the imperialists arrogantly divided the world among themselves, heedless of the wishes of the people involved; by the beginning of the twentieth century almost every feudal, semifeudal, and tribal country was either a colony or a sphere of influence belonging to a capitalist state. The inevitable response was the burgeoning of nationalism. Young people in many places formed groups, grouplets, and parties demanding national independence and the social reforms which had been denied them in large part because they were not independent.

In China native businessmen, students, peasants, and workers united in a nationalist movement that would eventually be known as the Kuomintang. Its leader, Dr. Sun Yat-sen, the son of a poor farmer, was graduated from medical school in Hong Kong in 1891 and soon thereafter turned his attention to revolution. Like the Italian nationalist Giuseppe Mazzini, he spent much of his time in exile in Europe, America, and Japan, proselytizing overseas Chinese for the movement and raising large sums to support it. There was no problem winning recruits, especially after the war between Japan and Russia (1904–5), in which two foreign nations fought over control of Manchuria and Korea, integral parts of China. From Hanoi, in 1907–9, Sun directed a half dozen uprisings against the Manchus, all of which proved abortive. But on October 10, 1911—celebrated thereafter by the Chinese as the Double Ten, the tenth day of the tenth month—the garrison at Wuchang mutinied, and revolt flared out of control through fourteen provinces. Sun returned from England three months later to become provisional president of a republic headquartered in Nanking. The Manchu dynasty passed into the limbo of history.

China at this point was in a state of confusion, much like Russia from March to November 1917, except that the period of confusion lasted not eight months but thirty-seven years. The left wing of the revolution was represented by Sun and the Kuomintang; the right wing by a consummate opportunist, Yuan Shih-kai, who at first tried to quell the uprising on behalf of the Manchus and then joined the revolution and replaced Dr. Sun as president. The foreign powers, though not always united, acted as they were soon to do in Russia and as the United States, a half century later, was to do in Vietnam; they either bought and subsidized puppets or, as in the case of Japan, overran choice territory with their armies. In April 1913 a consortium of British, French, Russian, German, and Japanese bankers gave Yuan a large loan, secured by a lien on China's revenues. Yuan repaid the favor by dissolving parliament and declaring the Kuomintang—its majority party—illegal.

Less than two years later, on January 18, 1915, Japan delivered a twenty-one-point ultimatum that shook China to its roots. Among other things the ultimatum demanded that China turn over to Japan former German concessions in Shantung, that Tokyo be given a monopoly of transport, natural resources, and capital investment in South Manchuria and Inner Mongolia, control over the province of Fukien, opposite Formosa, half ownership with the Chinese government in the largest iron mining and smelting company, and extension of the leases on Port Arthur, Dalny, and certain railways to ninety-nine years. Worse still, China was required to accept Japanese "advisers" for its army, police, schools, arsenals, and finance—in other words, permit Japan to run the government. Yuan secured a modification of the more onerous provisions, but it is interesting that the Western allies, then fighting a war to "save the world for democracy," raised no outcry against this wholesale brigandage. After a while the United States quietly recognized Japan's "special interests" in China, and at the Peace Conference of 1919 the Nipponese were permitted to hold most of their gains. By contrast, China's request for the removal of foreign troops, the abolition of spheres of influence, the turning over of foreign post offices, telegraph, and similar utilities to the Chinese government, and the cancellation of foreign concessions and settlement rights were all given short shrift.

In these circumstances the ancient state could not be glued together; a nationalist movement facing such towering odds was still too fragile to unite it. Yuan Shih-kai, a few months after the Japanese ultimatum, had declared himself emperor, but lacking popular appeal could not make the decree stick. One province after another seceded from the rule of the central government and fell under the sway of tuchuns—warlords—each of whom had his own army and his own alliances with this or that foreign power. The government in Peking was little more than a fiction. The only government that had long-term potential was the one in Canton, established by Sun and his Kuomintang. Even that one, however, was unable for the time being to unify the country against the combined power of the warlords and foreigners.

The inevitable result was further polarization—again, as in Russia in the eight intermediate months—with the revolution turning to the left, other elements to the right. After May 4, 1919, when the terms of the Versailles Treaty became known, tens of thousands of students took to the streets; millions more participated in an anti-Japanese boycott. The Peking government fell, only to be replaced by an equally spineless regime, equally pliable to foreign loans and blandishments. In this tenuous state of affairs, Sun Yat-sen sought outside help from the only place where it was available, Soviet Russia. He invited Bolshevik technicians and advisers to help him build a revolutionary army and a mass movement capable of solidifying the nation. Lenin was only too happy to oblige.

He sent Mikhail Borodin to advise the Kuomintang on civilian matters; Vassili Bluecher, later a marshal in the Soviet army, on military matters. An academy was established at Whampoa, where thirty Soviet instructors trained Sun's legions in the art of warfare; and Chinese Communists, who had formed their party in 1921, joined the Kuomintang as individuals to organize a mass base for nationalism. The Communists, advised by Borodin, enrolled millions into trade unions, peasant organizations, student groups. They created a propaganda machine which proved to be one of the revolution's most effective instruments. So close were Canton and Moscow that in 1926 the Kuomintang adhered to the Communist International as an "associate party," and Chiang Kai-shek, Sun's brother-in-law and successor, after Sun's death in March 1925, became an honorary member of the executive committee of the Comintern.

With aid from abroad, the Chinese revolution caught its second wind and in its second flurry came much closer to success than during the first. On May 30, 1925, a strike of textile workers who worked twelve hours a day, seven days a week, in a Japanese-owned mill, led to the famous Shanghai Incident in which British troops killed nine Chinese and wounded dozens more. In the strikes and demonstrations that followed, British forces killed eight Chinese in Hankow on June 11 and (along with French troops) slaughtered 52 and wounded 117 at Canton on June 23. The anti-British boycotts that followed—sponsored by the nationalist government at Canton—lasted fifteen months and almost put the British port of Hong Kong out of operation. With nationalist fervor sustained by Communist propaganda, Chiang Kai-shek's 100,000 troops moved northward against a million soldiers of the warlords to seize Hankow, Nanking, and Shanghai.

The Kuomintang was not a homogeneous force. It was, as Comintern theorists put it, a "bloc of four classes"—workers, peasants, petit bourgeoisie, and bourgeoisie—and it ranged in ideology from extreme left to extreme right. Chiang, son of a merchant, trained in a Tokyo military school, and for a time a small stockbroker, was the leader of the right. Early in the revolution, back in 1911, he had taken up with businessmen and bankers such as Yu Ya-ching and Chen Chi-mei, who bailed him out of penury and later made him rich. He was now their spokesman within the Kuomintang, less concerned about refashioning the social structure of China through land reform or the nationalization of industry than in achieving a national independence under which his native capitalist friends might prosper more easily. But national independence without social revolution proved to be a will-o'-the-wisp. Revolution was the only means of mobilizing the 80 or 90 percent of the population who were peasants and workers; without it Chiang could only fall back on the hated treaty powers for moral and material support and, in the process, become even more conservative, even more alienated from the bulk of the people.

Both Chiang and Chen Tu-hsiu, leader of the Communist Party, had been uneasy about the Kuomintang-Communist alliance. As early as March 1926, Chiang had taken the precaution of removing Communist political commissars from his army and disarming the Workers' Guard. Subsequently, as the revolution gained momentum, he forbade workers' strikes and sometimes sent troops against rebellious peasants, measures which of course were anathema to Chen. The Chinese Communist leader had agreed to the alliance grudgingly, only on orders from Moscow, and had sought on a number of occasions to break it. But Stalin, against the opposition of Leon Trotsky, had insisted that this was a "bourgeois revolution" and that therefore the Chinese Communists must accept Kuomintang conditions.

The denouement came as Chiang's troops prepared to take Shanghai. Inside the port city the treaty powers were holding excited consultations about whether to use force or seduce Chiang with material aid and recognition. The British had 9,000 troops on the scene, Japan and the United States sent in 1,500 soldiers apiece, and on the eve of the crisis Washington dispatched 5,000 more under the leadership of General Smedley Butler. Had Chiang failed, the great powers doubtless would have used the troops available to them—and more—for direct military intervention. The Kuomintang leader, however, was equal to his task.

On March 21, 1927, as Chiang's soldiers approached Shanghai, Communist-led proletarians organized by twenty-eight-year-old Chou En-lai declared a general strike, seized the police stations and arsenals, formed an armed detachment of 5,000 workers, and created a "Citizens' Government" which drove warlord Sun Chuan-fang from power. It was the largest working-class uprising in Asian history up to that time, and Chen Tu-hsiu was loath to surrender his bastion to Chiang. Again, however, Chen was over-ruled by the Kremlin, which ordered him to arrange for the workers to lay down their arms and submit. Three weeks later, on April 12, 1927, with the help of police from the French Concession, Chiang began a massacre of tens of thousands of Communists and militants.

Thus at the moment of its greatest triumph the "second revolution" was aborted. Trade unions were dissolved, the Communist Party liquidated. The leftist Hankow government, made up of Kuomintang leaders more friendly to the Communists, was so furious with Chiang it removed him as commander in chief, but he persevered in his repression, set up another government in Nanking, and proceeded to mop up the Communists—who in a rearguard action now adopted unrestrained revolutionary action. On November 7, tenth anniversary of the Russian Soviet victory, soviets were established in two villages near Canton, and a month later workers in Canton itself took political power, freed 3,400 political prisoners, and called a Workers', Peasants', and Soldiers' congress to proclaim "Soviet China." The event had some significance for Mao Tse-tung's future resistance, since it formalized a program to divide the big estates among landless peasants, to nationalize the major industries, and to abolish slavery and child labor. But for the moment it was a futile gesture. With the help of Japanese marines, Chiang's forces drowned the revolt in a sea of blood. As Hugh Seton-Watson observes, "the Kuomintang leaders had used Soviet support long enough to raise their nuisance value in the sight of the

Great Powers, and had then come to terms with the Great Powers at Moscow's expense."[3]

III

The Chinese revolution after 1927 split in two parts, each going in opposite directions. Chiang Kai-shek partly unified the country by taking Peking (renamed "Peiping"—"Northern Peace") in 1928 and by securing allegiance from the warlord in Manchuria. He established a government at Nanking, introduced a few minor reforms, and by 1937 pared down the number of foreign concession areas from thirty-three to thirteen. But as the spokesman for Shanghai bankers, who earned fabulous sums from rents paid by peasants in the hinterlands, and for the large landowners, Chiang was unwilling to free the peasants from usurious moneylenders or offer them the one great prize that most of the population hungered for—"land to the tiller." His regime moved steadily to the right. His bureaucrats grabbed for land and generally enriched themselves. Mikhail Borodin was not wrong when he said in the late summer 1927:

> From now on the imperialists will oppress China more than before. When the Kuomintang relied on the masses, the Chinese nationalists were top dogs; the workers of Hankow and Kiukiang took the foreign concessions back for China. Now that the Kuomintang suppress the masses, imperialist exactions will grow worse. The big business group of Shanghai cannot free China from foreign imperialists, for they are allied with them and profit by them.[4]

The native bourgeoisie, in other words, was totally incapable any longer of completing a bourgeois revolution.

The original impulse of the revolution by necessity, then, was carried forth by the Communists and the large numbers of Kuomintang intellectuals and army leaders who came to their side, convinced there was no other way for China to become independent. The tactics by which the Communists reached their objective in the ensuing two decades are too bewildering to sketch, as are the inner conflicts between Mao Tse-tung and Moscow or Mao Tse-tung and Li Li-san. But Communist strategy—whether it emphasized prime reliance on the proletariat, when Chen was the leader, or on the peasantry, when Mao became its spokesman—placed priority on mobilizing the desperate lower classes. Defense against the foreigner and defense against native reaction were both subsumed for Mao under the slogan "land to the tiller." By consolidating the great body of people—the tillers—for a revolutionary crusade, Mao tilted the scale for eventual victory. "Whoever wins the peasants," he told the American writer, Edgar Snow, "will win China. Whoever solves the land question will win the peasants."[5]

The "third" revolution was long, frustrating, and immensely costly in lives and resources—but it succeeded. Turning toward the villages in the spring of 1928, Mao and his chief supporter, Chu Teh, organized a "Soviet Border District" covering seven counties of Kiangsi and Hunan provinces. They confiscated land from landlords and distributed it to peasants; they built schools and hospitals. As of 1930 they had planted the Soviet seed in ten of China's provinces and had recruited a guerrilla army of 62,000 men—not a few of them deserters from the Kuomintang. On November 7, 1931, the fourteenth anniversary of the Russian Revolution, Mao proclaimed the Chinese Soviet Republic in a small market town called Juichin.

The details of the long struggle during the next seventeen years are too well known to be repeated here—the "annihilation" campaigns by Chiang Kai-shek, the famous 6,000-mile-long march to Yenan after the defeat in Kiangsi in 1934, the war with Japan, the postwar drive which brought victory in 1949. What is pertinent to this study is the role of the advanced nations in trying to prevent the revolution from reaching fruition. When they were not intervening directly, they were supporting whatever right wing they felt had a chance of survival—the Manchus against the Taipings, Yuan against Sun, the warlords against the Kuomintang, Chiang Kai-shek against an alliance of Communists and nationalists. The foreign powers did not always see eye to eye on how China should be exploited, but they were all agreed that it should serve *their* interests rather than its own.

At one pole was the United States, which was able in the Nine-Power Pact of 1922 finally to enforce an "open door" policy—equal trading and investment rights for all foreign states involved in China. The open door, however, was not an attempt to assure Chinese independence, as commonly believed, but to assure American predominance against its rivals. As Woodrow Wilson had pointed out long before, it was "not the open door to the rights of China, but the open door to the goods of America."[6] The liberal *Nation* magazine was eminently correct when it noted

> under the Open Door policy . . . we assume that we are giving all countries, and particularly Japan, an equal opportunity to do business in that market. But so vast are our natural resources and so highly developed is our system that the real advantages are all on our side. . . . The Open Door, paradoxically enough, stands in the way of [Japan's] expansion.[7]

At the other extreme was the Land of the Rising Sun, in a much less favorable situation than the United States. It had joined the industrial revolution late in history and was still woefully backward in many fields, especially heavy industry. As of 1929 its steel production was only 2.5 million tons annually; two thirds of its exports were in soft goods, textiles and silks. Its raw material situation was desperate: of the twenty-five raw materials experts considered essential for a modern economy, it had an adequate supply only in three. The worldwide depression of the 1930s, moreover, aggravated its problems. With the United States and its allies preoccupied with the economic slump, Japan decided this was a propitious time for territorial expansion. In September 1931 it seized the Chinese province of Manchuria and installed a puppet regime headed by Pu Yi, last of the Manchu emperors. Renamed Manchukuo, the 500,000-square-mile sphere of influence was one sixth the size of continental United States. Japan followed the Manchurian adventure with an attack on Shanghai in January 1932; it seized Jehol in 1933, Inner Mongolia and Northern China in 1935–36. Since tens of thousands of soldiers resisted its incursion, the Japanese tried to isolate them from the peasants by establishing "protected villages," surrounded by fences, ditches, and barbed wire—much as the United States was to do in Vietnam three decades later.

During these initial depredations Chiang Kai-shek tried to modernize China. He built roads and railroads, factories, airports, government buildings, and dikes. He also regained from the foreign powers the right to set tariffs—though the collection of customs still remained in outside hands. He unified the currency and promoted the so-called New Life movement based on the Confucian principles of "right relations": courtesy, honesty, service, honor. The nation gained a sense of pride as streets were cleaned, playgrounds built, sports activities encouraged. But none of this touched the common man at the bottom, who suffered from famines that sometimes affected as many as 57 million people (in 1929, for instance), or floods, or usury, or high rents charged by rural landlords. Professor Charles Hodges noted in May 1934 that

> big landlords are consolidating their position at the expense of the poor peasantry. . . . Through the connivance of corrupt military authorities, they acquire age-old state and community lands and entrench themselves at the expense of the poor and middle farmers. . . . An army of refugees, driven from home by banditry, civil war, flood, drought, famine, has become the visible sign of China's plight.[8]

Chiang Kai-shek himself admitted, in October 1930, that "We who staged the revolution have come to be regarded by the people as a privileged caste. They cherish toward us the same hate as formerly toward the Manchus." Every Kuomintang branch, he said, is "stigmatized for corruption, bribery, scrambling for power."[9] This was the lush harvest for those on the right wing of the revolution, who refused to proceed with its social objectives and who would rather spend 60 to 80 percent of the national budget on the military than on popular needs.

Supported now by Western loans and American planes, fliers, and advisers, Chiang placed higher priority on suppressing the "reds" than resisting the Japanese. His government in fact was ridden with pro-Japanese appeasers such as foreign minister Wang Ching-wei, and he himself was making all kinds of concessions to the Japanese such as granting them tariff benefits and permitting them to police northern territory. Toward the popular forces, however, Chiang's policies were inordinately tough, so much so that they sometimes backfired. In October 1935, for instance, Chiang dispatched an army to Sian under the Manchurian marshal Chang Hsueh-liang, to contain Mao Tse-tung. Unfortunately for Chiang this was at a time when anti-Japanese feeling was reaching a high pitch, and a National Salvation Union of students and others was conducting demonstrations everywhere against the foreign aggressors. General Chang's troops refused to carry out their assignment; indeed the general gave sanctuary to many Communists. For their part, the Communists were intelligent enough to capitalize on national sentiment; they had declared war on Japan after the first Shanghai incident and they called for a truce in the civil war to forge a joint resistance. But Chiang, still determined to exterminate Mao's soviets, arrested the National Salvation Union leaders and went to Sian on December 7, 1936, to buoy Chang's Tungpei army for another assault on the Communists. There he was "kidnapped" and held prisoner while the Tungpei generals forced him to discuss with Chou En-lai means of halting the civil war and conducting a joint campaign against Japan. Chiang remained obdurate for a while, until it became clear that he was in danger of being replaced by a pro-German government under Wang Ching-wei—who was then in Berlin negotiating with Hitler—and General Ho Ying-chin. Thereupon Chiang made the necessary promises to his captors, was released, and returned to Nanking to negotiate—in the ensuing months—the united front with Mao against the Japanese.

The agreement came none too soon, for on July 7, 1937, at the Marco Polo Bridge near Peking, the Japanese provoked another little incident, as pretext for initiating a full-scale war to subjugate all of China. With more than 150,000 troops, the bone-crushing Japanese machine steadily marched forward, adding Tientsin, Peking, Nanking, Hankow, Canton, and the richest and most heavily populated areas of China—except for Szechwan—to the vast territory already under Japan's control. It was a war that coalesced with World War II and ended only with Japan's surrender in 1945.

The united front proved to be a tenuous one, for while the Yenan regime agreed to subordinate itself to Chiang's leadership, it actually operated with relative independence and utilized entirely different tactics. Chiang, fearful of giving arms to small peasant groups lest they use them for land reform as well as resistance to Japan, engaged in stand-up battles typical of a traditional war-of-position. This not only favored the stronger Japanese but resulted in immense casualties, as many as 70,000 in a single battle. The Kuomintang was forced to retreat steadily until it fell back to Chungking, a site protected by the Yangtze gorges but lacking good rail or road communication.

On the other hand, the Maoists armed the peasants, recruited heavily from idealistic youth, and harried the Japanese through hundreds of effective guerrilla actions. Even such anti-Maoist writers as Harold Isaacs noted the considerable successes of the Eighth Route Army and praised Chu Teh as "one of the most remarkable military leaders in all history."[10] Military leaders with a cause, it became evident, were far more effective than those who fought merely for their own prerogatives. At war's end the Eighth Route Army had grown to 600,000 partisans, and another Maoist force, the New Fourth Army, to 300,000; simultaneously the Communist Party itself had grown from 40,000 members in 1937 to 1,200,000 in 1945. By that time the Maoists controlled one seventh of the Chinese territory and ruled 116 million people, one fourth of China's population. So alarmed was Chiang Kai-shek over the steady conversion of young nationalists to the Yenan cause that he used his best troops to surround the Soviet republic and failed to mount a single important offensive against the Japanese. He husbanded the vast supply of arms given him by the Americans for a future onslaught against the "reds." Chiang was reported to have said it was more important "that I have kept the Communists from spreading" than the Japanese. "The Japanese," he argued, "are a disease of the skin, the Communists are a disease of the heart."[11]

The rise and fall of Chiang Kai-shek ultimately proved that a nationalism lacking social revolutionary content was destined to be subservient to foreigners, impotent, and subject to corruption and defections. During World War II Wang Ching-wei and thousands of lesser Kuomintang figures deserted to the Japanese. When the civil war was openly renewed in 1945–49 the conservative nationalists disintegrated. Chiang had 4 million men at his disposal in August 1945, including thirty-nine supposedly "crack" divisions trained and supplied by Uncle Sam. He also had the largest air force any Asian nation, other than Japan, had ever seen. He controlled all the major cities and three quarters of the population. He received $3 billion in U.S. aid plus the weapons of a million disarmed Japanese soldiers, as well as titanic American help in transporting troops. Yet his regime tottered. From July 1946 to November 1947 Kuomintang armies lost almost 1.7 million men, two thirds of them made prisoners. Mountains of American guns fell into rebel hands. Chu Teh told a former *New York Times* man, Foster Hailey, "During the last few months of fighting we have annihilated thirty-five Nationalist brigades. In these operations we have seized much United States equipment. It is very good. We hope to get more of it."[12] After the Communists came to power, Western observers were amazed by the quantity of American weapons displayed. One can make a good case, it seems, that American supplies to Chiang helped the Communists more than Chiang.

Former Secretary of State Dean Acheson wrote:

> The broad picture is that after the war, Chiang Kai-shek emerged as the undisputed leader of the Chinese people. Only one faction, the Communists, up in the hills, ill-equipped, ragged, a very small military force, was determinedly opposed to his position. He had overwhelming military power, greater military power than any ruler had ever had in the entire history of China. He had tremendous economic and military support and backing from the United States. . . . No one says that vast armies moved out of the hills and defeated him. . . . What has happened in my judgment is that the almost inexhaustible patience of the Chinese people in their misery ended. They did not bother to overthrow this government. There was really nothing to overthrow. They simply ignored it throughout the country. . . . Added to the grossest incompetence ever experienced by any military command was this total lack of support both in the armies and in the country, and so the whole matter just simply disintegrated.[13]

IV

A hundred and ten years after the Opium War and a century after the Taiping Rebellion, the Chinese Revolution had finally established itself. By joining the national revolution with the socialist revolution it had effectively united the population against native reaction and foreign intervention. It was the most awesome victory for national liberation of this century. China, however, had suffered a staggering toll at the hands of imperialism. Its national income in 1949, according to the United Nations, was a mere $12 billion. Other experts claimed the figure was double that, but in any case it represented a pathetically low standard of living and development, both of which would have been immensely higher if the great powers had not inhibited and suppressed for so many decades China's revolutionary strivings.

Moreover, even after Mao's victory, the same nations, with America now as the vanguard, continued to array themselves against China. The fall of Chiang Kai-shek should have been the signal for rethinking relations with the ancient state and making amends for the many encroachments on its sovereignty. Instead it resulted simply in a change in the character of intervention. At the end of the civil war Chiang fled from the mainland, where more than 500 million people lived, to the island of Formosa, where only 9 million lived, and there established a government in exile which claimed to represent all of China. The United States concurred in this strange view and granted recognition to the Kuomintang government in Taiwan (Formosa) while denying it to Mao's regime in Peking. This was all the more startling since the wartime allies, Britain, the United States, and the Soviet Union, had agreed at the Cairo Conference that Formosa was to be returned to China, and in 1946 it had actually been recoupled with the mainland. Now Washington took the unique position that the small tail was in fact the big dog, that a separate Taiwan *was* China, and that for all practical purposes the most populous nation in the world did not exist.

Nonrecognition had unpleasant economic, political, and military consequences which undoubtedly slowed the pace of Chinese development by additional years, perhaps decades. An underdeveloped country seeking to modernize itself must, as we have underscored, build an infrastructure of roads, railroads, electricity, dams, sewers, and utilities, and it must educate its young people to assume the role of tomorrow's workers and engineers. All this requires considerable outlays of capital, far more, as we have shown, than was necessary when the United States or France was entering the industrial revolution. Moreover, though the infrastructure will lead to a much larger amount of producer and consumer goods in the long run, in the short run of five or ten years it brings no direct benefits. It is an investment in the future, not the present. It must wait for the factories to be built or the lands to be irrigated before it shows a harvest of more goods. An underdeveloped country, therefore, which can secure loans or gifts to build its infrastructure is far ahead of one which can't. China was not only denied credits and grants from the United States itself but from all U.S. allies, who had to agree to isolate the People's Republic on pain of losing their own aid from Uncle Sam. Except for some assistance from the Soviet Union for about a decade, until Sino-Soviet relations deteriorated, China had to rely on itself. After 1960 it was the only low-income country in the world that received no foreign aid from any source.

Another important pressure exerted against the Chinese Revolution was in the field of trade. The United States imposed an embargo on the sale of strategic goods to the People's Republic—and again forced U.S. allies to do the same. A developing country usually exchanges raw materials for foreign machinery. It cannot produce capital goods as cheaply as the developed nations can, and there is much, especially in sophisticated equipment, that it cannot produce at all. The Chinese found some ways around the American blockade, but it was a serious handicap nonetheless. That the Maoists were able to fabricate most of their own machinery and such complex weapons as nuclear bombs testifies to their ingeniousness. But the costs and sacrifices have doubtless been very heavy.

Beyond the embargo on trade and credits, the United States placed a military cordon sanitaire around China. During the Korean War, after General MacArthur had retaken Seoul on September 25, 1950, he proposed, along with an advance into North Korea, a naval blockade of the Chinese coast and bombing from the air of China's major industrial cities, supply depots, and other military centers. In addition, Chiang Kai-shek in Formosa was to be reinforced to take "diversionary action possibly leading to counterinvasion"[14] of China proper. The Joint Chiefs of Staff rejected MacArthur's plan as militarily unfeasible, and President Truman turned it down as politically impractical. But this did not prevent less extreme measures, such as the establishment and strengthening of 120 U.S. military bases around China, from the Philippines and Okinawa to Thailand. If the U.S. government did not undertake a preventative war, as extremists demanded, it nonetheless followed a course of severe containment. The argument was used that unless the Chinese could be stopped in Korea they would have to be stopped in San Francisco, a theme repeated with even greater regularity during the Indochina war, that if they were not stopped in Saigon they would move on Hawaii and Los Angeles.

To "stop" China, Washington interposed the U.S. 7th Fleet

between the mainland and Formosa, 130 miles away. It supplied Chiang with hundreds of millions in military aid and trained his troops for an eventual "return to the mainland." From Okinawa and Japan the American Strategic Air Command targeted nuclear bombs against China. The CIA, meanwhile, financed a contingent of 12,000 Kuomintang troops that in 1949 had fled to North Burma, from whose soil it conducted interminable raids against China until 1961. U-2s were sent over China for espionage, in clear violation of a host of international treaties. Toward the end of 1954 the United States and Taiwan signed a Treaty of Mutual Defense to guarantee the independence of Formosa and the Pescadores islands. In 1955, when two offshore islands, Quemoy (nine miles from the Chinese harbor of Amoy) and Matsu (about the same distance from Foochow) were in danger of being retaken by Peking, President Eisenhower let it be known that he would defend these two insignificant islands as part of the defense of Formosa. Three years later U.S. ships escorted Kuomintang ships to within three miles of the small islands, to break a blockade, and supplied Quemoy with howitzers. Chinese sources insisted that the 7th Fleet engaged in scores if not hundreds of forays against small Chinese craft in Chinese waters, a story which is not unbelievable in view of what the United States was later to do in Vietnam.

"The United States," summarized Chou En-lai in an interview with Felix Greene in 1960,

> has occupied China's territory, Taiwan, and set up many military bases and guided missile bases in regions close to China. It seeks in this way to form a military encirclement of China. The United States has carried out endless military provocations and war threats against China. Since September 1958, U.S. aircraft and warships have intruded into China's air space and territorial waters over a hundred times.[15]

In 1966 Anna Louise Strong claimed that China had sent four hundred "serious warnings" to the United States in the previous seven years for violations of China's air and waters. One can only imagine what would have happened if China had violated United States airspace and waterways even four times, let alone four hundred.

The effect, of course, was to force China to build and sustain a large military machine, complete with nuclear weapons, which diverted resources from the more important task of building the economy and improving living standards. Unable to overthrow the revolutionary regime by a frontal attack, the United States sought to undermine it by hundreds of acts of sabotage, small invasions, encirclement, and military and economic pressures. President Nixon's trip to Peking in 1972 may have signaled the end of such tactics, but by that time the damage wrought had been substantial. How much it affected the internal quarrels within the Communist movement and some of its economic setbacks we do not as yet know, but if the experience of the Soviet Union is any guide, it must have been considerable. It is clear, in any case, that imperialist intervention to inhibit, smash, and warp revolution has been not only fierce and persistent but a dominating factor in shaping the character of revolution even after the underclasses seize power.

CHAPTER FOUR

The Background of Stalinism

I

It would be wrong to assume that foreign intervention against revolution was the only drama being enacted during the century-long tumult of imperialism. History is never that schematic.

Overlapping the events in China, Asia generally, Africa, Latin America, and parts of Europe were three other developments of high significance. One was the completion of the bourgeois revolution in Britain, France, the United States, and elsewhere. Despite the political changes wrought by 1642, 1688, 1776, and 1789, the plight of people in capitalist countries remained miserable and such lower-class aspirations as the right to vote, the right to form unions, the right to an education, and similar prerogatives only partly fulfilled. It remained for Chartism and the emergence of a trade union movement to enlarge the democratic front in Britain; for the Democratic-Republican Clubs of Jefferson, the workingmen's parties, the loco-focos, Jacksonian democracy, and innumerable labor struggles to deepen capitalist democracy in the United States; and for the 1830 revolution, the 1848 revolution, the Paris Commune of 1871, and many incidental struggles by the lower classes to create the modern capitalist society in France.

A second drama was the extension of the bourgeois revolution

69

to certain parts of Europe, notably Italy and Germany, where it had not yet taken root. Napoleon's armies had shaken the old structure at the beginning of the nineteenth century, but Napoleon in due course had been defeated, and from 1815 to 1848, as already noted, Prince Metternich of Austria headed a Holy Alliance of reactionary states which tried both to undo national revolutions after they had occurred (for example in Latin America) and to prevent others from succeeding (for instance in Poland). Nonetheless the revolutionary spark could not be extinguished; it was fed by such patriots as Giuseppe Mazzini and by a host of men whom historians have called Romantic nationalists. Their agitation culminated in the wave of uprisings that spread in 1848 from France to Prussia, Austria, Hungary, Italy, and elsewhere. It was a complex revolution with different objectives in different places: constitutional government in Prussia, unification in Italy and Germany, relief from serfdom in many countries, freedom from Austrian rule in Hungary, in a few areas socialism. By and large the revolution failed, but it swept Metternich and his alliance from the scene, and in its backwash a decade or two later Germany and Italy were unified and transformed into capitalist states.

The third drama, concomitant with industrialism, was the intensification of the class struggle between workers and capitalists. The condition of laboring people during the nineteenth century seemed to justify the thesis of Marx and many others that a proletarian revolution was imminent. "What distinguishes the present from every other struggle in which the human race has been engaged," wrote America's leading radical, Frances (Fanny) Wright, in November 1830, "is that the present is evidently, openly and acknowledgedly a war of class and that this war is universal."[1] Two studies by Eugène Buret and Dr. Réné Villermé in 1840 on the poverty of the French and British working class showed that the average laborer worked twelve to sixteen hours a day, sometimes from 5 A.M. to 9 P.M., that he was allowed no holidays or vacation with pay, that he toiled under abysmal sanitary conditions, and that he seldom earned more than half of what was needed to keep body and soul together.[2]

A French tailor named Grignon wrote in his *Reflections on the Impoverishment of Working People in General* (1833) that

we work from fourteen to eighteen hours a day in positions so physically exhausting that our health is soon ruined and our limbs lose their suppleness and vigour, and become stiff until finally we are taken from the workshop to the hospital. How are we to find a few hours a day for our instruction? How are we to exercise our intelligence, enlighten our minds, or improve our morals?[3]

Indeed the health of the French working classes was so bad that in industrial areas four out of five conscripts for the army had to be rejected for poor physical condition. In one section of Lille, difficult as it is to believe, 20,700 of 21,000 children died before the age of five. Two thirds of the million Parisians in 1846 lived in inhuman hovels, and between 260,000 and 300,000 earned so little they had to depend on public and private charity to subsist. Circumstances in England and America were slightly better but not substantially so.

When workers sought to ameliorate their plight by forming trade unions, they were met with stark repression. Under English and American common law, unions were deemed to be conspiracies and on dozens of occasions were dissolved by the courts. In America literally hundreds of workers were killed by soldiers and constabularies in the miners' strike of 1875, the national railroad strikes of 1877 and 1894, the harvester strike in Chicago in 1886, the Homestead strike in Pennsylvania in 1892, the metal mining strikes in the Rockies, the needle trades walkouts, the Ludlow Massacre of 1914, and the great steel strike of 1919, and tens of thousands were either injured, jailed, incarcerated in bullpens, or deported from their homes.

There certainly was a class struggle, as Fanny Wright and Karl Marx had observed. And it was quite understandable why Marx and Engels should have predicted in the 1840s that the expected "bourgeois revolution" in Germany would be "the immediate prelude to a proletarian revolution"[4] or why, in a letter to Abraham Lincoln congratulating him on his reelection, Marx should have made a similar evaluation relative to the United States. "As the American War of Independence," he wrote, "initiated a new era of ascendancy for the middle class, so the American Anti-slavery War will do for the working class." Yet none of this came to pass. After each depression, capitalist nations enjoyed new bursts of economic energy and attained higher peaks of affluence. Working-

72

class problems, though far from solved, were sufficiently ameliorated to take the steam out of revolutionary agitation. Strikes remained militant and bitter but with few exceptions seldom came
close to a general uprising. Under certain circumstances, perhaps,
the Pullman strike of 1894 in the United States or the general
strike of 1926 in Britain might have flared into political revolt;
and strikes in Germany, Austria, and elsewhere after World War I
did have revolutionary potential. But by and large capitalist countries were far more stable than colonial and underdeveloped ones.
Oddly enough, the United States, which was the most stable, was
wracked by more strikes per year and more violence than any other
country—often more than all the others combined. But in the six
decades from 1875 to 1938, the years of the fiercest "labor wars,"
its class struggles were not a prelude to revolution as much as a
partial humanization of capitalism.

Thus the outstanding feature—the central thrust—of the present
historical cycle has not been the class struggle within the advanced
nations, important as that has been, but the conflict between imperialism and the people of less-developed states. It is this conflict,
more than any other, which has shaped the politics of the last century. Initially imperialism was impregnable. With Britain as the
stabilizing agency of a world order called Pax Britannica, the great
powers easily suppressed the aspirations of hundreds of millions
of people for national independence and social viability. Aligning
themselves with feudal and tribal reaction, the imperialist states
either inhibited revolutions that were already on history's agenda
(as in Asia), prevented them from maturing where conditions
were not yet ripe (as in Black Africa), or kept them in limbo unable to restructure their institutions after gaining national independence (as in Latin America).

In time, however, worldwide capitalism was wracked with a
series of crises—world war, depression—that enervated it and
gave the masses of "backward" nations their opportunity to settle
accounts. The third phase of the cycle we have outlined began with
uprisings in Mexico and China (1910 and 1911), neither of which
reached fruition immediately, and the revolution in Russia (1917),
which finally reversed the trend. Henceforth international capitalism and the international revolution were to be locked in a see-
saw battle, with the former forced to give ground, the latter taking
it. The Great Depression and World War II were the background

for the most extensive social upheaval in all history, embroiling more than two billion people in six dozen countries. It is still a difficult revolution to sort out, because in many countries, after national independence was wrested from the foreigners, it stopped short of *social* transformation. The foreign powers, in other words, were able to halt its momentum, hold it in suspended animation. Elsewhere, however, notably in the Communist countries, the revolution has moved more rapidly and much farther. Regardless, what is significant is the fueling of a new worldwide conflict between social systems in which capitalism, once rampantly on the offensive, is now in retreat. Its area of control has shrunk and continues to shrink, despite an episodic victory here and there for Pax Americana; and its hold, even over countries clearly under its domination, is loosening. The contenders this time are better matched.

Yet even in retreat, capitalism continues to practice the art of intervention. It has not been able to prevent millions of nationalists and socialists from coming to power, but it has slowed the tempo of progress in the new nations and has been a major factor in shaping the character of their leadership. This new form of intervention is universally downplayed by critics of socialism, who picture the United States, Britain, France, Japan, et al. as innocent bystanders with no desire or inclination to hinder the Russian, Chinese, Cuban, Mexican, Congolese, Kenyan, Indian, Indonesian, Vietnamese, or other revolutions. The inability of such peoples to attain comparable living standards to those of the West is due, according to the critics, to their own failings; the emergence of corrupt or inept regimes, they say, is simply a byproduct of the inherent totalitarianism of socialism or the inherent immaturity of native peoples, not foreign intervention.

The truth is, nonetheless, that every single country-in-revolution is and has been seriously affected by subtle—sometimes not so subtle—capitalist pressures from the outside. If the Ivory Coast, though independent, is ruled by an entrenched conservative, it is in no small measure because France continues to fish in its troubled waters. If Bolivia has fallen under rightist dictatorship, it is because the American Central Intelligence Agency has undermined the leftist regimes that preceded the dictatorship. And if Malaya is governed by an unpopular ministry, it is because the British were able to set on its heels the guerrilla movement that fought it for so many years. The one country most affected by outside pressures, and most severely modified by them, has been the nation that engineered the first successful revolution and was so long isolated from potential allies, the Soviet Union. It is here, I think, we can gain the clearest insight into the role of foreign intervention during the third phase of the historical cycle we have been discussing.

II

As noted earlier, the most difficult problem the Left has to overcome in winning a hearing for socialism, even today, is the memory of Stalinism. There is just no way to justify the murders, ordered by Joseph Stalin, of most of the leaders of the Russian Revolution as well as hundreds of thousands—perhaps millions—of others. According to the Soviet author Roy A. Medvedev, "the NKVD arrested and killed, within two years [in the 1930s], more Communists than had been lost in all the years of the underground struggle, the three revolutions and the Civil War."[5] There is also no way to justify the forced labor camps in which so many people worked under killing conditions, or the frame-up trials of the 1930s, or the totalitarian features of Stalin's regime. In all history there is no parallel to these crimes committed by a proclaimed revolutionary against his revolutionary associates.

The present Soviet leadership, beginning with the late Nikita Khrushchev in 1956, has admitted—what it denied previously—that the murders, tortures, and slave labor did in fact occur. Its explanation that they were due to a "cult of personality" is shabby, however, for it does not explain how and why a single man could gain so much power *under a socialist system* and hold the fate of so many people in his hands. The capitalist explanation of Stalinism —namely, that it inheres in the system, that once you eliminate the free market, private enterprise, and competition, totalitarianism is inevitable—is equally weak. There is ample evidence that the socialist revolution could have gone in directions other than Stalinism and that in fact it has done so in Yugoslavia, Cuba, and China.

A brief review of Russian history proves, as I see it, that, while Stalinism had many internal causes, external pressures played an equal or greater role. In other words, had the great powers been neutral or benevolent, the Soviets would still have had difficulties, but not of such a nature as to sire Stalinism; almost certainly, a more relaxed and tolerant Soviet leadership, perhaps under Bukharin, Trotsky, or Zinoviev, would have guided the nation on a less stormy course.

That foreigners decisively affected the fate of Russia has been evident at least since the turn of the century. Russia was neither an occupied colony like India nor a multiply shared sphere of influence like China. But it was a backward country, in which 80 percent of the population lived from agriculture and in which the industrial revolution came a century late, under the aegis of foreign capitalists. Serfdom had been abolished in 1861 after the Czar was defeated in the Crimean War and after peasant revolts became ominous. The peasant secured a measure of personal freedom, in that he was no longer the property of his lord to be bought and sold with the villages, but in most respects his 1861 victory was pyrrhic. He was required to pay a redemption fee for his "emancipation" and to pay rent in money and kind—up to half the harvest—to his old master. In addition he often worked on the landlord's holdings a specified number of days, without wages, and was subject to fines and floggings for any breach in his duties. At least a third of the peasants did not even own a horse; from year to year ever more became landless. The city dweller, if he worked in a factory, was treated no better. Wages for the majority of proletarians in the 1880s and 1890s were $4 a month. Large numbers lived in company barracks, sometimes housing as many as ten or twelve people in relatively small quarters. Strikes were ruthlessly smashed, their leaders almost invariably jailed or exiled. All in all the Czarist regime was a self-proclaimed autocracy, one of the most tyrannical of existing governments.

Onto this semifeudal hulk was grafted, toward the end of the century, a modern factory, railway, and mining system which gave employment to almost three million proletarians but was essentially foreign-owned. By the time World War I broke out, the great powers had a stake of 2 billion gold rubles ($1 billion) in Russian industry, the largest share accruing to France (648 million rubles), followed by Britain (500 million), Germany (317 million), and Belgium (311 million). Foreign capital dominated 60 percent of the sizable petroleum industry, 70 percent of coal mining, 67 percent of cotton textiles, 90 percent of copper and manganese, and 32 percent of the railways. In addition the Russian government was indebted to foreign banks to the tune of $2.5 billion, a very large sum at the time. "We can say without exaggeration," Leon Trotsky wrote, "that the controlling shares of stock in the Russian banks, plants and factories were to be found abroad."[6]

It cannot be said that Czar Nicholas was a puppet of the Western powers, for he ruled a great empire. But he was strongly attuned to their wishes, and they reciprocated with a solicitude which was in marked contrast to the hostility they would show the Soviet regime after 1917. On more than one occasion they bailed him out of difficulty—in particular, during the 1905–7 revolution which shook the monarchy to its roots.

In mid-January 1905, on the heels of Russian military defeats at the hands of Japan, a strike broke out at the largest plant in St. Petersburg, the Putilov Works. Six days later, on January 22, 1905, some 200,000 laboring men, women, and children marched behind a priest who had been active in union affairs, Father Gapon, to present a petition to the Czar. In humble terms they beseeched their monarch to grant an eight-hour day, free speech, press, and association, and a Constituent Assembly. They never got to see the Czar. His reply was a volley of gunfire on an unarmed crowd, in which somewhere between 500 and 1,500 people were killed and 3,000 wounded. For the next two years Russia was a bedlam of strikes, general strikes, small peasant revolts, a mutiny in the navy, and a short-lived soviet (council) of workers' delegates. The Czar made minor concessions to the rebels, pledging for instance elections for a Duma, whose powers would be limited to consultation. Alternately, however, he crushed the strikes, arrested Soviet and leftist leaders, including Trotsky and Lenin, and encouraged Black Hundred mobs to commit pogroms against Jews. By the end of 1905, the Czar and his entourage seemed to have matters under control. They had forcibly dissolved the St. Petersburg Soviet and successfully quelled an uprising in Moscow. The resistance, however, did not abate; the revolution gathered a second wind. At this critical junction, in the spring of 1906, the Western powers came through with a loan of $450 million, half of it from France, the largest international loan ever made up to that time. "It was enough," writes historian D. F. Fleming, "to finance the suppression of the revolution and to make the government independent of the new Duma before it could meet."[7] Fortified by the loan, the

Czar reneged on promises of civil liberties and changed the election laws so as to eviscerate the Duma and render it useless. The "great democracies" had saved autocracy.

Eleven years later they tried again to save it, but this time to no avail. The Czar had been in trouble even before World War I broke out. Fully a million workers engaged in strikes during 1914, climaxing their efforts in July—coincident with a visit by French prime minister Raymond Poincaré to St. Petersburg—by erecting barricades and challenging the authorities in street battles. A more prudent monarch would have taken this as a signal to stay out of the fray. But Nicholas was bewitched by secret Allied promises to incorporate into his empire Constantinople, the Dardanelles, Galicia, and parts of Prussian Poland. He soon found to his dismay, however, that fighting a modern war with an antiquated social system behind him was an exercise in futility. Though 15 million men were mobilized for the armed forces—the largest army ever assembled up to that time—supplies were so inadequate that troops sometimes went into battle with one rifle for three men. A fourth of the army, 3.8 million soldiers, was lost through death, injury, or capture in the first ten months alone. In three years—despite a few successes against Austria—the musclebound and incompetently led Czarist military suffered almost 10 million casualties, not to mention 2 million desertions. In addition, on the home front the economy was in utter chaos—railroads operating sporadically, shortage of bread and almost everything else, a 400 percent inflation of the ruble in just two years. The Allies tried to bolster the Czar with loans of $4 billion, but it was like applying a tourniquet to a dead limb. Russia was a society without checks and balances, without democratic prerogative, without *countervailing* power, and when it began to crumble its class struggle revealed itself naked and unmitigated, in classic Marxist form. There was nothing in the middle to hold it together; it could either pass from one rightist dictatorship to another or succumb to social revolution.

On March 8, 1917, women waiting in long queues for bread besieged the St. Petersburg bakeshops. Next day police fired on them, and in retaliation workers declared a general strike in factories and schools. When the local garrison refused to shoot at demonstrators and instead deserted to the people, the second Russian Revolution was virtually over. The demise of Czarism was accomplished with a few telephone calls. The Czar abdicated, a provisional government was formed based on the official Duma, and parallel to it a dual power emerged around the Soviet of Workers and Soldiers' Deputies.

This was one of those grand moments in history, like 1776 in America or 1789 in France, when leaders and nations must decide which fork of the road serves their purpose. Lenin and his Bolsheviks debated an ideological problem: their previous theory held that in a backward country such as Russia the subject on the agenda was a bourgeois revolution on the model of France, 1789. Yet in 1905 the capitalists had not only been unwilling to make a revolution but had joined with the autocracy against the people. Lenin had concluded from this that the working class would have to lead Russia in that bourgeois revolution and then wait for some time, short or long, to carry out its own, proletarian, revolution. Whatever the symmetry of this strategy, it was unwieldy, a point already noted by Trotsky in 1909. The flexible Lenin, noting the emergence of Soviets everywhere in 1917, jettisoned the old strategy in favor of compressing the two revolutions into one, under the slogan "All power to the Soviets." It was this decision, made against the advice of many Bolshevik leaders, which propelled the Leninists to power.

For the Allies, the problem posed by events in March was not ideological but practical: if Russia were to be consumed by revolution, who would hold the eastern front against Germany? How could the Russian people transform their institutions and fight a war at the same time? And just as the practical issues of trade and access to raw materials had lit the fuse of imperialism a long time before, so the mundane issue of conducting a war sparked the hostile intervention against Bolshevism. To galvanize the people around his party, Lenin had put forth the slogan "peace, bread, land." It conformed precisely to the wishes of Russian citizens, but to the Allies it was treason—land reform because it could not be undertaken during hostilities without disrupting the war effort, and peace because it meant that Germany could withdraw troops from the eastern front to fight on the western front, where the war was not going too well anyway. All types of delegations were dispatched from the West to encourage Russia to honor the Czar's promises, including one from America, among whose members were James Duncan, vice-president of the American Federation of Labor, and Charles Edward Russell, a prominent pro-war socialist. For a few fleeting months misgivings in London and

Paris melted away, as Alexander Kerensky, a "socialist of sorts" who headed the provisional regime, declared his intention to continue the war. In June, Kerensky ordered a military offensive, which unfortunately turned into a rout, a fiasco that ended within a few days. It confirmed for the tired but desperate Russian people that the only road to peace was through Bolshevism. On November 7 they helped the Bolsheviks seize power in St. Petersburg, with virtually no bloodshed, and ten days later in Moscow, though not quite so nonviolently.

For the Allies what had been an irritant now became a terrifying menace. They had closed their eyes to Czarist tyranny and had applauded the Kerensky regime, even though it was at odds with its people on the substantive issues of peace, bread, land. But it was no longer a matter of saving a military front; with the entry of America into the war the tide shifted toward victory in any case. It was now a matter of saving the capitalist system itself, its colonies, its spheres of influence, its power at home.

"The whole of Europe," wrote David Lloyd George in a memorandum to the Peace Conference, March 1919,

> is filled with a spirit of revolution. . . . If Germany goes over to the Spartacists it is inevitable that she would throw in her lot with the Russian Bolshevists. Once that happens all Eastern Europe will be swept into the orbit of the Bolshevik revolution. . . . Bolshevik imperialism [sic] does not merely menace the states on Russia's borders. It threatens the whole of Asia and is as near to America as it is to France. It is idle to think that the Peace Conference can separate, however sound a peace it may have arranged with Germany, if it leaves Russia as it is today.[8]

A distraught Winston Churchill wrote sometime later that "we may well be within measurable distance of universal collapse and anarchy throughout Europe and Asia."[9] His prescription for the Bolshevik regime was that "the baby must be strangled in its crib." Throughout the West there was traumatic fear in establishment circles that the contagion of revolution would spread to Germany, Austria, Bulgaria, Hungary, Finland, and the colonies in Asia and Africa. Four years of war for the preservation (or winning) of empire would end in vacuous victory if capitalism were uprooted in half of Europe and the colonies set free elsewhere. It was necessary to crush, or at least isolate, the Russian Revolution if capitalism itself were to survive.

Only a few hundred people had been killed in the November uprising, mostly in Moscow. In the first seven or eight months thereafter there was opposition from Kerensky, the cossacks, and the White Guards, but it was containable; so too the sabotage, small uprisings, and assassinations later committed by the Left Social Revolutionaries (including the attempt on Lenin which left him seriously wounded). These were storms the Soviets could have weathered. "Had this trend [of minimal violence] continued," writes D. F. Fleming, "the revolution in Russia might have taken a far milder course than it did."[10] But the revolution which changed the history of the twentieth century was not permitted to continue on its own momentum; it was attacked on all sides by an alliance of reaction that severely modified its course.

III

There is no question that the Allies could have had peace with the Soviet Union in 1917-21. There was certainly no military threat emanating from Moscow; even if the Kremlin had wanted to—and it obviously didn't—it was in no position to invade Europe. Lenin and Trotsky, moreover, took a surprisingly moderate position both toward the great powers and, at first, toward opponents at home. They were aware of their weakness, their isolated position, their need to win over some of their enemies or at least neutralize them. They saw their revolution, in one respect, as a holding operation—until it could spread elsewhere, particularly to Germany, from whom the Soviets might expect the loan of capital and know-how to spur its development. "We have always and repeatedly told the workers," Lenin was to write a few years later, "that . . . the basic condition of our victory lies in the spread of the revolution at least to several of the more advanced countries."[11] The mood of Bolshevism, therefore, was by necessity and disposition one of conciliation.

By way of example: Only a few days after the Communists came to power they had to deal with an assault by General Krasnov and his cossacks, who, in an effort to restore Kerensky, attacked at the gates of Petrograd. With the help of old Czarist officers, such as colonels Muraviev and Valden, Trotsky was able to assemble a defensive force and defeat Krasnov. The general was taken prisoner, but instead of having him shot or imprisoned the Bolsheviks released him on parole after a promise he would not sin again—a promise he soon broke by organizing a new resistance. Similarly, the Leninists took a moderate attitude to the Mensheviks and Social Revolutionaries who had opposed their revolution, inviting them to return to the Congress of Soviets and take their seats on its central executive committee. Overtures were made as well to bourgeois elements to help in the management of the banks and industries. In this first period the Bolsheviks proceeded cautiously even with their program of nationalization. They confiscated the lands of the church, the nobility, and the landlords and distributed them to the tillers, but they did not form the peasants into collectives or operate the farms themselves. They were content for the moment to tolerate individual proprietorship. It was not until May 1918 that any industries were nationalized—petroleum, sugar, tobacco, matches, spices, tea, coffee. But even then, in the opinion of *New York Times* man Walter Duranty, these "were acts of self-protection, adopted unwillingly or at least prematurely, to prevent 'sabotage' from stopping the wheels of industry and trade."[12]

Neither native reaction nor the foreign powers, however, could be assuaged. Scarcely a month after the November uprisings, White Guards, commanded by four rightist generals, launched a drive against the government with the avowed purpose either of reinvesting the Czar or, if that proved impossible, establishing a military dictatorship of their own. Simultaneously in Paris Marshal Ferdinand Foch, supreme commander of the entente, proposed direct Allied intervention to seize the Trans-Siberian Railroad and reform the eastern military front. The plan was temporarily shelved because of hesitancy in London and Washington. But this did not prevent the French and British from granting large-scale military aid to the anti-Bolshevik factions. In fact they divided the duties; by a secret agreement arrived at in mid-December 1917, France pledged to finance counterrevolution in the Ukraine and Britain in the Caucasus.

Thus the Soviet regime from its very inception was always in a precarious state. Its economy was all but shattered. It was under attack from rightists within the country who were abetted by forces outside, and it was finding it difficult to extricate itself from the war. On the day it took power the Soviet government proposed to all belligerents that they declare an armistice and enter into a democratic peace agreement, with no annexations and no indemnities. Not even Wilson, however, was ready to accept so ideal a solution, even though it appeared to mesh with his famous Fourteen Points for peace. On March 3, 1918, therefore, after temporizing for some time, the Bolsheviks were forced to sign a humiliating treaty at Brest-Litovsk which gave Germany Russian territories containing 62 million inhabitants, one third of the major crop areas, and half Russia's industrial resources. In May the internal attack on the regime was stepped up as 50,000 Czech deserters, in the process of being repatriated through Vladivostok, seized a large part of the Ural region, almost all of the Trans-Siberian railway and—encouraged, as Frederick L. Schuman points out, by "British, French and American agents"[13]—installed two anti-Soviet governments in Siberia. The British, having reversed themselves on the subject of direct intervention, landed troops in Murmansk and Archangel, while French, Japanese, and American forces disembarked at Vladivostok, heading for the interior of Siberia. Before it was over there were fourteen foreign armies on Russian soil—according to a French foreign minister, Stéphen Pichon, 850,000 troops in South Russia alone—and hundreds of thousands of White Guards trying to push the Red Army into a tightening circle bounded by Petrograd and Moscow. A million and a half Red forces were fighting off enemies along fronts stretching thousands of miles.

Originally the Allied justification for intervention was to reestablish a military front in the east. There could be no such pretense after the war ended on November 11, 1918. It was now simply a matter of overturning a government, in a sovereign country, which they could not abide. The Allies were never in a position to loose a full-scale assault, because they themselves were exhausted after so many years of hostilities and because some of their troops showed a disturbing tendency to mutiny—the French, for instance. But their participation was not insignificant, and their help to the rightists was prodigious. A week after the armistice in Europe, Admiral Kolchak took charge of the rump government in Omsk, Siberia, declared himself ruler of all Russia, and sent his armies on the long trek toward Moscow. If his army was shattered (and he himself later captured and shot) it was not for lack of weaponry and money. The British sent him seventy-nine shiploads of maté-riel, enough to equip 100,000 men. "We have given real proof of our sympathy for the men of Russia who have helped the Allied cause," Lloyd George told the House of Commons, "by sending them one hundred million sterling [$500 million] worth of material and support in every form."[14] Simultaneous with the Kolchak drive, General Denikin, mobilizing forces from southwest Russia, moved to within two hundred miles of Moscow, and General Yudenich, beginning in Estonia, advanced to within ten miles of Petrograd. Both, like Kolchak, were sumptuously supplied with tanks, artillery, rifles, and instructors by the French and British. According to Churchill, Britain gave Denikin alone "A quarter of a million rifles, two hundred guns, thirty tanks, and large masses of munitions and equipment" supplemented by "several hundred British officers and non-commissioned officers, as advisers, instructors, store-keepers, and even a few aviators."[15] That none of this largesse was given without economic consideration is clear from the agreements signed between the French and White Guard leaders, whereby France was assigned the management of railways in the Ukraine and Crimea, and by similar agreements which gave Britain future control of the oil facilities in their particular zone of occupation.

The Soviet Union was the Western world's first Vietnam—and like Vietnam it caused suffering on an unbelievable scale. Indeed the Russian travail was greater, for there was as yet no Soviet Union or China to resupply the Red Army or provide food for civilians. Moreover, Russia was already exhausted before the civil war began—it was, as Duranty observed, "a wilderness of disorder, disease, and hunger."[16] Intervention made matters much worse. The bread ration in the big cities in 1918 was one eighth of a pound per person every two days, and it was often skipped. By late 1920 and early 1921, the situation was catastrophic. Millions had died from hunger and typhus, many thousands on the battlefield. Not less than a million, for instance, perished from disease and other causes during Kolchak's retreat across Siberia. The grain harvest of 1920-21 was only 40 percent of prewar levels; industry was operating at only 15 percent of "normal." Pig iron and steel production was less than a twentieth and coal less than a tenth of what they had been in peacetime. The situation in transport, where three fourths of the locomotives and two thirds of the freight cars were out of commission, was so woeful that the Soviets could dispatch a mere 300,000 men to the Polish front, though they had 5 million available. Foreign trade was so immobilized that in the first year of its renewal, 1921, the Soviets imported $104 million of goods (as against $750 million to $1 billion prewar) and exported an insignificant $10 million. George F. Kennan comments:

> What six and a half years of foreign war, revolution, civil war, and foreign intervention had done to Russia is something most of us here, happily for us, are probably incapable of imagining. One of those situations had been achieved . . . where civilization seemed largely to have broken down . . . where people took on the qualities of wolves, and man often became the enemy of man in the most intimate physical sense, as in a jungle.[17]

To add to the problem, a crop failure in 1921 caused widespread famine. Had it not been for the daily food rations supplied by Herbert Hoover's American Relief Administration to 10 million children and adults, as well as the aid of the Soviet Relief Committee, which gave aid to an equal number, millions more would have died of actual starvation.

IV

In these circumstances, Lenin tried repeatedly to make peace. In the four months from November 1918 to February 1919 the Soviets sent seven notes to the Allies, written—as William Henry Chamberlin says—"in the most conciliatory language."[18] But the West refused to be conciliated. In March 1919 William C. Bullitt, then with the American peace delegation in Paris, was dispatched to the Soviet Union to seek a modus vivendi. Within a week he had come to a tentative understanding with Lenin that was highly favorable to the Allies. The Bolsheviks agreed that all existing governments in Russia, White as well as Red, would retain jurisdiction over the areas they then occupied—thus depriving the Bolsheviks of their claim to Siberia and other large areas. Debts owed the Allies from Czarist and Kerensky days would be assumed as a joint obligation of all "governments" in Russia. Troops would be demobilized and a general amnesty declared for political prisoners. In return the West would lift its blockade, withdraw its soldiers, and reopen communications. Bullitt was jubilant over his pact, but the plan was given short shrift even by Wilson, who had sent him there. Admiral Kolchak at that point was marching toward Moscow, and the Allies evidently felt that they didn't have to make any kind of agreement; they would soon have their own people in power. "Never, surely," writes Kennan, "have countries contrived to show themselves so much at their worst as did the Allies to Russia from 1917 to 1920."[19]

The absence of peace forced the Bolsheviks to take much sterner measures than they had intended and engage in certain practices—such as the red terror—they had originally eschewed. When bourgeois elements, despite many appeals, continued passive resistance against the revival of industry and banking, a Supreme Economic Council was formed to operate the large plants, and banks were nationalized. Beginning in May 1918 key industries, starting with sugar, oil, coffee, and tobacco and then the basic ones, were also nationalized. Resources were so scarce there was no alternative but for the state to directly manage the economy. Private trade was prohibited, worker detachments were sent into the rural areas to requisition food for the army and for city residents, millions of banknotes were printed to cover government expenses. This total control was a planned economy of sorts, but not the kind of planning the Bolsheviks had intended; it was war planning, heedless of costs, the demand of the market, or orderly development. It concentrated only on providing supplies for a war effort, any way they could be provided. It was not true socialist planning; appropriately enough it was called War Communism. Workers received their basic pay in food and clothing; normal trade union activity was limited, strikes prohibited.

War Communism, though necessary and inevitable under the circumstances, consigned the Russian Revolution to a false start toward economic viability. The crisis also drove the Communists to political exigencies they would have preferred to avoid. In July 1918 the Left Social Revolutionaries, who had joined the government, broke with Lenin over the signing of the treaty with Germany and initiated a small insurrection. The insurgents arrested Dzerzhinski, head of the Cheka; occupied the post and telegraph offices; assassinated the German ambassador (in order to ignite, as they hoped, a revolutionary war with Germany); killed the head of the Petrograd Cheka; and tried to murder Lenin himself. Such actions could not be disregarded, even though the Bolsheviks took reprisals with considerable misgivings. The terror on the right, by the White Guards—far worse than anything by the Left Social Revolutionaries—also called for retaliation. The Whites regarded anyone not explicitly on their side as an enemy. They executed thousands of people for no other reason than that they were neutral. On one occasion, in August 1919, fifty-two carloads of prisoners were unceremoniously slain in a rightist orgy of vengeance. The Cheka answered these acts of terror with a terror of its own that included the taking and killing of hostages and resulted, according to William Henry Chamberlin, in the death of 50,000 people.

After nearly three years of War Communism, conditions became so stifling that a faction within the Bolshevik movement, The Workers' Opposition, demanded a return to "proletarian democracy," including free functioning of the trade unions. Anarchists openly called for a Third Revolution. Early in 1921, in the midst of the war with Poland and after a series of strikes in Petrograd, the sailors at the Kronstadt naval fortress rose in revolt against "Bolshevik tyranny." The exponents of a Third Revolution were suppressed in mid-March with heavy casualties. On the heels of these events, Lenin jettisoned War Communism and introduced a New Economic Policy which legalized free trade in shops and markets and permitted private business to function in small and middle enterprises.

But in the wake of chaos and catastrophe, the Communists also suppressed opposition parties. Isaac Deutscher quotes Trotsky to the effect "that he and Lenin had intended to lift the ban on the opposition parties as soon as the economic and social condition of the country had become more stable."[20] From 1917 to 1921 their attitude had been ambivalent—first permitting the Mensheviks and Social Revolutionaries to function openly, then outlawing them, only to repeat the process, depending on

the vacillations of those parties in which some groups leaned towards the Bolsheviks and others towards the White Guards. The idea, however, that these parties should be suppressed on principle had not taken root before the end of the civil war. Even during the spells of repression, those opposition groups which did not plainly call for armed resistance to the Bolsheviks still carried on all sorts of activities, open and clandestine.[21]

But in the midst of famine, economic distress, cries for a Third Revolution, and the Kronstadt mutiny which the two parties had applauded, these opposition groups were permanently dissolved. At approximately the same time, the Communists, on Lenin's motion, passed a resolution prohibiting ongoing factions within their own party. Dissidents might still express their views in the press and in special discussion bulletins, as well as speak to each other openly, but they were prohibited from forming permanent groupings.

Clearly, the economic and political path that the Soviet Union would follow depended on peace with the outside world, on the relaxation of tensions. The extent of repression grew or abated in accordance with the pressures exerted against the Moscow government—in other words, on how tenuous was its prospect of survival. In 1917-21 its position was precarious. In the face of 10 million war casualties, a battered industrial machine, immobilized railroads, the starvation of millions, and a war against fourteen foreign armies and a half-dozen native counterrevolutionary armies, what was remarkable was not that there was repression or restriction of dissent but that it was not more extensive. Outside intervention forced the Soviet Union to modify its political structure in the direction of tighter discipline. It also forced it to alter its economic planning in the direction of self-sufficiency—with consequent mutations for its whole way of life.

CHAPTER FIVE

The Causes of Stalinism

I

It is axiomatic that a nation embroiled in war cannot live a normal life. The effects are minimal, perhaps, in "little wars" such as Korea or Vietnam—minimal, that is for the great power, the United States. But in major wars countries reshape their economic and political physiognomy to the point where they are often unrecognizable. Thus, for instance, "free enterprise" America found it necessary during World War II to abrogate, in effect, the free market which it had always advertised as the backbone of its system. The government imposed price controls, set wage standards, rationed gasoline, meat, and cigarettes, froze workers to their jobs in defense industries, allocated scarce materials, drafted 16 million men to a new kind of "work"—military "work"—and recruited millions of women and older people to take their place. Such items as new automobiles became unavailable, their place in the production schedule taken by tanks and airplanes. On the political front legislation was enacted against "subversion" (the Smith Act), Japanese-Americans were unceremoniously and illegally incarcerated in detention camps, and the government partly emasculated the labor movement by demanding, and receiving, a no-strike pledge for the duration of hostilities.

All this was done by a nation with unparalleled resources, a highly developed infrastructure, and an industrial capacity such as man had never known before. It was a nation, furthermore, untouched by a single bomb or a single act of sabotage in a factory. In other countries, Britain, for instance, the austerity was far more severe and the political climate bordered on dictatorship.

The Soviet Union has been in this sort of emergency situation almost uninterruptedly from 1917 to the present. Though it has been under military attack only twice in that period, it has been under economic and political pressures so intense they had the effect of a shooting war. As a consequence, normal and orderly development in the U.S.S.R. has been impossible. The war between capitalism and socialism not only caused modification of its institutions but influenced its internal struggles, including the one which led to Stalin's victory. Anti-Communist theorists invariably disregard this point, for they are determined to show that the failings of socialism stem from its own logic. Communist theorists, on the other hand, underplay the point because they find it impolitic to tell their people that there might have been other and better roads to socialism. Nonetheless it is patently obvious from the historical record that foreign pressures have warped the development of socialism in Russia and that without such intervention the Soviet course would have been much different. The capitalist world is thus in the position of a vandal who, after disfiguring a famous painting, calls it a poor work of art.

II

If we dissect the process of revolutionary change, either bourgeois or socialist, we find it to be composed of two overlapping phases, one of which may be called negative, the other positive. The negative phase consists of restructuring economic and juridical institutions so that a mechanism emerges for the formation of capital. Most important in this phase usually is land reform, for to the extent that land reform is completed the positive tasks of revolution can be pursued more effectively. In the positive phase, the central question is how rapidly to accumulate capital and how to put it to use.

If the *tempo* of capital formation is too slow, progress is minimal; if it is too fast, it may exact such high sacrifices from the population that the revolution loses its popular support. If the capital is invested primarily in consumer industries, it may satisfy immediate needs but fail to satisfy the long-term objectives of a balanced development; if it is invested too heavily in an infrastructure and the producer goods industries, the popular quest for a better life is unrequited and measures must be taken to keep the people "in line." In addition, of course, there is the matter of equitable distribution of the national income, all of which makes the implementation of revolutionary goals highly complex. Even under the best of circumstances, with the most selfless of leaders at the helm, the process is likely to be fraught with error. For the Russian revolutionaries of 1917 there was the corollary difficulty that there existed as yet no body of previous experience to guide them.

The Bolsheviks were well versed in the subject of capital formation, but not capital formation in a socialist society. Karl Marx had written a classic three-volume work on capital, in which among other things he explained the process of primitive accumulation under capitalism. "In actual history," he wrote, "it is notorious that conquest, enslavement, robbery, murder, briefly force, play the great part." In the twenty-seventh chapter of the first volume he showed how original capital was accumulated in England by the "wholesale expropriation of the agricultural population from the soil . . . the spoilation of the church's property, the fraudulent alienation of the clan property."[1] A socialist society obviously could not resort to such methods—robbery, fraud, usurpation. But if not, what then? Neither Marx nor other leftist thinkers had discussed the matter in any detail. There was a *general* feeling of how it should be done, but little else.

The original expectation of Lenin and Trotsky was that capital would flow into the Soviet Union from advanced nations such as Germany, after the revolution had spread to their boundaries. "The work of [socialist] construction," Lenin said in 1919, "depends entirely upon how soon the revolution is victorious in the most important countries of Europe. Only after this victory can we seriously undertake the business of construction." A year later he was still pointing out the dependence of the Russian Revolution on others; "We have always emphasized that we look from an international viewpoint and that in one country it is impossible to accomplish such a work as a socialist revolution."[2] In 1921, however, when hopes for international revolution ebbed in the face of setbacks in Germany, Hungary, and Finland, Lenin stated that "as long as there is no revolution in other countries we will have to creep out of this in decades."[3] By 1923-24 the wave of social upheavals had spent itself. Bolshevism was forced to look elsewhere for nascent capital, either to the capitalist states, which invariably demanded that it breach its socialist structure as a condition for receiving aid, or to its own internal resources, which were terribly limited.

The weakened economies of Europe were given adrenaline by the United States, one of the two nations (the other being Japan) which had come out of World War I in better shape than it went into it. Had it not been for the $13 billion in loans by Uncle Sam from 1918 to 1929, it is doubtful that Western Europe could have stayed afloat. Germany was saved by $2.5 billion of U.S. money, as well as the paring down of its reparation bill through the Dawes and Young plans. But no such gestures were made to the Soviet Union; on the contrary, there was a determined effort to strangle it by denying it long-term credits and capital and by placing impediments even on normal trade. What could not be done by military intervention—to strangle the baby in its crib, as Churchill had put it—would be accomplished by economic isolation.

The policy of the United States, expressed by Secretary of State Bainbridge Colby in August 1920, was that "we cannot recognize, hold official relations with, or give friendly reception to the agents of a Government which is determined and bound to conspire against our institutions." When the Russians asked that trade be resumed, Charles Evans Hughes, Colby's successor, rejected the offer in March 1921 on the grounds that the Soviet Union did not recognize the rights of private property, free labor, and the sanctity of contracts. "I do not propose to barter away for the privilege of trade," said President Coolidge in December 1923, "any of the cherished rights of humanity."[4] At the very time that the United States was seeking more commerce and pouring billions of loans into the sclerotic veins of the rest of the world, it was denying them to the socialist state.

Other governments, beginning with Britain in 1924, did recognize the Soviet Union. But they demanded, as a condition for normal economic relations, that the Kremlin repay debts incurred by the Czar and Kerensky (at the very time, ironically, when they themselves were defaulting on wartime loans from the United

States) and that Russia restore to foreign entrepreneurs their prewar properties. Moscow was willing to pay some of the debts, but only if the Allies reimbursed Russia for damages inflicted during the 1918-20 intervention. A compromise was worked out with the Labor government of Britain in 1924, but it was not put into effect because Tories returned to power in the meantime and from 1927 to 1929 severed diplomatic relations with the Soviets.

Try as they might the Soviet leaders were unable to reestablish normal trade or lure long-term loans and capital to their country. In 1918 Lenin offered generous terms to foreign companies willing to build factories or undertake other business enterprise on Soviet soil; in reply to critics who feared he was filling capitalist coffers, he said we "need not mourn the billions of rubles we pay to capitalism." The long-term benefits to the Soviet Union would be much greater. But the results were negligible: as of the end of 1927 only twenty-three foreign firms were engaged in manufacture and seventeen in mining, accounting for less than one half of one percent of Soviet gross output in industry. The best Moscow could accomplish in this period was a few hundred million dollars of *short-term* commercial credit to finance a limited amount of trade. In the back of many Western minds was the conviction that Bolshevism was near collapse anyway. Frederick L. Schuman lists twenty-one headlines in the *Chicago Tribune* from October 26, 1925, to November 26, 1927, that gave vent to this wishful thinking—"Claim Starving Poor Threaten Doom to Soviet," "Siberia Tries to Shake Off Moscow's Yoke," "Secret Report Shows Russia Near Collapse," "Rumania Hears of Widespread Russian Revolt," "Odessa Troops Mutiny Against Moscow Regime," "Russia Calls Soldiers Home as Revolt Rises," "Hundreds Die in Ukraine Riots."[5] None of it was true, but it reinforced a widespread hope and gave a measure of justification to the policy of economic suffocation.

III

In this hostile climate the Russian leaders had no choice but to go it alone; the capital they needed would have to come from their own people. The question was How? Contrary to present impressions the Communists had few fixed ideas on how to operate a socialist economy, and they quarreled constantly among themselves on how to proceed. There were disputes, for instance, over who should control the nationalized industries; some argued that they should be run autonomously by the workers of each factory, others that they should be managed by appointees of the central government. There were disputes on how to plan production, whether to have separate plans for each industry, uncoordinated with the others, or a single plan for the whole country. Most of all there was the overriding dispute from 1922 to 1928 that embraced three or four interrelated issues: how to form nascent capital, how rapidly to industrialize, how to deal with the peasantry, how to raise living standards. The ultimate decision, as is now well known, was to drive the peasants from private farms into collectives, industrialize at an excessively rapid tempo, and accumulate capital by depriving the population of consumer goods—all of which was accompanied in the political realm by centralizing power in the hands of the state and a small group around Stalin. But none of this was preordained; it came after an intense internal struggle which, but for the maladroitness of the opposition and foreign pressures, might have been decided differently.

At the end of the civil war Russia desperately needed funds for reconstruction. Limited amounts were available from taxes on private businessmen who had reemerged during the New Economic Policy and from profits in state-owned industry. Additionally there was the time-honored device of printing unbacked paper money. These sources, inadequate though they were, brought industry and agriculture close to prewar levels by 1926. But prewar levels had been primitive; the problem remained of where to find the large sums of capital for a major advance.

For a brief time in 1922 Trotsky urged that the working class adopt a policy of "self-exploitation,"[6] that it forego improvements in living standards so that the extra profits gained thereby might be used for industrialization. In a sense this approach was similar to that of Mao Tse-tung and Fidel Castro today: that workers who believe they are working for their own future can be spurred by "moral" (as against "material") incentives. The laborers of Russia, however, had suffered enough privation; they were in no mood for further sacrifices. Indeed, as Kennan notes, "the spirit of sacrifice was giving way to lassitude, weariness with causes and ideals, a yearning for return to the reassuring preoccupations of private life. . . . There comes a time when people want to eat and sleep and mend their clothes and think about their children."[7]

In these circumstances the Communists—including Trotsky—found it expedient to appease the working class rather than exhort it to "self-exploitation." By 1927, according to Manya Gordon, a critic of communism,

> wages actually stood above the pre-war level . . . notwithstanding the eight-hour day, the two-weeks holiday, and a number of other privileges which the workers received as a result of the revolution. . . . It is important to note . . . that such betterment in the condition of the workers was not due to the natural economic well-being of the country. . . . In 1926-27, the Soviet wage earners were much better situated than they had a right to be.[8]

The Communist leaders of all factions—including Stalin's—still felt that in a "workers' state" the first obligation of the government was to cater to the needs of the proletariat.

But if large sums of capital were not to be squeezed out of the working class, there was only the peasantry left. This posed both economic and political dilemmas. Land distribution had been the first order of business on the Bolsheviks' agenda when they seized power. All land was nationalized and distributed to peasants and landless rural workers for their private use. This was not socialism, but it was necessary both for economic and political reasons. "We achieved victory," said Lenin in 1921, "because we adopted not our program, but that of the Social Revolutionaries," with the result that "nine-tenths of the masses of peasantry, within the course of a few weeks, came over to our side." Afterward the Communists reconciled themselves to "capitalism" in the villages for a long time to come. Stalin even proposed partial denationalization. "Would it not be expedient in the interest of agriculture," a journalist asked Stalin in 1925, "to deed over to each peasant for ten years the parcel of land tilled by him?" To which the Soviet leader replied, "Yes, and even for forty years."[9]

Private agriculture, however, presented problems. One of them was that the farmer consumed more than previously, leaving that much less grain to be sold on the market. Another was the tendency of the well-to-do peasant to take over the land of less fortunate tillers when the latter defaulted on loans. Nine percent of the farmers in White Russia were evicted from their holdings because of such defaults and 21 percent in Siberia. More ominous than anything else was a phenomenon that Trotsky called the "scissors." Periodically the farmers would refuse to take their grain to market or to put more land to the plow simply because there wasn't enough finished goods in the city to buy with their money. In 1926-27, when agricultural output was close to prewar levels, a mere 14 percent of the grain harvested was being sold on the market—as against 26 percent in the past. Thus not only were the cities in danger of being starved but, if insufficient grain was collected for export, the Soviet government would be unable to import vitally needed machinery. This was the dilemma to which the various factions addressed themselves.

The question of socialist accumulation soon centered on which classes to appease, which classes to squeeze. Nikolai Bukharin's views, which dominated Soviet thinking for most of the decade, were based on the political consideration that the alliance between worker and peasant had to be maintained at all costs. The working class, Bukharin argued, could not hold power by itself, particularly in a country as undeveloped as Russia. If that meant delaying capital expenditures or importing consumer rather than capital goods, so be it. The important thing was to make the peasant secure and keep his allegiance. "There are many capital outlays," said Bukharin's collaborator, A. I. Rykov, "which must be postponed until such time as industry has won the possibility of increasing its revenues on the basis of an extended peasant market and increased mass production." Stalin too scorned rapid industrialization on the grounds that "there is a great lack of capital in this country." With unconscious prescience, he predicted what was to occur under his own rule some years later. Arguing against Trotsky in 1925, he stated that "the future development of industry will probably not be so rapid as up to the present," because rapid industrialization "will certainly ruin us . . . undermine our currency . . . inevitably lead to . . . a great increase in the price of agricultural produce, a fall in real salaries and an artificially-produced famine." The first draft of a five-year program prepared in 1927 called for an increase of 9 percent in industrial output the first year, tapering down to 4 percent the fifth year. Anticipated industrial progress was so low that the government budget was pitched at 16 percent of national income—as against 18 percent in Czarist days. A more rapid pace of development, said Stalin, "would certainly be a fiasco."[10]

In Bukharin's thinking—and Stalin's—if the peasant refused to deliver his grain, the state would coax it from him by offering higher prices. If there were not enough consumer goods for the peasant, the state would import them. "We must tell the peasants, all the peasants," said Bukharin, "to enrich themselves, to develop their business and not to fear spoilation."[11] Naturally all this would reduce the rate of capital formation, but Bukharin was content with an annual rate of 7 or 7½ percent of national income—a very low figure when one considers that it was 9 or 9½ percent under Czarism. The Bukharin-Stalin policy was so moderate, one foreign writer observed, that it might be acceptable to "a group of Manchester liberals."

Trotsky took a more sanguine view, though not so extreme as the one Stalin eventually adopted. The former leader of the Red Army also predicated his position on the need for an alliance between workers and peasants—but not all peasants, only the poor and middle ones. The repository from which extra capital could be sought was the kulak, the wealthier peasant who had been permitted after 1925 to hire labor and rent additional land. According to Trotsky, 60 percent of the grain destined for sale was in the hands of 6 percent of the peasant class, and it was these 6 percent who were doing the hoarding. The kulak was the obvious source to be tapped for industrial capital. If in the process of raising his taxes or levying loans against him the government alienated him, that was unfortunate, but it would not disturb the basic alliance of workers and the rest of the peasantry—still a vast majority of the population. As a first step Trotsky proposed a compulsory grain loan of 200 million poods (a pood is 36 pounds), slightly more than the annual grain export of Russia in each of the previous two years. By squeezing the kulak, Trotsky expected the rate of capital formation to be doubled, industry to flourish, and the so-called "scissors" to be closed.

IV

Whether Bukharin's or Trotsky's strategies were workable, they had the merit that neither would require extraordinary police measures against the population. Since both anticipated a steady rise in living standards for the majority of Soviet citizens, opposition would be muted—except perhaps from a relatively small segment, the kulaks, if Trotsky's plan had been put into practice. Both approaches were consistent with a high degree of internal democracy. Both, and certainly Bukharin's, would have been conducive to what the Czechs much later, in 1968, would call "socialism with a human face."

But while it is interesting to speculate on what might have happened if either of the main opposition groups had guided Soviet destiny, the cold fact is that by 1928-29, after a half dozen years of raging factionalism, Stalin emerged the unchallenged master of the Communist Party and the Soviet Union. Trotsky's group was expelled en bloc in late 1927, Bukharin and his followers somewhat later. In the process of winning the factional war, however, Stalin executed a breathtaking 180-degree turn in his economic program. Instead of a slow pace of industrialization, he ordered one far more rapid than even Trotsky had suggested. Instead of an agriculture based on individual farms, he made a volte-face to total collectivization. The consequences were monumental.

This complete reversal of direction by a national leader is one of the most intriguing questions of modern history. Why did Stalin do it? It is sterile to attribute it to his lust for power (with rare exceptions all politicians lust for power), or the "cult of the individual" that Nikita Khrushchev referred to in February 1956 as an explanation for Stalin's murders and purges. The concept that men make history in a vacuum has long ago been repudiated by leftist thinkers. The individual certainly makes some contribution, large or small, but there are circumstances and happenings that favor the rise of one leader as against another. As George Plekhanov pointed out in *The Role of the Individual in History,* back in 1898:

> In order that a man who possesses a particular kind of talent may, by means of it, greatly influence the course of events, two conditions are needed: First, this talent must make him more comfortable to the social needs of the given epoch than anyone else. . . . Second, the existing social order must not bar the road to the person possessing that talent which is needed and useful precisely at the given time.[12]

This thesis is confirmed by the Russian Revolution itself. Lenin was an unknown figure outside Russia until the March 1917 events opened the door to his talents. Once opportunity beckoned, his personal traits fit exactly the necessities of the time. Historians generally concede that Lenin's leadership was a major, if not indispensable, factor in making the 1917 revolution and preserving it from 1917 to 1923. He was that rare person who commanded respect from all sides; he could heal the wounds after each factional feud as no one else in his movement. His solid self-confidence made it possible to admit mistakes, shift course, compromise, improvise. In 1922 he said:

> It is certain that we have done and will do a lot of stupid things. No one knows this better than I. Why do we do stupid things? In the first place, because we are a backward country. Secondly, education in our country is minimal. Thirdly, we are getting no help. Not one civilized state is helping us. On the contrary they are all working against us.[13]

Other leaders, including especially Stalin, were not capable of such forthrightness, a quality demanded of a chieftain at that particular juncture. Had Lenin lived he might have staved off the Stalinist debacle. But that is far from certain, because he was above all a product of revolutionary upsurge, not decline.

The Stalin familiar to history, by contrast, was a product of downsurge, isolation, fear. He reflected the shift in popular mood from the buoyancy of 1917 and the heroism of the civil war to fatigue, demoralization, confusion. The revolution in Russia, it was clear by now, was isolated; capitalism, as already noted, had upset the revolutionary wave of 1918-23 in Germany, Hungary, Finland, and Italy and had crowned its victory with Chiang Kai-shek's rout of the Chinese Communists in 1925-27. As Russia drew inward, Stalin's theory of establishing "socialism in one country" rather than Trotsky's reliance on "world revolution" seemed reasonable. Why spend time and money on foreign revolutions that have little chance of success anyway when there is so much to do at home? The theory of socialism in one country implied less risk, less involvement in the adventures of other peoples, more concern with pregnant domestic problems.

Pessimism was also fostered by the problems arising from

political and economic encirclement. In 1928 there was another "scissors" crisis—peasants were hiding their grain, the granaries were empty, bread was in short supply even in Moscow, and actual famine prevailed in some places. In a six-month period there were 150 small peasant revolts that were put down by force. In June there was a confrontation between unemployed and militiamen in the capital after some shops had been vandalized. And if this were not enough, Stalin and many others had the gut feeling that a second military intervention by the Western powers was imminent. The Sixth Congress of the Communist International, meeting in Moscow in June 1928, proclaimed that the capitalist nations, "with England at their head," were preparing an invasion of the Soviet Union. The new program of the Comintern, adopted a few months later, stated that "expeditions against the colonies, a new world war, a campaign against the USSR are matters which now figure prominently in the politics of imperialism." The prognosis was eleven years wrong, but it was not all fantasy, for there *had* been a war scare in Europe in 1927.

Pessimism therefore encouraged a sense of emergency, a feeling that unless something drastic were done the "workers' state" would disintegrate from within or succumb to attack from without. Stalinism was the coefficient of this sense of emergency. Where Bukharin had based his politics on a modus vivendi with the West, and Trotsky on undermining Western capitalism by extending the revolution, Stalin assayed the role of "realist"—Russia must prepare to defend its borders with its own guns, its own manpower. It was naïve to dream of revolution in China and Germany, or an understanding with London and Washington, when the enemy was, in Stalin's opinion, already outside the gates. Russia needed steel, electricity, factories—and quickly—not evanescent dreams. The answer to both the threat of intervention and the threat from within was rapid industrialization, the fabrication of a heavy industry capable of producing steel for cannons and steel for power dams. Rapid industrialization would require heavy sacrifices, the kind of "self-exploitation" that Trotsky had urged in 1922, though much greater. But Stalin postulated that when a social system is threatened with extinction it must take whatever steps are necessary to survive—no matter what the cost. He must have known that the sacrifices necessitated by rapid industrialization could not be exacted by persuasion, that some amount of force would be necessary. But it is doubtful that he expected the terror to get as far out of hand as it did, or that he planned it out of pure ruthlessness. He may have been as rude and power-hungry as Lenin said. Rude or not, however, no political leader sets out deliberately to alienate his whole constituency. It is something that springs from the logic of a particular crisis and the policy fashioned to meet it.

The logic of the 1928–29 situation, in Stalin's view, called for a pace of industrialization four times as rapid as the one advocated by Bukharin, twice as rapid as the one advocated by Trotsky. It is from this taproot that Stalinism poured out, not the "cult of the individual" or defects in socialism per se.

V

The rate of capital formation under Bukharin's stewardship had been around 7 percent a year, which means that out of every dollar of national production 7 cents was put aside for factories and infrastructure, while 93 cents remained for private and public consumption. Trotsky's plan called for doubling the rate of capital formation, still leaving 86 cents out of every dollar for consumption. But Stalin's five-year plan, initiated in 1928, diverted more than a fourth of national income for capital investment, leaving only 70 or 75 cents of each dollar for consumption. The same man who had said in 1925 that rapid industrialization "will certainly ruin us" now pulled out all the stops. Not only was the tempo of development to be excessively rapid but lopsided as well. It was to emphasize basic industry and relegate consumer industry to secondary importance, thus adding to the burden of the average citizen that much more. Millions of peasants, for instance, were to be drawn into city factories, but there was no adequate housing program to meet their needs; they would have to double up in the existing flats, very often a whole family to a single room. The percentage of capital allocated to heavy industry in the first two five-year plans was 85 to 86 percent. "We must catch up and surpass the most advanced countries," Stalin said, "or perish. Full steam ahead or perish."[14]

Where did the capital come from for this forced march? Some of it came from a slight improvement in the credit situation. General Electric in the autumn of 1928 gave the Soviets five years to pay for electrical machinery, and the Labor Party of Britain, on returning to office in 1929, reopened diplomatic and economic relations. These, however, were negligible sources, and dried up anyway when the great depression engulfed America. Mostly the new capital was generated by squeezing the whole population—all workers, all peasants, not just the kulaks—through heavy taxes, forced loans, low wages, rationing, high prices for many commodities, a staggering inflation, the seizure of crops and livestock, and forced collectivization. Particularly onerous was the turnover tax, a sales tax that fell especially hard on the lower-income groups. It brought in more than 42 billion rubles during the first five-year plan and 219 billion during the second. Forced loans and deliberate inflation also cut real earnings to shreds. The government printed nearly 4 billion paper rubles from 1928 to 1933, tripling the number in circulation and reducing the purchasing power of money to 40 percent of what it had been in 1926.[15]

The primary source of capital was from the village, whose agricultural products were to be exchanged for foreign machinery. It was capital taken out of the hide of the peasant by ruthless coercion. Lenin had stated over and over again that "It would be the greatest absurdity to try to introduce communal agriculture work into such backward villages, where a long education would be necessary before the preliminary attempt." Socialists, he wrote, "have no thought of expropriating the small farmers, but rather seek to show them by force of example the advantages of socialized and mechanized agriculture."[16] In July 1928 the head of the government, A. I. Rykov, asserted that "the chief task of the party" is "to develop individual farms"—a thesis to which Stalin fully subscribed. "There are people," said Stalin, "who think that individual farms have exhausted their usefulness. . . . These people have nothing in common with the line of our party."[17]

But within a few months the party and the army were dispossessing millions of individual farmers and dragooning them into collective farms. The shift in policy was not so much ideological as pragmatic. If Russia were to make a big leap it needed machinery it did not have and could not as yet produce, and if it were to buy machinery it had to export more grain. It was as simple as that. The fly in the ointment, however, was that the peasant was loath to deliver his grain if there were so little to buy with his money once he sold it. Thus a furious though silent war began between the village and the regime, a war the outside world learned about only years later. The village was hoarding its foodstuffs and refusing to sow more acreage. Stalin decided, therefore, to take what he could not buy; the army was sent into the village to expropriate food reserves. Inevitably the peasant hid what he had, and equally inevitably the government made it a crime to conceal food. Like a chess match each move led to a countermove, but the end result was that the cities found themselves short of bread and the foreign trade program, by which Stalin hoped to exchange grain for machinery, was placed in extreme jeopardy.

The indicated answer for a government that was in a hurry was to replace individual farms with the collective (kolkhoz). It did not matter that the state lacked technicians, machinery, fertilizer, or capital to develop the kolkhoz; the immediate need was to get the grain and get it by whatever means possible. In the collective, control of the crop would be in the hands of a manager beholden to the party, not the individual farmer. And since the grain could not be concealed in the kolkhoz the state no longer would have to cajole the farmer with the offer of better prices or the promise of consumer goods. It was not an ideal way to increase output—food production in fact went down—but it was an effective means for the state to make its collections.

Stalin's announcement that individual farming would be replaced by collectivization came as a complete surprise, yet it was fully in accord with his determination to modernize the economy at any cost. At first it was envisioned that one fifth of the peasants would be collectivized in five years, but having opened the spigot a little, Stalin soon turned it on full force. In November 1929 he accelerated the pace so that by 1932—in three years, not five—61.5 percent of the 25 million peasant families had been pushed, almost bodily, into 211,000 collectives. As might be expected, they joined unwillingly and sullenly, and though they had neither the weapons nor the leadership for armed resistance they found other ways for venting their fury. One of the jokes making the rounds in the Soviet Union, quoted by John Gunther, expresses better than any statistic the feelings toward collectivization: "Stalin had lice in his hair. No means, mechanical, medicinal, chemical, could extirpate them. Desperate, Stalin called [Karl] Radek into consultation. Radek said: 'Simple. Collectivize one louse. The others will run away.' "[18] Instead of bringing their animals into the common pool, peasants slaughtered them for meat and hides or sold them for a song to neighbors not yet collectivized. They ate the seed put aside for the next crop; they destroyed equipment. It would be decades before Russia recovered from this silent war. From 1928 to 1933 the number of horses declined from 23 to 14 million, long-horn cattle from 70 to 38 million, cows from 31 to 20 million, sheep and goats from 147 to 50 million.

The villages turned into chaotic nurseries of defiance and repression. Grain production, far from rising, plummeted downward. In 1931 the crop was 69.5 million tons—as against 96.6 million tons in 1913. But the state more than doubled its collection of grain. Before collectivization it had averaged 8 to 10 million tons annually; from 1930 to 1932 it averaged 25 million tons. And these were famine years, when incredible numbers actually starved to death, even in the rich Ukraine. Despite starvation, however, the government shipped abroad 203 million rubles of foodstuffs. While the production of sugar dropped and sugar had to be rationed for the population at home, exports of the commodity rose from 127,000 tons in 1929 to 320,000 in 1931. Import of consumer goods was cut drastically—in 1932 it was only a sixth of what it had been in 1913; but import of industrial goods, such as machinery, rose sharply—in 1932 it was three times as much as in 1913. The lowered standard of living of the people was reflected in the reduced imports of necessities such as rice, tea, coffee, herring, cotton. The purchase of coffee, which is not grown in Russia, fell from 1,417 tons in 1913 to 710 tons in 1927–28 and a trifling 58 tons in 1933. Tea imports slid from 75,811 tons in 1913 to 28,134 tons in 1927–28 and 19,307 tons in 1933. Cotton imports in 1933 were only one sixth of the 1927–28 level and one ninth of the 1913 level.

Needless to say, the staggering and costly rearrangement of the economy caused mass disaffection. The French author Victor Serge, who lived in the Soviet Union during this period, wrote that "these years are a nightmare. Famine comes to the Ukraine, the Black Lands, Siberia, to all the Russian granaries. Thousands of peasants flee across the frontiers to Poland, Rumania, Persia or China."[19] Serge quotes a number of letters he received which indicate how badly the situation had deteriorated. A factory worker complains: "They are squeezing us, and how! Five men to the brigade instead of six, without change of equipment. The system of bonuses is applied in such a way that . . . no one hopes to receive any. We live on 55 rubles a month." A kolkhoz member reports that members of his collective have received no pay for two months. "In a neighboring village, forty women have recovered their cows by force, shut them up in the houses, and said to the authorities of the rural Soviet: 'You can fire, but you can't have our cows.' However the cattle is taken. . . . It is hard to believe that such abominations are done in the name of socialism." Another kolkhoz member advises Serge that

> presidents of the *kolkhozes* have been assassinated in the vicinity. Everywhere the women demand and take their cattle. . . . In the cities there is neither butter, meat, eggs, nor potatoes, and even the capitals are on microscopic rations. For a long time we have seen neither meat nor fish. During the last few days the cooperatives have at last received some horse sausage.[20]

How was the government to deal with the hostility that enveloped it—the women trying to steal back their cows, the killing of animals, the sabotage, the spontaneous strikes, the low quality of work, the deliberate absenteeism, the widescale petty theft? It closed the circle with totalitarian repression. The war, the civil war, the foreign intervention, the economic strangulation, the fear of another invasion from abroad—all this fanned the flames of internal factionalism, until Stalin emerged the victor to implement a hysterically rapid industrialization program. Rapid industrialization required rapid collectivization and, in the face of peasant resistance, widespread jailings and banishment.

The 25- to-30-percent annual rate of capital formation, backbone of the new plan, demanded high taxes, forced loans, speed-up on the job, low wages. Strikes, therefore, could not be permitted because higher wages meant more consumption, more consumption reduced capital formation. And if strikes were prohibited, speech, dissent, opposition must also be curbed, lest the agitation for freedom upset the "plan." The worker must be tied to his job and the peasant to his village, because free movement and job turnover meant less production; but, ironically, they could not be kept in place except in an atmosphere of fear, imprisonments, exilings, thus causing a considerable turnover anyway.

Every now and then Stalin loosened the reins a little. Perhaps he did it to gain time to enlarge the organism of repression—the secret police. Perhaps he did it in the hopes of regaining some popular support, muting defiance. But it never worked too well. On one occasion Stalin criticized the bureaucracy for "the abominable, the criminal, the exceptionally brutal conduct of the secondary officials" and decreed that peasants could leave the collectives voluntarily if they wished. But in one two-week period during March 1930 many millions availed themselves of this opportunity; the epidemic was stopped by strengthening the police apparatus and resuming the drive for full collectivization. In 1935, the first year of recovery, when living standards began to rise again, the government abolished food cards and permitted peasants to work a small piece of land and own a horse or cow within the kolkhoz.[21] There was a sigh of relief everywhere, like taking off a tight shoe. But the relaxation was of a modest nature, insufficient to bring masses into the streets in shrieking jubilation; anyway, by now repression had become and would remain institutionalized. The very process of improving matters whetted the appetite, an appetite which the Stalin regime could not appease if it were to go ahead with its program, always stressing basic industry as against consumer goods industry, steel mills as against housing, production as against better living standards.

Intended or unintended, total state control of the individual became the way of life. Wherever the state ran into threat or potential threat, it replied with stark repression. To get the message across on collectivization, it uprooted millions from their homes. Thus in sixty-five days from December 27, 1929, to March 2, 1930, the government, according to Duranty, deported 2 million peasants to remote places. Others put the figure at 5 million. As late as 1933 the Rostov press reported on the exiling en bloc of 50,000 people who lived in three cossack settlements. Tens of thousands of former Trotskyites and Bukharinists, around whom opposition might have coagulated—not to mention ordinary people with no such background—were unceremoniously jailed, held without bail or trial, and sent into forced labor camps.

The lopsided economic program could not be sustained without shackling the individual so as to serve the state's interest above his own. The internal passport, designed by Stalin, effectively kept him rooted to his designated place of employment. Even a short stay from home required a GPU visa, not unlike travel to a foreign country. Railroad workers were frozen to their jobs, subject to as much as ten years in jail for breaking discipline. On August 7, 1932, Stalin proclaimed the death penalty for theft of merchandise belonging to the state transport industry, a sure sign that many people were living by their wits, stealing and selling government property when they could. Workers were required to carry labor books, devilish devices for tying them to their factories and permitting easy blacklisting for economic or political dereliction. Absenteeism and tardiness were punished by fines and imprisonment. The trade unions were shorn of all independence, converted into company unions for the government. The membership card in the union obligated the laborer to "set an example, bring all workers to participate in socialistic emulation and to become shock workers. He must help to increase production, remembering that, according to Lenin, it is production which decides in final instances the success of the new social form." Strikes were of course totally prohibited. The secret police, tightly controlled by Stalin, became a power unto itself, and opposition of any kind, even speaking privately against a party policy or leader, was adjudged a criminal offense.

The Russian Revolution, as the circle leading from isolation to repression was completed, turned against itself, away from its original ideals. Production, not people, became its primary concern. Stalin was ready to sacrifice a generation or more to lay the foundations for a modern economy—and a modern defense system. How deep was the turnaround is indicated by the purges of the mid-1930s, the like of which was not seen even during the French Revolution a century and a half before. In the three years after Sergei Kirov was assassinated in 1934, 98 of the 139 members and candidates of the central committee—according to Nikita Khrushchev—were arrested and shot. All the old Bolsheviks who had led the 1917 revolution, with the exception of those dead and a few such as Stalin and Molotov, were purged and most of them killed, among them Bukharin, Zinoviev, Kamenev, Rakovsky, Radek, and Piatakov.[22]

VI

The revolution certainly did not live up to its original intentions. Considered as a thing-in-itself it apparently was aborted. Yet it is vital to put the turnaround in broader context, just as one would do with a military setback—for instance, the Battle of the Bulge in World War II. Was it the precursor to new setbacks or to a readjustment? Was it the expression of permanent weakness or of a momentary failing of leadership and outlook?

The abortion theory is vulnerable to three disclaimers: first, that despite a quarter of a century of Stalinism, Soviet Russia's material, cultural, educational, and scientific achievements are enormously impressive; second, that like other nations the Soviet Union has been subject to the whims of historical accident; and third, that the evolution of Stalinism was part of an opening salvo in a long war between two social systems that cannot be assessed except in the framework of that war.

There is no need to dwell at length on the first point. The Soviet accomplishments in schooling, literature, science, theater, music, medicine, and social insurance either exceed those of the West or are comparable. Even in areas where the Russians have been unable as yet to catch up, such as in material blessings and GNP, the Soviet performance has been creditable. Before World War I per-capita income in the United States was eight to ten times higher than in Czarist Russia. During and after the war, when Russia was devastated, the disparity grew wider, more favorable to America. But today the American income level, though far higher than in 1914, is only twice that of the Soviets, and that despite the vastly greater losses in men and money the U.S.S.R. endured during World World II. In static terms America is on a loftier plateau, but in dynamic terms the Soviets have been moving closer with remarkable tenacity. Admittedly the Soviet development lacks balance: in 1971, for instance, it outstripped the United States in steel production for the first time but was decades behind in providing housing for its people. With all that, however, it has come a long way in narrowing the gap.

What this suggests is that, far from being inherently defective, the socialist system, even in its least attractive form, possesses inherent promise. We can only speculate how much greater would have been that promise if Lenin had lived, if Trotsky or Bukharin or someone else had taken the helm in 1928–29, if a less obstructive policy had been pursued by the capitalist states, or if some of them had joined the socialist cavalcade in 1919–23 or after World War II. Accidental factors of leadership, geography, diplomatic or military success, and technological breakthrough often change a nation's course. "Accidents" of one kind or another account for the differences between, say, Japanese capitalism and British capitalism, Scandinavian capitalism and Austrian capitalism. A different set of accidents from those that occurred might have propelled the Soviet Union to a different form of socialism.

The effect of "accident" is poignantly evident in American history. The 1776 revolution might not have taken place without the leadership of Sam Adams or the activity of groups such as the Sons of Liberty, and the War of Independence might have been lost but for the "accident" that France was at war with Britain and therefore willing to aid the thirteen colonies. Consider, too, the more subtle results of the limited naval war with France, 1798–1800. Alexander Hamilton, perhaps the most influential man of his times, proposed a full-scale war in the course of which the United States would seize some of the territories in the Western Hemisphere belonging to France's ally, Spain. Had Hamilton not been frustrated by the Jeffersonians and, later, President John Adams, relations with France might have been so embittered as to preclude the sale of the Louisiana Territory to the United States in 1803. And without that purchase the road to expansion westward might have been barred.

There are innumerable other "accidents" that changed the destiny of America: the Napoleonic wars, which kept Britain embroiled in Europe rather than here; the failure of the great Indian chief, Tecumseh, to effectively unite the Indian tribes during the war of 1812; the defeat of Henry Clay by James Knox Polk in 1844; the defeat of Charles Evans Hughes by Woodrow Wilson in 1916. There is something of a parallel, incidentally, between Polk's victory in the 1840s and Stalin in the 1920s—though it should not be stretched too far. The eleventh President of the United States, a man lacking either the stature or charisma of those who preceded him, had no intention of running for the Presidency in 1844 and would have been elated if the front-runner, Martin Van Buren, had chosen him as vice-presidential candidate. But Van Buren was opposed to war with Mexico, whereas the mood of the country was for "manifest destiny." "Dark horse" Polk, who talked of seizing all of Oregon and the "immediate *re*annexation" of Texas, fit that mood and was eventually nominated (on a ninth ballot) and elected. The man he defeated, Henry Clay, was far his superior in intellect, experience, and color, but he too did not fit the national mood of the moment. The war with Mexico that followed Polk's victory at the polls was as immoral as the one with Vietnam long afterward, but it confirmed the annexation of Texas and enlarged the United States boundary to California and the Pacific. Would the outcome have been the same if Van Buren or Clay had won? Would Britain have been prevented from taking upper California and establishing a protectorate over Texas? No one can say for certain; all that is clear is that Polk was an "accident" and that the war he brought on might not have taken place, or might not have taken place at that time or with those results, if that "accident" hadn't occurred.

Stalin's ascent in the Soviet Union must also be described in part as accident. Lenin, on December 25, 1922, after suffering one stroke and before his second, wrote a letter which the Communist Party suppressed for decades and which has become known in history as his "testament." In it he evaluated the party leadership. Bukharin, he said, was "the most valuable and greatest theoretician" but too "scholastic." Trotsky, though "the most able man in the present Central Committee," was distinguished "by his too far-reaching self-confidence and a disposition to be too much attracted by the purely administrative side of affairs." Stalin had "concentrated an enormous power in his hands; and I am not sure that he always knows how to use that power with sufficient caution." Lenin concluded that "these two qualities of the two most able leaders [Stalin and Trotsky] of the present Central Committee might, quite innocently, lead to a split." Ten days later the founder of the Russian Communist Party dictated a codicil to his testament which indicated that had he been well he would unquestionably have fought to remove Stalin as general secretary. He wrote:

Stalin is too rude, and this fault, entirely supportable in relations among us communists, becomes insupportable in the office of General Secretary. Therefore, I propose to the comrades to find a way to remove Stalin from that position and appoint to it another man who in all respects differs from Stalin only in superiority—namely, more patient, more loyal, more polite and more attentive to comrades, less capricious, etc. This circumstance may seem an insignificant trifle, but . . . it is such a trifle as may acquire a decisive significance.[23]

It is altogether likely that had Lenin recovered his health (he died after a long illness in January 1924) Stalin's role in history would have been much curtailed.

Other Soviet leaders were less adroit than Lenin in dealing with Stalin or in foreseeing the consequences of his role as general secretary. In the interests of spurious party unity, for instance, they agreed to withhold Lenin's letter from the public and to retain Stalin in his position. Before Lenin's death and for some period thereafter, Trotsky probably could have established his position as Lenin's successor had he appealed to the military and the people over the head of the party. He was still "so popular in the army and throughout the country," writes Victor Serge, "that he might, with good chances of success, have attempted a *coup*."[24] Perhaps. Perhaps not. A regime installed by a coup, in any case, might have been as bad as the one it replaced, or it might not; there are a number of instances—Peru for example—where a coup has led to better government. Again, no one can say. All that is clear is that the Russian Revolution had many choices of leadership, many paths open to it—other than Stalinism.

More important than the effect of accident, however, on the fate of the first socialist state was the impact of continuing foreign pressures. The Russian Revolution was not only an upheaval in one country but the first battle in a long war between two *international* social systems. Other elements aside, it was bound to be warped—to an extent large or small, depending on how well it fought back—so long as it remained isolated. It was bound to be hampered until it could strengthen its internal foundations and spread itself to other countries, preferably the advanced ones. Put in another way, Stalinism was part the result of the special internal circumstance that the Soviet people were exhausted, but even more, it was the result of hostile pressures by the capitalist West in a continuing international war between two social systems. It is against the background of that international war that we must assess the promise and the pitfalls of revolution—as well as the destiny of capitalism.

CHAPTER SIX

The
Middle
Years

I

The five and a half decades during which capitalism has tried to roll back socialism can be broken down into distinct phases, each of which signifies that during the previous one capitalism has partly failed, partly succeeded, but on balance has lost ground. During the first six or seven years of the confrontation the old system limited the revolution to one bastion but failed to overrun it. In the next decade the single bastion was isolated and its character warped, but it took root, like a young tree that finally shows sign of life. In the following phase both adversaries suffered serious setbacks; like two punch-drunk fighters, neither was able to deliver the coup de grace.

In the early 1930s socialism was beaten in Germany when Socialists and Communists failed to unite against Hitler. Socialism was beaten again in Austria when Otto Bauer's Social Democrats were torn to shreds during the four-day February 1934 revolution. And it was beaten a third time in the terrible civil war that engulfed Spain from 1936 to 1939 and left a million corpses. On the other hand, capitalism too had little to celebrate. It was felled by the worst economic depression in history and was beset, even while recovering, by an international trade war that grew fiercer each year. For both sides it was an anxious decade, and conditions would soon get worse.

In the 1930s, unlike the 1918–20 civil war period, when the capitalist states joined hands for military intervention, the great powers were divided on how to deal with the Soviet Union. President Franklin Roosevelt, among others, was convinced by now that the Soviet Revolution had lost its thrust and was no longer a serious danger to the status quo. He based this belief on the fact that Stalin readily offered deals to moderate local Communist activity in return for a relaxation of international tensions. Not long after the United States granted diplomatic recognition to Moscow, for instance, American Communists shifted from bitter antagonism to left-handed support of the New Deal. Concurrent with the Franco-Soviet Pact of mutual assistance in May 1935, French Communists entered into a Popular Front government with Socialists—whom they had called "social fascists" not long before—and middle-of-the-road capitalist parties. In this period fear of the "Communist menace" abated in most of the capitalist states.

On the other hand there were still important pockets of intransigence towards the Soviets, centering around Nazi Germany. In his *Mein Kampf* Hitler had proclaimed Germany's need for *Lebensraum*—living space—and openly asserted that "if we speak of soil in Europe today, we can primarily have in mind only Russia and her vassal border states."[1] Hitler's hysterical anticommunism was a fig leaf for the *Drang nach Osten* against the "giant empire in the East," which he claimed was "ripe for collapse," and though his policy received no official endorsement from London, Washington, or Paris, it was heralded by many influential political figures in those capitals who were ready to give Hitler at least limited encouragement. "In a very short time, perhaps a year or two," David Lloyd George told the House of Commons on November 28, 1934, "the Conservative elements in this country will be looking to Germany as the bulwark against Communism in Europe."[2] In November 1937 Lloyd George, joined by Winston Churchill, Lord Halifax, and others, glowingly advised the Nazi leader of their awareness "that the Fuehrer had not only achieved a great deal inside Germany herself, but that, by destroying communism in his country, he had barred its road to Western Europe, and that Germany could rightly be regarded as a bulwark of the West against

Bolshevism."[3] Many such people changed their minds subsequently, when they realized that Hitler's grandiose schemes, if successfully implemented, would give the three Axis powers control of the Euro-Asian heartland and cause the eclipse of Britain, France, and the United States as great empires. Even so, not a few prayed that the Germans and Russians would bleed each other to death. "If we see that Germany is winning the war," said Senator Harry S. Truman after Nazi armies had invaded the Soviet Union, "we ought to help Russia, and if Russia is winning we ought to help Germany, and in that way let them kill as many as possible."[4]

The inability of capitalist leaders to compose their differences in 1939 ranks as a turning point in the struggle against socialism; there would never be another opportunity to uproot it. In the war that followed, Hitler was unable to defeat the Soviet Union on the battlefield; Winston Churchill, as junior partner to Franklin Roosevelt, was unable to contain it. The aging British leader tried time and again to convince the American President that the "second front" should run from south to north, through Italy and Central Europe, rather than west to east, across the English Channel into France and the Low Countries. Under Churchill's plan, Allied armies could be placed flush against Soviet borders, confining the Kremlin to its former territory. Roosevelt, however, demurred— not because he loved communism but because he believed that American expansion after the war depended on containing the inevitable social upheavals. He was willing to enter into an "arrangement," called "coexistence," whereby Russia would widen its influence into border states and be given postwar credits for reconstruction, in return for helping assure worldwide stability.

Whether "coexistence" could have muted the conflict between the two systems is not at all certain, for no one could have prevented the native revolutions in China, Indonesia, Indochina, India, Kenya, or the Gold Coast, for example. They sprang from long-nurtured discontents, not the manipulation of leftists, either native or foreign. It was a moot question anyway, since the Allied victory over the Axis and the temporary American monopoly of the atom bomb nourished a new Western arrogance not unlike that of 1918–20. With Roosevelt gone, there was much talk in the late 1940s and early 1950s of a "preventative war." Even so august a figure as former Secretary of State James Byrnes, in his 1947 book *Speaking Frankly*, suggested that if the Russians "go to the point of holding eastern Germany and vetoing a [United Nations'] Security Council directive to withdraw occupation forces, we . . . must make clear to all that we are willing to adopt those measures of last resort if, for the peace of the world, we are forced to do so."[5] Byrnes made it clear beyond doubt that the words "measures of last resort" meant an all-out atom attack. Though cooler heads—or more timid hearts—sidetracked the "preventative war" strategy, there was no doubt that official Washington was determined to put the socialist system out of operation. The war against communism was viewed as a permanent one. In a National Security Council Paper of April 1950 (NSC–69), described by Dean Acheson as "one of the great documents in our history," the council foresaw, in the paraphrase of the *New York Times,* a conflict between the two systems "into an unforeseeable future."[6]

In the mythology of the cold war, the statement by Nikita Khrushchev at a United Nations meeting that "we will bury you" is taken to mean that socialism intended to mount an unrestrained offensive to destroy capitalism. From the focus of long-term strategy there is no question that such is its goal. But in the short term, from 1945 to 1972, it was the other way around: capitalism was making another desperate effort under the heading of "containment" to emasculate its nemesis. It applied new pressures, which continued to warp Soviet—and bloc—development, and inhibited progress toward "socialism with a human face."

II

On May 8, 1945, after being in office less than a month, Harry Truman abruptly ended lend-lease shipments to the Soviet Union and offered nothing in its place. A request by Molotov, made four months earlier, for a $6-billion thirty-year loan, and recommended by Ambassador Averell Harriman on the grounds that "the sooner the Soviet Union can develop a decent life for its people the more tolerant they will become,"[7] was gruffly pigeonholed. This was not yet the cold war, but it marked the beginning of the containment phase in the relationship between the two systems.

What was containment? The author of this historic policy, George F. Kennan, writing under the pseudonym "X" in a 1947 issue of *Foreign Affairs,* expressed it thus:

The United States has in its power to increase enormously the strains under which Soviet policy must operate, to force upon the Kremlin a far greater degree of moderation and circumspection than it has had to observe in recent years, and in this way to promote tendencies which must eventually find their outlet in either the *break-up or gradual mellowing* of Soviet power.[8]

Apart from what the word mellowing means, the American intention here is precise—and Moscow understood it precisely. It meant, in the words of A. G. Mileykovsky, writing about it years later, that "the socialist area would first be pushed back to its frontiers of 1939 and then fully liquidated."[9]

In line with the containment policy the United States made a number of overtures to the Soviet Union and its allies which, if accepted, would have meant the end of socialism in Russia. When they weren't accepted, Washington increased "enormously the strains upon which Soviet policy must operate." Behind a poisoned carrot was brandished a potent stick. The Kremlin was invited to become part of the Bretton Woods monetary system, but that would have meant accepting the open door in foreign trade and the free convertibility of all currencies into dollars. Had the Soviet Union agreed, its monopoly of foreign trade would have been breached and its economy would have become dependent on the whims of the world market rather than its own planning. Socialism would have been bludgeoned to death under the high-sounding slogan "free trade." The so-called satellite nations—except for Czechoslovakia—would have remained backward producers of raw materials, without any hope of building a viable industry. If, for instance, American steel, chemicals, and bulldozers had been permitted unchecked into the Bulgarian market, they would easily have undersold the primitive Bulgarian industry and have driven it into the ground. For Washington and George Kennan this might be a "mellowing"; for Bulgaria it would be suicide.

The results since 1947 confirm this judgment. Whatever one may say of the authoritarianism in Bulgaria, its refusal to join the "American system" has saved it from the fate of its neighbor, Turkey. Before World War II, Bulgaria and Turkey were at approximately the same stage of backwardness. Today Bulgaria's per-capita income is more than double that of Turkey's ($800 against

$347) and its progress in industry, education, health, and many other fields far more imposing. Prior to World War II the output of electricity in both nations was negligible; Turkey's continues to be small, 30,000 villages still lacking electricity, whereas the kilowatt production in Bulgaria has jumped thirty to forty times and all but the most remote mountain villages are electrified.

In March 1946 Washington advised Moscow that it was ready to grant it a billion-dollar credit on condition that the Kremlin join the International Monetary Fund and World Bank and abide by their rules on foreign commerce. The Soviets were also invited in 1947–48 to join the Marshall Plan, but with similar unacceptable conditions. The United States, of course, was demanding specific "considerations"—as James Forrestal put it—from every nation to which it gave loans or grants, sometimes being quite arrogant about it. But while Britain, for example, could accept conditions, such as rescinding its empire preference system, and still retain capitalism, the Soviet Union could not dissolve its monopoly of foreign trade and retain socialism.

In subsequent years conventional wisdom held that the cold war began because Moscow refused to permit democratic elections in Poland, refused to withdraw from Iran, and threatened to overrun Europe. In fact, as correspondent Howard K. Smith observed at the time, the shoe was on the other foot. Containment, he said, was "an excellent excuse for extending American control everywhere by establishing military bases, financing and thereby dominating threatened governments, and tying down other nations' power by standardized arms agreements."[10] The myth had no substance, except to camouflage an offensive under the defensive term containment. A nation that had lost perhaps a tenth of its population and even more of its physical resources was hardly in a position to overrun Europe—and, in fact, American leaders were well aware of it.

"I do not know any responsible official, military or civilian, in this government or any government," said John Foster Dulles in March 1949, "who believes that the Soviet government now plans conquest by open military aggression."[11] This was an estimate made at various times by Ambassador Walter Bedell Smith, Forrestal, Kennan, and others. The Russians did refuse, for a time, to withdraw from Iran, but Britain, France, Holland, and others were simultaneously refusing to withdraw from Greece, Syria, Lebanon,

Indochina, and the Dutch East Indies. And while democratic elections were not permitted in Poland, neither were they tolerated in Greece, where British troops held sway, or Madagascar, which was under French occupation.

Stalin, in fact, was more than willing to live by the rules of coexistence. The French and Italian Communists, leaders of the wartime partisan forces, permitted themselves to be disarmed and gave up the factories they held. Later they joined bourgeois governments in much of Europe and worked feverishly, as Joseph Alsop pointed out, to reconstruct the economies of the old system. Stalin not only withdrew the Red Army from Iran, Manchuria, Hungary, and Czechoslovakia but actively worked to prevent Mao Tse-tung in China and Tito in Yugoslavia from taking power. By any standard Stalin's communism was already "mellow," so mellow that French Communists refused to endorse nationalist movements in Madagascar, Tunisia, Algeria, and Morocco. But the United States was in no mood for coexistence.

III

Thus, in the absence of loans or grants from the only available outside source, the United States, the postwar Soviet regime was once again confronted with the familiar dilemma associated with capital formation—where to get it? Where was the money to come from for reconstructing a debilitated country, let alone further expansion? According to official Russian sources, 15 to 20 million people had been killed during the war and 15 large cities, 1,710 towns, and 70,000 villages lay in total or partial ruin. Six million buildings, affording shelter to 25 million citizens, had been demolished; 31,859 industrial plants, 90,000 bridges, 4,100 railway stations, 40,000 miles of railway track, 56,000 miles of highway, 10,000 power stations, and 40,000 medical centers and hospitals had been ruined or looted. The losses in cattle, poultry, and farm machinery were equally immense.[12] Recovery from this paralyzing state of affairs obviously involved a staggering sum of money— which the Soviets did not have.

Once again the Stalin regime acquired capital by squeezing the people under its rule, both those in Russia and, even more, the 110 million in the seven buffer states which were now part of the Soviet sphere of influence. Under the Yalta and Potsdam agreements, Moscow was entitled to reparations from former enemy countries—Germany, Hungary, Bulgaria, Romania—and it took them now with a harsh hand, most of it from the eastern zone of Germany.[13] Mountains of machinery were dismantled and shipped to the Soviet Union. One calculation by an anti-Soviet economist, J. Wszelaki, puts the value of such seizures, from 1945 to 1956, at $20 billion, $15 billion from East Germany, $2 billion from Romania, $1 billion from Hungary, and $2 billion from Poland.[14] Whether this figure is correct or not, the reparations were certainly substantial. Romania and Hungary alone were required to make annual payments of $500 million between them—calculated at *1938 prices*, which means the real value was probably twice that sum. Two fifths of the Romanian budget in 1946-47 and one fourth of the Hungarian went to satisfy reparation exactions. Beyond that, in East Germany, Moscow operated factories accounting for one fourth the industrial output of that zone. While these burdens were eventually relaxed and abolished, they delayed by years the recovery of Eastern Europe but they made possible a more rapid recovery in Soviet Russia.

Another source of capital was from the special agreements with nations that had been wartime allies, such as Poland and Yugoslavia. Through a complicated arrangement, Poland was compelled to deliver 8 million tons of coal to the Soviet Union in 1946 and 12 to 13 million tons in subsequent years, at below-world-market prices. The loss to Poland by 1956 was said to be $500 million. In addition the Kremlin reaped a harvest from dozens of joint companies formed with bloc countries, on a fifty-fifty basis, to exploit petroleum, quartz mining, bauxite, transportation, and shipping. The joint companies were joint only in theory. A Soviet-Yugoslav undertaking for transport on the Danube, for example, charged the U.S.S.R. 38 cents for every ton-kilometer shipped and Yugoslavia 80 cents. Milentije Popovic, in his *Economic Relations Among Socialist States*, estimated that, in its joint ventures with Bulgaria, Russia received the equivalent of 2.7 man-days of labor for one day of its own labor.

These severe methods of accumulating capital raise some interesting questions. Admittedly, they were forced on the Soviet leadership by the policy of containment; if the Lord himself had been at the helm in the Kremlin he would have had to exploit somebody to secure the funds for reconstruction. But how does one justify one socialist country seizing billions in machinery from another socialist country under the guise of reparations? Lenin, in 1917, it will be recalled, demanded a peace with "no annexations and no indemnities." If it were necessary to make sacrifices, and clearly it was, why couldn't they have been shared equally by the eight socialist countries rather than exacted in such a way as to favor the Soviet Union? The injustice of reparations was compounded by the injustice in terms of trade: what the Soviet Union bought from its allies was pegged at low prices, what it sold at high prices. This is exactly the relationship between capitalist United States and its satellites in Latin America; the coffee from Brazil keeps going down in price or goes up slowly, whereas the tractors from the United States go up steadily and considerably. Conceding that the unfavorable terms of trade dictated by the Soviets was short-lived and has since been favorably adjusted, the question still remains: Why did one socialist government seek advantage against other socialist governments?

In part the answer lies in Stalin's methods and style—of placing burdens on people as far away from his own source of power as possible. In part it rests with the innate tendency of all sovereign states, whatever their social complexion, to defend themselves at the expense of others. The inequality of sacrifice that Stalin demanded, however, was not the overriding injustice in the situation. The overriding injustice was the American effort—as Kennan put it—"to increase enormously the strains under which Soviet policy must operate." There is no question that without Soviet participation the war would have lasted considerably longer and perhaps ended somewhat differently. Certainly, of those in the Allied camp, the Russians made far and away the largest sacrifices, both in terms of men lost and of property lost. Yet the United States felt no strong obligation to help in Soviet recovery; on the contrary it used the crisis as an opportunity to try and break up or "mellow" socialism. Aid should have been forthcoming without *any* conditions, simply as repayment by one ally to another for the greater contributions it had made to the common effort. Instead, aid was dangled before the Kremlin under condition that, in effect, it jettison its socialist character. Whatever the injustices against the bloc countries, therefore, the much greater injustice was the pressure applied on the Soviet Union by the West generally and the United States in particular.

Given this situation, there was no other course but to squeeze someone, and Stalin chose to squeeze primarily the people of the socialist bloc. Again, as in the 1930s, what is interesting is not only *how* capital was formed but that once it was formed the socialist system was able to utilize it effectively. Having reached what economists call the takeoff point, Soviet industry pushed ahead from 1947 to 1950 at a growth rate of 20 to 26 percent annually. Steel production, as good a barometer as any to measure material development, jumped from 18 million tons in 1940 to 27 million tons by 1950 and 45 million tons by 1955. Output of electric power leaped in the same time span from 48 billion kilowatt hours to 91 billion to 170 billion.[15] Considering the tensions and costs of the cold war and the sums diverted for military preparedness, this was no small achievement—even if the consumer industries still were starved and the bloc countries paid much of the price.

There was, however, a negative aspect to this saga, moving almost in cadence with foreign pressures. No one as yet has written a definitive study correlating Stalin's terror to the hardship of a recovery pursued without outside aid. But it is obvious even to the naked eye. "In the first phase" of Soviet rule in Eastern Europe, writes Hugh Seton-Watson, an unabashed critic, "government was by a genuine coalition of parties of left and left center."[16] These governments included non-Socialist peasant parties in Hungary, Romania, and Bulgaria, and peasant-supported parties in Czechoslovakia. The November 1945 election in Hungary was by all accounts the most democratic in many decades, if not in its whole history. The Small Landholders' Party captured 59 percent of the vote as against 18 percent for the Socialists and 17 percent for the Communists. No one can be sure what might have happened if Stalin and Truman had reached a détente; the spiral of Stalinist authoritarianism might have been reversed, as it was to be after 1953. But the cold war placed a steel fence around the socialist bloc and foisted a heavy burden on it. Stalin might have responded to this challenge by an idealistic call for equality of sacrifice or a cogent explanation as to why self-exploitation was necessary. Instead he tightened the controls and sought scapegoats to deflect attention from his own responsibility for an unpopular course.

In one country after another, the non-Communist parties were driven into merger with the Communist parties or were obliged to yield power to them. The policy reached a climax in February 1949 when the Czech Communists managed a bloodless uprising against the government of Eduard Benes. The next step, purging of nationalist elements within the Communist parties, was virtually inevitable. Many Communist leaders, especially those who had fought in the underground or with partisan forces, responded to popular sentiments by urging more consumer goods and less coercion. One of the "crimes" listed against Wladyslaw Gomulka in Poland, for instance, was that he had promised the peasants they would not be collectivized. Such leaders, by and large, were the ones purged. Politburo member and Minister of Interior Laszlo Rajk was tried in Hungary in September 1949 on the farcical charge of being an American and Yugoslav agent—and executed. (Like most of the major purgees he was later "rehabilitated.") Traicho Kostov, a Deputy Prime Minister in Bulgaria, suffered a similar fate, though he repudiated his alleged confession in open court. Foreign Minister Vladimir Clementis, Deputy Prime Minister Rudolf Slansky, and many others in Czechoslovakia fell in 1950–51, and more than half the ninety-seven members of the party's Central Committee were removed. In Romania, Poland, and East Germany the number of executions was small, but key figures such as Gomulka were removed from office and imprisoned. A U.S. Department of State estimate—probably exaggerated, but indicative nonetheless—put the figure of Communists ousted from their party in six East European countries at 1.75 million. Within Russia itself the followers of Andrei Zhdanov were similarly eliminated, how many thousands of them is anyone's guess.[17]

As with the Stalinist purges of the 1930s, these were gross injustices that were morally reprehensible. The institutionalized Stalinist schema, however, demanded rapid industrialization; the average citizen in the Soviet area, therefore, had to pigeonhole his hopes for a better life and submit to discipline and austerity as if he were at war. In fact, this was part of Stalin's rationale. He was convinced, as he had been in 1928, that an invasion by the West was imminent. The Hungarian dissident, Imre Nagy, subsequently criticized the "overemphasis of the war danger" in the "years 1949 to 1952." But whether it was overemphasized or not, it was there, especially after the Americans established a separate West Germany and the Russians replied with a blockade of Berlin. A year later the Korean War broke out, and with it, according to a bitter critic, Professor Zbigniew K. Brzezinski, came an even greater intensification of the monolithic pressures inherent in Stalinism. The threat of a total war . . . obscured internal differences and created a unity born of fear. The conflict, no matter who began it, seemed to bear out the Stalinist position that America had been preparing for war against the Soviet camp. If it had not, then why should it intervene in an area [Korea] which it had previously disclaimed as being of no political or strategic significance?[18]

Both the feverish pace of industrialization, with its attendant austerity, and the terror that followed in its wake are linked to the fear of war with the United States. This fear does not justify the execution of innocent people whose only crime was to differ with Stalin's plans and estimates. But it makes clear that they came about not because of the venality of a single man (although that too played a part) but much more because of the interaction of two hostile social systems.

IV

Why the hot war did not come about is a matter of speculation. Perhaps it was too soon after the previous catastrophe. Perhaps the acquisition of the atom and hydrogen bombs by the Russians made such a step too risky. But the cold war had many effects on the course of socialist life similar to what a hot war might have had. The pressures from without propelled the Soviet bloc into emergency-type improvisations which distorted its system of economic planning to a caricature.

On March 26, 1948, Truman banned the sale of aircraft to Eastern Europe. In November more items were added to the proscribed list and special measures were taken to prevent American merchandise, sold to Latin America, from being resold to the Soviet bloc. The big blow came with the passage of the Export Control Act of 1949, which prohibited the sale of military or strategic goods to the socialist states on the grounds it was a threat to Uncle Sam's national security. The words "military" and "strategic" were so broadly construed that in the month of September the United States shipped only $100,000 worth of cargo to the U.S.S.R. In March 1950 six hundred types of goods were listed as requiring special export licenses, including heavy machinery, industrial machinery, industrial chemicals, alloy metals, and electronic equipment. In the case of China, North Korea, and later North Vietnam and Cuba, the embargo was total. Moreover, as a corollary to its Marshall Plan aid, the United States required all recipients to join the embargo on penalty of being denied American grants and loans themselves.

To make matters worse, the embargo embraced not only equipment and materials but technical know-how. American firms were prohibited from supplying the socialist nations—directly or indirectly—with classified

> information of any kind that can be used, or adapted for use, in the design, production, manufacture, utilization, or reconstruction of articles or materials. The data may take a tangible form, such as a model, prototype, blueprint, or an operating manual; or they may take an intangible form such as a technical service.[19]

Needless to say, supervising such curbs was so wide-ranging a task it was never total. But the United States pursued it with vigor. Two Italian firms, for instance, were sued for $182 million because they applied technical knowledge, supplied them by an American company to build a plastics factory in Sicily, for similar construction in Poland and Czechoslovakia. "Not only must foreign firms meet the problems of segregating their technical knowledge by source," wrote Samuel Pisar, "but they are also required to submit written assurances that know-how of American origin which has come to their attention will not pass into the hands of communist users, without prior authorization."[20] To make the trade and technical restrictions complete, the United States effectively barred or reduced Soviet exports to America through discriminatory tariffs many times higher than what other nations were charged. Had the United States conferred equal status to Soviet imports, the tariff on a gallon of vodka, for instance, would have been $1.25; but in fact it was $5.

A Czech economist once explained to me the ripple effect of the ban on one item, sulfur. With the foreign supply cut off, the Soviet bloc had no choice but to reactivate certain Czech mines that provided a very low grade ore at a cost two and a half times the world price of sulfur. Thus every product in which sulfur was used was that much more costly than—and that much less competitive with—similar products in the capitalist world. If the example of sulfur is multiplied by hundreds, one gets an idea of the nightmarish problem faced by the socialist countries both in cost accounting and competition with the West. In many instances Soviet and East European factories either used inferior substitutes for what they couldn't buy from Uncle Sam and his friends or did without. That explains, in part, why so many commodities they fabricate seem unfinished or are of low quality.

Cut adrift from the world market by the American-sponsored embargo and by discrimination against its exports, the socialist world turned inward. What could have been bought elsewhere—and cheaper—had to be reassigned for production to bloc countries, at higher cost. Planning programs had to be coordinated to limit duplication, and since there could be no thought of free trade, a new mechanism had to be established for commercial intercourse. In January 1949 the Soviet Union and five Eastern European nations formed the Council for Mutual Economic Assistance (Comecon), later adhered to by East Germany, Outer Mongolia, North Korea, North Vietnam, and Cuba. Here business was conducted on a semibarter basis, with each nation entering into a host of bilateral agreements to exchange so many rubles' worth of one item for so many of another. It was an unwieldy and insular arrangement, but inevitable under the circumstances. By 1953 more than four fifths of Soviet commerce was within its own bloc, its trade turnover with Comecon states having grown from $777 million to $4,773 million. A similar change occurred in the trade patterns of the rest of the bloc.

Stalin hailed this parallel market as a giant stride forward. "The disintegration of the single all-embracing world market," he wrote, "must be regarded as the most important economic consequence of the second world war." It was, he said, a great advance for communism and simultaneously "has had the effect of further deepening the general crisis of the world capitalist system."[21] In truth, of course, it was nothing of the sort; it was an emergency measure, a defensive step, and while it did ameliorate some of the commercial problems of the East, it gravely aggravated others.

Comecon's plan for a self-sufficient "socialist international division of labor" resulted in many maladjustments. Czechoslovakia, to take one example, had once been one of the most efficient industrial economies in the world, noted for the high-grade engineering at its Vitkovice ironworks and Skoda auto factories, as well as the high quality of its textiles, glassware, shoes, and chinaware. Forced into a market system with a low level of quality, however, Czech products also deteriorated toward the low common denominator. Since it could not buy the higher-grade machinery of the West, it lost its place as a marvel of efficiency and product excellence. The standard of the Soviet bloc as a whole lagged behind that of the West. As one East German economist delicately put it, "In certain cases the limited scope of the existing international division of labor [within Comecon] leads to a situation in which production is not always equipped with modern techniques, especially in machine-building."[22] As of 1970, according to *U.S. News and World Report,* the Soviets had only 5,000 computers in operation while the United States had 60,000—and much more sophisticated ones. Russia was producing 1,000 computers annually as against 25,000 by the United States. Nor could this gap be closed by imports, because the NATO nations and Japan continued an embargo on the more complex computers.

To an extent, the gap in technology was compensated for by throwing ever larger numbers of workers into the factories. Since there was a vast redundancy of agricultural labor, millions of peasants could still be drawn from the villages into the textile mills and chemical plants. The socialist states did not have to worry that their costs were higher than those of the capitalists, or that efficiency per man-hour of labor was lower. On their own *parallel market* they did not have to compete with the West. Suppose, for instance, that it cost $8 to produce a pair of shoes in Prague which could be manufactured for $6 in Rome, and suppose further that it cost $2 to produce a bushel of wheat in the U.S.S.R. that could be produced in France for $1.50. Czechoslovakia and the Soviet Union could exchange shoes for wheat at the $6 and $1.50 prices—the world market prices—without harm to either one. A pair of Czech shoes "bought" four bushels of Russian wheat, whether you figured it at world market prices or internal Soviet bloc prices. Since the levels of inefficiency were probably fairly similar, and since each socialist government had a considerable amount of leeway because of its monopoly of foreign trade, the parallel market could function without undue concern for efficiency and quality. The relatively small amount of trade with the capitalist states could be effected by selling below cost and the losses absorbed by the rest of the economy.

Nonetheless, despite Stalin's brave words—and those of some of his successors—the "second" world market remained uncompetitive with the real world market. It had to accept second-class status. As late as March 19, 1970, three Russian scholars wrote to Brezhnev, Kosygin, and Podgorny that

> comparing our economy to that of the United States we find that we are behind not only on the quantitative plane but also —and this is much sadder—on the qualitative plane. The gulf between the United States and us is all the greater in the newest and most revolutionary sectors of the economy. We are ahead of America in coal extraction, but behind in oil, gas and electric energy; we are ten years behind in chemicals and infinitely behind in computer technology. . . . We simply live in another era.[23]

The three scholars were dissidents who differed with the official view on many things, but there is little doubt that their estimate was valid.

The second market operated under enormous handicaps, not the least of which was that it reinvigorated state domination over the individual and was a much less effective form of planning. The state set wages and prices, allocated materials, and exercised a veto power even on minor decisions of individual plant managers. This was certainly a form of planning, but not a very desirable one— the worst kind possible, in fact, for it not only undercut political freedom but grossly limited individual initiative. More, by continuing to stress heavy industry and by downgrading consumer industry, it accentuated inferior quality and *under*consumption. There were always long lines in the stores for certain wares, always shortages, always insufficient concern for consumer wishes. I once asked the manager of a dress factory employing thousands of workers in Moscow how he knew what women wanted to buy. He replied that it didn't matter because there was never enough to meet demand, anyway, and no other manufacturers in that area from whom to buy. "Unless a woman wants to make her own dresses at home," he said, "she has no choice but to take our product."

The vice of poor quality is built into the very structure of over-centralized planning. The price of goods is set by the state; and since that price, as often as not, is likely to be artificial and unreflective of true value, it is a poor measuring rod for economic results. The plan, therefore, sets goals in terms of units or weight—so many tons of steel, so many lathes, so many yards of cloth. The plant manager is judged not by the quality of his products—as he would be if he had to sell on an open market or had to make an accounting to consumer groups—but by his *quantitative* accomplishments. The result is that he skimps on a vital safety gadget, he uses a poor dye in coloring cloth, he transfers inspectors who ordinarily check quality to jobs on assembly lines. Almost everyone who has written on the Soviet economy—and not a few Soviet observers, as well—has commented on the inferior grade of its products. One can see it to this day just walking through Moscow —new buildings, for instance, with cracks in the concrete or electrical fixtures amateurishly installed. A few years ago I saw nets on the outside of some relatively new housing projects, placed there to catch bricks insecurely held by low-grade mortar. Since there is a shortage of apartments in Moscow, the Soviet government does not have to worry about finding tenants, even for buildings with loose bricks.

The defects of socialist planning in the first dozen years after World War II, like those of the 1930s, had distasteful consequences for the people of that part of the world and tarnished socialism's image for the tutored and untutored elsewhere. But whether those defects might have been avoided or mitigated—as I personally believe—they were in the final analysis the bruises of battle between two social systems. In the long run those bruises will heal and be forgotten; for in the same period socialism broke out of three decades of isolation and made an extraordinary leap into the economic stratosphere. As of the mid-1950s it was no longer confined to a single country but embraced twelve nations with more than a third of the world's population and a quarter of the world's area—not counting the many nations in the Third World which also considered themselves socialist. The Communist bloc produced half the world's coal, three tenths of its steel, one fifth of its electric power. As of 1957 industrial output of the capitalist countries was twice that of 1937; that of the Communist countries 8.7 times higher. American production in 1958, following a similar pattern, was double that of 1940; Soviet production 4.3 times as great.[24] Admitting that the socialist states started from a much lower base, they still had many feathers for their caps; and if they lived "in another era" compared to the United States, as the three Soviet scholars averred, they were also in another era much more bountiful, compared to their recent past.

V

Though it is difficult to tote the balance sheet in the ongoing war between capitalism and socialism during this period—for capitalism, too, made breathtaking economic strides—two developments offered important clues for the future. If we are interested in determining which *direction* the world is going, these developments are most informative. One was the semicollapse of European capitalism for a time in the 1940s, revealing both its vulnerability and the pivotal role of America in rescuing it. Another, of equal portent, was the evolution of an anti-Stalinist socialism in Yugoslavia, the first major step toward worldwide humanistic socialism.

Not only the vanquished but the victors of World War II—except for the United States—were in desperate circumstances at the end of hostilities. Britain, the linchpin of capitalism until not too long ago, was in dire straits despite billions of wartime lend-lease and a $3.75 billion postwar loan from the United States. Traditionally, the British economy depended on exports and on earnings from its merchant marine and foreign investments to keep it afloat. Less than 5 percent of the population was engaged in agriculture. Farm products and raw materials such as cotton, rubber, wool, iron ore, and oil had to be imported in large quantities. But Britain was no longer in a position to pay for them. She had sold outright $3 billion of her overseas holdings and had mortgaged most of the rest, about $9 billion, against her debts. War damage and shipping losses had depleted her capital assets by another $9 billion. If British citizens were to enjoy 1939 living standards, the country's exports, it was estimated, would have to climb by 75 percent; but actually they had declined by two thirds. Each day John Bull was being depleted of precious dollars, a circumstance that threatened him with imminent bankruptcy. Bread was still being rationed, austerity was still severe, yet the crisis refused to abate.

Conditions elsewhere were as bad or worse. France was producing only half as much iron and steel as before the war, and farmers were withholding food from the market—as in Russia in the late 1920s—because there were insufficient consumer goods to be had in the cities. Germany lay in rubble, its major cities—Cologne, Essen, Berlin, Frankfurt, Hamburg, Munich, and Mannheim—immobile ghost towns. Food was scarce, money almost worthless. One could sell a pack of cigarettes on the German black market for the equivalent of a worker's pay for a whole month. There was no fuel for heating, the food ration was below 1,500 calories a day, apartments were unavailable, jobs few and far between. As Dean Acheson, Undersecretary of State, summarized the global situation, "the world needed and should receive in 1947 exports from the United States—the only source—of sixteen billion dollars (four times our prewar exports), and could find imports to the United States with which to pay for them of only half that sum."[25] A balance-of-payments deficit of $5 billion faced Britain, France, Italy, and the western zones of Germany. "It is now obvious," said William Clayton, Undersecretary of State for Economic Affairs, "that we have grossly underestimated the destruction to the European economy by the war."[26]

The emergency was aggravated in the winter of 1946–47 by an unexpected natural disaster, when the continent suffered one of the worst snowstorms and cold spells of this century. Like a bulldozer tearing through the countryside, the storm made a shambles of what was left of the British economy. As of February, half the factories were inoperative, transport was at a standstill, coal mines were closed, gas and electric service vastly curtailed, and millions out of work. When the cold spell ended and the thaw arrived, the nation was hampered by floods which worsened matters for months more. A financial editor of Reuters observed that "The biggest crash since the fall of Constantinople—the collapse of the heart of an Empire—impends." It was not due, he said, to "a couple of snowstorms" but to "the awful debility in which a couple of snowstorms could have such effects."[27]

In this emergency, Britain not only was unable to police its empire—it was forced to cut India, Burma, and Ceylon adrift and to withdraw troops from Greece—but to appease its populace at home. The prospect of revolution in the advanced countries—

Britain, France, Italy, Germany—shifted from a long- term theoretical potential to something more immediate. Clayton told a New York audience in December 1947 that unless Washington provided help, and quickly, "the Iron Curtain would then move westward at least to the English Channel." Europe, in other words, would fall to the Communists or some other leftist force, and this in turn would mean "a blackout of the European market [that] could compel readjustments in our entire [U.S.] economic structure . . . changes which could hardly be made under our democratic free-enterprise system."[28]

Stalin and his Communists, let it be noted, did not take advantage of capitalism's travail. On the contrary. Still hoping for coexistence and still oriented on "socialism in one country," he helped stabilize the old system. "Near the end of the war," writes historian D. F. Fleming, "Stalin scoffed at communism in Germany, urged the Italian Reds to make peace with the monarchy, did his best to induce Mao Tse-tung to come to terms with the Kuomintang and angrily demanded of Tito that he back the monarchy, thus fulfilling his [Stalin's] bargain with Churchill."[29] In France and Italy, on the morrow of liberation—while De Gaulle was still in Algiers and Italy was in monumental confusion—the Communist-controlled partisans and *garibaldini* took over the factories in both countries. With their stockpile of armaments and their mass followings they might have gone further, to a full-scale revolution. But General De Gaulle took a plane to Moscow and talked with Stalin, and French Communists evacuated factories and submitted to the disarmament of the partisans. Another word from Moscow and revolutionary danger abated in Italy. So moderate was Communist policy that French Communists refused to endorse the nationalist movements in the colonies; the upheavals in Madagascar, Tunisia, Algeria, and Morocco occurred despite them, not because of them.

Communists also entered "bourgeois governments" throughout Europe—willingly, even enthusiastically. For almost two years Maurice Thorez, veteran Communist leader, was vice-premier of France, and Palmiro Togliatti held a similar position in Italy. Europe was distressingly vulnerable to internal revolt—yet the followers of the Kremlin armed no guerrilla detachments, engineered no uprisings. They worked avidly instead to revive capitalism. Joseph Alsop, writing for the *New York Herald Tribune* on July 12, 1946, was struck by the cooperation planner Jean Monnet was getting from Communists in reconstructing France:

> The key to the success of the plan to date, which has been considerable, is the enthusiastic collaboration of the French Communist Party. The communists control the most important unions. . . . Communist leadership has been responsible for such surprising steps as acceptance by the key unions of a kind of modified piecework system. . . . Reconstruction comes first, is the Party line.

Had Stalin sought to intensify the crisis, matters would have been far worse for the West. As it was, the United States saved Europe and Japan unhindered by revolt. Truman proclaimed his famous Doctrine and received from Congress $400 million to aid Turkey and Greece. The Marshall Plan pumped $12.3 billion into Western Europe over the next four years to revive its economy and close the dollar gap. Whatever the shortcomings and injustices of the plan (it imposed many conditions on the recipients), it did work. By 1950, when the Korean War broke out, the seventeen nations were operating at an economic level 25 percent higher than prewar and the dollar gap had been reduced from $12 billion to $2 billion. The heartland of capitalism was reclaimed. It has survived in the last two decades on a plane of prosperity never reached before.

Confounding critics who predicted another enervating depression, capitalism showed considerable resiliency. Nonetheless, it also revealed its vulnerability: the minuses, in other words, outweighed the pluses. The British, French, and Dutch empires decomposed. The Dutch East Indies, one of the richest and most populous of colonies, became the independent nation of Indonesia after a brief period of guerrilla war and political confrontation. Britain not only lost the pearl of its empire, India, but its influence in such places as Greece—and soon the Middle East—as well. Mohammed Naguib and Gamal Abdel Nasser led a revolt in Egypt which effectively took it—and the Suez Canal—out of the British orbit of control. Kwame Nkrumah broke the British shackles in the Gold Coast, initiating an upheaval that would soon sweep almost all of sub-Saharan Africa.

The same decay infected the French empire: Madagascar broke loose from French moorings, revolts lashed at Algeria and the rest of North Africa, and the Vietnamese defeated France at Dienbienphu. Most important of all, China, with 600 million people, finally became independent, under the aegis of communism.

Within ten or fifteen years dozens of nations comprising more than half of humanity were embroiled in the most extensive revolution of all history. Some limited their sights to national independence, but many coupled independence with socialism as twin objectives. The subsequent development of these revolutions, most of them under leadership other than the Communists, was far from homogeneous. In certain places—Malaya and Morocco, for instance—the governments effected little social change and were content to hitch themselves to the American chariot. But in others —Guinea and Tanganyika, to cite two examples—the leadership instituted significant changes and took a neutralist position. Not a few of the neutralist countries eventually veered toward the Soviet Union and China as their friends and protectors—India, Bangladesh, Pakistan, Tanzania, Algeria, Iraq, Syria, and Egypt, to name a few. Thus, though the United States saved the heartland of capitalism from socialism, it steadily lost influence around the periphery, in the former colonies. Such countries as Iran, Bolivia, Taiwan, Ivory Coast, Guatemala, and the Dominican Republic were held by the West. But it was a shrinking sphere in which a few nations went Communist, many more neutralist and leftist.

Back in 1951 John Fischer, liberal editor of *Harper's Magazine*, boasted that "the Line of Containment has held, under great pressure, in Korea, Greece, Indochina, Turkey, Berlin and Yugoslavia. We have suffered one major defeat—China—but that may yet be recovered."[30] Fischer's optimism, however, was more synthetic than real. The fact was that containment had failed to hold the line and there was no hope whatsoever that socialism could be rolled back or China "recovered." Capitalism, while not yet in rout, was certainly in retreat.

On the other side of the international social equation, the results were also inconclusive. For while socialism had burst out of its isolation and made considerable advances, it still had not penetrated the bastions of the capitalist system. Moreover, the Communist nations had been hurt by American cold war pressures, and what might have been a fairly rapid movement toward humanistic socialism proceeded more slowly. Nonetheless, along with socialism's economic successes, the counteraction to Stalinism did begin and "socialism with a human face" did make its first appearances. Yugoslavia, though a small country off the beaten path of world affairs, opened a chapter in the history of the capitalist-socialist confrontation of unique and perhaps decisive significance.

CHAPTER SEVEN

Socialism
With a
Human Face

I

It is not particularly original to point out that history is a cauldron of conflicts in which individuals, groups, classes, subnations, and nations seek power (privilege and/or riches) against other individuals, groups, classes, subnations, and nations. But original or not, it is necessary to restate this thesis if only to emphasize that there can be no coagulation of power on the one side without the emergence, either openly or subrosa, of a countervailing power on the other. The needs and wishes of inarticulate masses somehow find advocates or spokesmen even in the most monolithic of systems.

In some instances the opposing strains in a given nation's development are easily delineated. The United States always seems to have had a Hamiltonian strain and a Jeffersonian one, the former striving to concentrate power in the hands of the "rich and well-born," as Hamilton put it; the latter trying to disperse power to a broader spectrum of the population. The Jeffersonians—from the Democratic Clubs through Jacksonian democracy, the Abolitionists, Grangers, Populists, Progressives, New Dealers, and present-day liberals—did not try to overthrow capitalism but, in answer to the stirrings of the "injured and oppressed," to humanize it.

The humanistic strain is not so clearly delineated in the saga of socialism, because its history is bisected by twenty-five years of Stalinism, when all dissidents were severely dealt with. Even during that quarter of a century, however, and certainly in the first few years, there were pockets of opposition to Stalin's ruthlessness. A Soviet Marxist, Roy A. Medvedev, tells in his book *Let History Judge* of antagonism so widespread in 1933–34 that a move was made to replace Stalin as party secretary with Sergei Kirov.[1] Significantly, at the congress of the party that year Stalin received less votes for the Central Committee than any other candidate. It is widely believed in non-Communist circles that Kirov was assassinated in 1934 to emasculate the opposition, a charge that was given some credence by Khrushchev in his famous 1956 speech when he referred to the "many things which are inexplicable and mysterious" in Kirov's death.[2] Whether sub-rosa opposition continued after 1934 or how extensive it was is not yet known. But it is inconceivable that it was entirely extinguished. That conclusion is reinforced by the fact that on the morrow following Stalin's death in 1953, the collective leadership that replaced him liberated hundreds of thousands of people from the forced labor camps and Premier Georgi Malenkov won approval for a New Course which was a wide-ranging repudiation of the Stalinist course. It is difficult to believe that these "new" ideas came to Malenkov and others in the bloc countries during a grand moment of inspiration; it is more credible that they nursed them for a long time, waiting for the propitious moment to put them forward.

In any case, whatever Stalin's success in repressing the humanistic strain within the Soviet Union, it tended to reappear in Eastern Europe very soon after World War II. And in Yugoslavia it established an enduring base which merits greater attention than it has yet been given.

II

Tito's quarrel with Stalin began on the issue of national autonomy and expanded from there into the broader area of how socialism should be constructed.

The Yugoslav Communists, unlike East European Communists who had been installed by the Soviet army, had come to power on their own efforts. They had organized a Partisan movement of 800,000 guerrillas that withstood everything Hitler had thrown at them; they were not likely to stay supine for anyone. In their memory was a smoldering resentment against Stalin for having tried, during the war, to force them into a united national front with Drazha Mihailovich's Chetniks, a right-wing guerrilla force loyal to King Peter's government-in-exile. They had refused afterward to share power with the king, though Stalin had given pledges to Churchill that they would.

Josip Broz (Tito) himself was a man of considerable stature, who had fought in the Spanish Civil War and had stayed with his guerrillas on Yugoslav soil throughout the perilous years. Now he and his former Partisans were appalled by the demands made on them by a "fraternal" socialist country. They chafed at the bit over the joint stock companies. They resisted Stalin's urging to industrialize slowly, so that they might provide raw materials and agricultural products to the Soviets. And they were particularly bitter over the strutting behavior of Soviet military specialists and Soviet intelligence agents who threw their weight around as if they were in conquered territory. Red Army officers stationed in Yugoslavia received $600 to $800 a month pay, as against $180 to $220 for men of comparable rank in the local forces. Soviet intelligence was recruiting agents within the native army and throughout the civilian population as if it were in an enemy country.[3]

The issue that brought the conflict to a head was a flirtation between Tito and Georgi Dimitrov of Bulgaria, which had as its goal the federation of their two countries. In August 1947 the two men signed an agreement to form a customs union and abolish frontier formalities. "We shall establish cooperation so general and so close," said Tito, "that federation will be a mere formality." Dimitrov set his sights even higher, to include all six Balkan states, plus Greece, in the federation.[4] Needless to say, Stalin was not enthralled with the idea of a power center that might someday challenge his own authority. He gave Dimitrov a severe tongue-lashing, enough to make him buckle, and as reprisal against Tito held up a $40-million trade agreement which just then was of vital urgency for Yugoslavia. In the ensuing exchange of letters, the Yugoslav made it clear that while he wanted to remain an ally of the Soviet Union he refused to accept for his country the role of satellite. The fissure widened with each letter until June 1948, when the rupture was finalized at a conference of the Communist

Information Bureau (Cominform), which excommunicated the Titoists for alleged "anti-Party and anti-Soviet" behavior.[5]

Yugoslavia was now isolated, much as the Soviet Union had been in the 1920s, except that the trade and credit boycott against it was Soviet-sponsored, not capitalist-sponsored, and the danger of invasion originated from Moscow, not Washington. For a year or two Tito cherished the hope that Stalin would reconcile himself to an independent Communist state. At the 1948 convention of his party, the Yugoslav leader ended his speech with the ringing words: "Long live the Soviet Union, Long live Stalin!"[6] He dismissed as slander the possibility of receiving aid from the capitalist West. Stalin, however, did not relent, and Tito was forced to readjust his perspectives. If Yugoslavia were to survive it had to turn to the West and the Third World to market its exports—one sixth of everything it produced. Changing from one market to another, moreover, was not just a matter of soliciting new customers. It demanded a quantum jump in efficiency to meet international standards of price and quality, and that in turn was impossible without tapping the initiative of the producers—managers, workers, peasants. In the cloistered confines of the parallel market in which the Soviet bloc functioned, price, quality, and unit cost could be partly disregarded by applying the heavy-handed methods of state manipulation—what Tito called "administrative socialism" and "bureaucratic centralism." But in present Yugoslav circumstances that was no longer feasible. More, it was now necessary to guard against a possible Red Army attack (as was to happen later in Hungary and Czechoslovakia), and that also could not be done without consolidating popular allegiance by involving the mass of Yugoslavs in decision-making. Out of these necessities was born the system of "self-management" which became the cornerstone of Titoist socialism.

The Soviets had progressively centralized economic and political power; the Yugoslavs, beginning with the Workers' Council law of 1950, progressively decentralized. They opened their economy to the checks and balances of the market, competition, and popular involvement. As outlined by Tito, "self-management" called for Yugoslavia to "inaugurate the process of the withering away of the state," to keep the party "at a safe distance from the state apparatus," and to supplant nationalized industry with "social ownership."[7] These were to be the guidelines of the new socialism.

Under the principles of "social ownership" and "self-management," the enterprise—mine, mill, factory, department store, hotel—is deemed to be under the collective control of those who work in the particular enterprise, not the "nationalized" property of the government. It is managed by the workers themselves, not by a centralized state through a central plan—much in the tradition of Louis Blanc's workshops or William H. Sylvis' producer cooperatives. In each enterprise the Workers' Collective elects a Workers' Council, which in turn chooses a small Management Committee to decide matters of policy—subject to approval or veto by the council every few weeks or months and by the collective every year. The Management Committee hires, fires, and sets the salary of the director. It determines what products to manufacture, how much and from what bank to borrow, the sales and advertising budget, the price ranges, what to export and import, and whether to merge or work out pooling agreements with other enterprises.

The Management Committee, charged with earning a profit, is given a large measure of autonomy in sales as well as production. Unlike the Stalinist system in which a bureaucracy determined the purchaser and price in advance, the self-managed enterprise in Yugoslavia can sell to anyone it pleases at whatever price it can get. A yard of cloth or a pack of cigarettes may sell at one price in one store and a higher or lower one in another. The enterprise hires salesmen, makes marketing surveys at home and abroad, places advertising on radio, television, billboards, and in newspapers—all aimed at increasing sales and profits. Often it employs foreign experts to improve styling and production techniques. If this mode of operation seems similar to that of capitalism, it has the fundamental difference that the surpluses go to the worker and society as a whole, not the individual entrepreneur or shareholder.

Within the enterprise there is a further decentralization of decision-making. Each department is organized as a separate unit with the right to do its own hiring and firing and organize some of its own work. Its earnings depend not on preset wage scales but on how well the department meets quotas approved by the Management Committee and Workers' Council. In a number of factories I visited a few years ago there was a dispute between individual departments and management over the question of tardiness. The supervisors held that lateness was reducing production; the workers insisted that it was their own affair and that they themselves could be depended on to invoke discipline if they felt that lateness actually cut into their earnings.

At the end of the year the government takes its share of the profits, the workers theirs. Until the mid-1960s the division was about 70 percent for the state and 30 percent for the workers. With the reform of 1965, however, the percentage was reversed to 30 percent for the state and 70 percent for the Workers' Council. The profits can be used by the Council in one of three ways: for new equipment, for social improvements such as housing or medical facilities, or to pay a bonus to the employees. In effect the members of the Workers' Collective do not receive wages, as such, but a share of earnings—as in any partnership. Weekly wages are merely a down payment on the final annual accounting. If there happens to be a loss, the workers are required to cut their earnings to a certain minimum, below which the state subsidizes them.

This system may appear to be anarchistic, subject to the whims of an impersonal market and the efficiency levels of each group of producers. But in fact it isn't. The federal government and each of the six republican governments do have a plan and retain many levers to enforce it. Without spelling out the minute details, the government sets targets—so much steel, so much minerals, so much agricultural goods—but instead of using direct compulsion to achieve these targets, as in the Stalinist system, it applies *in*direct pressures. It determines, for instance, when and approximately where a new plant or hotel should be built and allocates capital for the project. One of the republics and its local administrative agencies takes over from there to plan the actual construction and operation. If the national regime is not satisfied with either the quantity or quality of production in an enterprise, it imports competitive products from abroad; to force its own soda water industry to improve, for instance, it may import soda water from Italy. The government also directs the flow of capital and production through its tax policy—higher taxes on less needed goods, lower taxes on those more vital to the economy. It denies or approves import and export licenses, sets the rates on foreign exchange, and in an emergency, though this has become less frequent with the years, mobilizes the League of Communist members in a particular enterprise to push for a particular policy. So that, while each enterprise is theoretically free to fabricate, say, luxury automobiles rather than trucks, or television tubes rather than electric bulbs, in practice its prerogatives are more limited.

Concomitant with self-management in industry, mining, and commerce, the Titoists decided to abandon collectivization of agriculture. It would have been both inconsistent and uneconomic to retain compulsion in the village while relaxing it elsewhere. The collectives therefore were permitted to disband, and 5.5 million farmers were allowed a maximum of 25 acres each (as of 1968) for personal use. To help them toward greater productivity, the government formed Scandinavian-type service cooperatives in each village to provide seed, machinery, fertilizer, and credits as well as to market the crops. The hated buy-up is long gone. If you ask a Yugoslav theoretician how he expects to introduce socialism in agriculture, he tells you that the 2,300 socially owned farms, which operate on self-management principles and are presumed to be more efficient than small individually run farms, will eventually draw the latter into their ranks. The private farmer will not be *forced* to give up his holdings but will be *persuaded* to do so by the lure of greater earnings.

The Yugoslavs, ever pragmatic, also opened a small chink for private enterprise, in areas where they felt social enterprise needed to be prodded. A few hundred thousand people were permitted to operate small repair shops, own a few trucks, run small restaurants, shops, roominghouses. The only limitation was that they could not hire more than five people each. Many of these entrepreneurs became well-to-do—by Yugoslav standards—evoking considerable antagonism from young militants. But private enterprise is still a long way from being a threat to socialist enterprise.

Self-management has not been without its flaws, no country with a $600 to $700 annual per-capita income can avoid imbalances and inequities. But it has nonetheless proven singularly successful. In 1960 Denis Healey, a leader of the British Labor Party, acclaimed Yugoslavia's rate of economic growth in the previous five years as exceeding that of any nation anywhere with the exception of China. "But unlike China," he noted, "Yugoslavia has also enjoyed a staggering increase in personal consumption."[8] When he had been there in 1955, he observed shops almost bare and a "wartime look" to many towns. Now in 1960 the crowds in major cities seemed to Healey to "look almost indistinguishable from those in other cities" and while there was no middle class comparable to those of major Western nations, "there is none of the squalor which disfigures the south of Italy or Spain, and none of the hopelessness which accompanies that squalor."

My own observations both before and after 1960 confirm this estimate: there has been a balanced development in this Slavic nation that endowed it not only with a modern industry but an impressive growth in consumption. A Yugoslav press service report of July 12, 1964, claims that from 1953 to 1963 the increase in "industrial production varied between 12 to 13 percent, which placed Yugoslavia among a group of countries with the highest rate of economic growth in the world." Agriculture, says this report, forged ahead after 1957 when it began to grow by 6 to 7 percent a year—"three or four times quicker than the average." National income per capita, according to the same source, "became almost five times greater, rising from 110 to about 500 dollars" by 1963. Some of the credit for this accomplishment must go to the United States and other Western nations which came to Tito's aid when he was shunned by Moscow. In the first decade of the Titoist experiment, to March 15, 1959, American aid totaled $888 million, of which about half, $414 million, was in the form of agricultural surpluses, wheat, cotton, fats, and oils. To widen the schisms in world communism, Washington opted to help Tito. Without that help Yugoslavia could not have progressed as it did. The determining factor, however, was not so much the money but a system of socialism capable of using that money more beneficially.

III

In addition to more and better goods, the principle of self-management has had corollary effects in every sphere of Yugoslav life. It has vastly widened popular participation, as the state transferred more and more of its prerogatives to the grass roots. Each local area is constituted as a "commune" and elects a People's Committee to coordinate economic matters and manage the political system. The powers of this committee are much more autonomous than one would find in the Soviet bloc and can be gauged by the fact that it receives a major, if not the largest, share of the tax money. Most of the taxes exacted for education go into a special local fund supervised by a self-management committee composed of representatives of the commune, teachers, students, and others with a stake in education. That committee authorizes the building of new schools and sets education policy, subject only to broad directives from the national and republican governments. Similar committees function one notch lower, at the single school level. The national minister of education told me in 1968 that his staff had been cut by nine tenths as a result of decentralization. Similarly, self-management is applied to housing, where apartment buildings are "socially owned" and self-managed by committees of tenants, and to science, where research funds are administered by an autonomous committee of scientists.

Four other aspects of the system reveal the substitution of participation for compulsion. One is the modified role of the trade union. Unlike unions in capitalist countries, the trade union is not primarily oriented toward setting wages or conducting strikes. It handles grievances on such items as safety or the assignment of housing, and it supervises cultural activities, vacation resorts, and sports programs. But unlike the Stalinist unions it does not try to enforce production standards; that is left to the Workers' Councils, the Management Committee, and the workers themselves. The Yugoslav unions, in other words, are not an instrument of "socialist speed-up."

Another divergence from the Soviet system is the role of the party, called the League of Communists. The party does not manipulate every decision by applying mechanical discipline so that all members vote alike. On the contrary, except on overriding issues, party members are free to disagree with each other in public and at all Workers' Council, union, or national and republican assembly meetings. Party members are frequently defeated in balloting by other party members, and since election laws provide that there must be at least twice as many candidates for every post as are to be elected—whether in the legislature or in the shop—party members often lose to nonparty members. Indicative of the changed status of the Party was the part it played—or didn't play—in the 1968 demonstrations by university students against corruption, growing inequality in incomes, bureaucracy, and unemployment. The demonstrations, which culminated in the seizure of the university at Belgrade, were unique in three respects: first, that they were led by the party's own youth groups on the campus; second, that leading Communist professors openly sided with the students despite the fact that they bitterly criticized the government; and third, that Marshal Tito himself eventually appeared on television and radio to endorse the students' objectives.

One night, while dining with Najdan Pasic, editor of the party's monthly organ, *Socialist*, and a member of its central committee in Serbia, I asked him hesitantly what he thought of the student revolt. I was surprised to learn that both he and his wife, a professor, had participated actively on the side of the young people. Neither husband nor wife knew what the party's or Tito's position would be, but they felt the demonstrations were justified, and though holding high positions they joined the student cause. Pasic told me that the adult Communists at the university, himself included, called off a meeting of the party faction lest the students conclude the party was conspiring against them. Needless to say, party members could not have acted with such independence in most of the other socialist countries.

Another aspect of the withering of state compulsion has been the decentralization of the government structure. The six republics that comprise Yugoslavia—Slovenia, Croatia, Serbia, Bosnia-Herzegovina, Montenegro, and Macedonia—have acquired considerable autonomy. Within established federal guidelines they set political and economic policies in their territories and are in charge of implementing national programs assigned to their domains. If, for example, the federal plan calls for a new steel mill, the national government decides only how much money to allocate and what republic will assume responsibility. The republic itself, and its communes, choose the site and do the job.

Another innovation of Titoist socialism though presumably a temporary expedient, has been the principle of rotation in high-level jobs. With the single exception of Tito, most leading Communists are shifted from one post to another—say, from editing *Borba* to a diplomatic job—every couple of years, to prevent formation of bureaucratic cliques. Zealots have criticized the rotation system on the grounds that it is inadequate and that it is often a game of musical chairs. Some charge it is meaningless since Tito's power—and prestige—remain sacrosanct. Yet, allowing for such defects, the decentralization of the party and the constant shifting of the leadership cadre reflects a wholesome desire to widen popular controls.

A third change brought on by self-management has been the evolution of a unique legislative system. There are five chambers of parliament in Yugoslavia in addition to the federal assembly. There is a chamber of nationalities, elected by national minorities; an economic chamber, representing the social enterprises throughout the country; a chamber for education and culture; another for social and health organizations; and a fifth for political and miscellaneous groups. Before a bill becomes law it must secure approval by the chamber whose area of competence is affected most —a bill on medical care must go to the social and health chamber, on planning to the economic chamber—as well as approval by the federal assembly. There is much uninhibited discussion and dispute in these chambers and not a little contention between republican and federal assemblies.

The most important change fashioned by Titoism has been in the sphere of personal freedom. In the West there is a naïve assumption that democracy is synonymous with the multiparty system and elections. But while these give the average citizen in capitalist countries certain limited control on political representatives—limited because it takes large sums of money to run for office and because much of the electoral system is institutionalized —that citizen enjoys no rights whatsoever in choosing the more important figures who run the economy, the bankers, businessmen, landlords. The Yugoslav citizen, by contrast, though his control over the political levers is restricted to an extent by the one-party system, enjoys considerable economic prerogatives. Imperfect as self-management may be, it permits the average person a much greater voice in how the factory should be run and his own work organized than under capitalism or Soviet socialism. It is a more meaningful form of democracy than one confined to casting a periodic ballot.

The Yugoslav government does not sanction political factions, but people generally are free to say what they like, and the press is full of controversy. Even the party press enjoys a fair degree of independence; except for publicizing major decisions the editor publishes what he pleases. Personal movement, too, is subject to few restrictions. A man may change his job or move around the country without reprisal. He may accept work outside the country, in West Germany, say, without fear that he will be denied a passport. According to the *Nation's* correspondent, Claude Bourdet, there were almost a million Yugoslavs working abroad in 1971, sending home $500 million a year. Here again the enlargement of freedom is not just a whim of officialdom but a built-in feature of the system. If the state wants the social enterprises to be efficient it must permit them to dismiss redundant laborers. Unlike other Communist countries, Yugoslavia eschews hidden unemployment. It is not happy with the fact that 7 to 10 percent of its labor force is jobless, and it periodically debates whether to absorb them into special service industries or New Deal-type work projects.

The country, however, cannot achieve maximum competitiveness on the world market if it employs unnecessary labor in unnecessary jobs. If it must tolerate a certain amount of unemployment for the time being, then it must also allow the unemployed free movement inside and outside the country. And if it is to grant passports to job seekers going abroad, it must also grant them to anyone else who wants to travel. Its system can survive only in an atmosphere of noncompulsion. Yugoslavia loses thereby the services of many urgently needed technicians and experts who are lured abroad by the promise of higher salaries. But the Titoists insist that the answer to the problem is not to curtail movement or build Berlin walls but to bring wages and salaries up to the general European level.

It would be wrong to overstate the case for self-management in Yugoslavia, for there is a tentative character to it, much as there is to the socialisms of all other countries. It is constantly seeking a golden mean between centralism and decentralism, coercion and persuasion. The nation began its experiment, it should be recalled, with a devastated economy—on a proportionate basis, as devastated by the war as the Soviet Union had been—and in a state of backwardness that few critics appreciate. Thus, while Titoism set itself humanistic norms to encourage participation and popular prerogative, it has not always been able or willing to live up to them. If one thinks of democracy both in political *and* economic terms, there is no country of a comparable economic level which enjoys more of this scarce commodity; its people determine their own destiny to a greater extent than the peoples of Greece or India or Mexico or any socialist country. Nonetheless Yugoslavia has made its share of mistakes and committed its share of injustices—such as the imprisonment at one time of Milovan Djilas, once the third highest figure in the Communist movement, for his espousal of more political liberty.

By and large, Titoism has run into two kinds of problems during the period of self-management: one relating to the market mechanism, the other to a tendency inherent in that mechanism to cause glaring inequality. Though the Titoists have paid fealty to the market as a means of gauging demand and assuring a high quality of goods, they have been forced to tinker with the market more often than they wanted to. For example, in order to encourage infant industries the regime decided to reduce the price of raw materials. Necessary as this step may have been, it discouraged the development of mining and other primary industries and lowered the earnings of workers engaged in those industries. Another example was the heavy investments made in underdeveloped republics, such as Macedonia and Montenegro, not because they were economically sound—they weren't—but to provide jobs. By state fiat, too, food prices were held down so as to sustain the living standards of workers; but this in reality was a tax on peasants. Similarly, subsidies were given to export industries, while penalties were placed on import industries. All this subverted the competitive élan and impeded, to that extent, efforts at improving productivity; it also placed heavier burdens on some sectors of the population than others.

To approach their goals, therefore, the Titoists have had to adjust and readjust their methods constantly. In the West this has usually been interpreted either as a sign that everything was falling apart or, as some Leftists contend, that Yugoslavia was returning to capitalism. "Yugoslavia," writes Barry Rubin of the Mao-ist *Guardian*, "is a model of the transition from socialism to capitalism."[9] Actually, however, the Titoist saga has been one of inevitable improvisation along a designated path. The Yugoslavs divide their postwar history into three parts: six or seven years of "administrative socialism," a dozen years of limited self-management, and after 1964–65 a second stage of self-management called "de-statization." The economy was booming in 1964–65 when the new plunge was taken—national income was rising 10 percent a year, industry even more, and personal living standards were appreciably higher than before self-management. But there were danger signals ahead. The dinar, at 750 to the dollar, was soft currency. Progress in agriculture was slow, primarily because lower prices drained incentive. Too many state investments were politically motivated rather than economically feasible. The competitiveness of manufacture was being sustained by artificial means that could not continue indefinitely.

A wholesale reform was legislated in 1965 to remove the state still further from the economy—to allow economic forces, in other words, to work on each other without government interference. Price ceilings were lifted on many raw materials and farm products. The dinar was devalued to approximate its true buying power. Subsidies to exports were abolished. The social enterprises were given added incentive by being permitted to keep the lion's share of their profits. And the banks were removed from state control and transformed into "socially owned" institutions, "self-managed" by the various enterprises which were their major depositors. The purpose of this latter change was to guarantee that loans would be made on sound economic criteria rather than political favoritism. The reforms obviously were anathema to many (consumers, for instance) and a blessing to others (farmers, for instance), but the Titoists felt they had to make a readjustment to prod their economy toward greater zeal.

Titoist socialism has evoked criticism from some Marxists, as already noted, that it is "restoring capitalism." Reliance on a market mechanism and competition is said to be a step backwards. But this is simply a genuflection to Stalinist economics; there is nothing in socialist theory that obviates the use of the market as a means of determining what the consumer wants in terms of both quantity and quality. Neither Lenin nor Trotsky nor anyone else, in the early days of Bolshevism, equated the market with capitalism. Used intelligently it can effectively serve socialism in its formative decades without plunging it into a depression. For the state can always step in to correct imbalances. This is what happened in 1972–73 when the Yugoslav economy was faced with a "liquidity crisis." With cash in short supply and almost 1,000 enterprises in the red to the tune of $300 million, the state applied heavy pressure on the populace to pledge 5 to 10 percent of their earnings for three-year loans bearing 10 percent interest. Taxes were raised on luxury items, some prices boosted, some wages cut in unprofitable enterprises. Detractors offered this crisis as proof that self-management doesn't work. In fact, all it proved was that a nation that rose from nineteenth-century standards in so short a time still has a long way to go to meet Italian, German, or French competition. Doubtless there will be other spurts and spasms in the Yugoslav saga, and at one point or another Titoism may take the wrong turn. But any nation that must make two revolutions in one must of necessity improvise. The only question is whether that improvisation exacts a heavy or a light toll from the average citizen, and whether it is accompanied by extreme or moderate compulsion.

Another criticism of Yugoslavia has been that it has sired inequality. This is certainly true, as one can see from the periodic exposés in the Belgrade press of high living and "socialist millionaires." Quite a few people engaged in private enterprise, such as the service industries or professions, have been able to accumulate sizable fortunes by Yugoslav standards. There are doctors, by way of example, who invest their savings in fleets of trucks registered in the names of children and relatives; or small businessmen who get around the laws limiting ownership by illegally inscribing the names of family members as owners. These manifestations of inequality have been a source of constant friction and protest. When the charges became widespread in December 1971 Tito ordered an investigation of profiteering and the "unjustifiable amassing of wealth," and some steps were taken to curb the profiteers. Doubtless these measures will only be partly successful and will have to be followed by new restrictions; in an economy of scarcity there will always be some people ingenious enough to circumvent the spirit and letter of the law. Only vigilance can keep it within manageable proportions.

A more disturbing type of inequality has been the inequality in earnings and living standards from one republic to another and from one enterprise to another. Because of the emphasis on "profitability," each republic tends to grow at a different tempo, one more rapidly than another. Some enterprises show large profits, others much smaller ones, and still others take losses, so that the worker in a successful enterprise may earn much more than workers earn in unsuccessful ones. The result is a push and pull between those who benefit and those who don't—sometimes taking a reactionary, selfish form, sometimes an idealistic form. Thus in 1971 student strikers at the University of Zagreb demanded that the foreign exchange earned by the relatively rich republic of Croatia be held for development there instead of transferred by the federal government for development of the poorer republics. Tito, addressing union officials in January 1972, wondered out loud in the face of such protests whether "the socialist character of our society has been lost." Certainly it is always in danger of being distorted. But on the other hand, discontent over inequality sometimes explodes into strikes—2,000 in 1968—and demonstrations that seek to correct it. The demands of 40,000 students who closed Belgrade University in June 1968 included abrogation of special privileges for high party officials, jobs for the unemployed, an increase in earnings for lower-paid workers, higher student grants, and stern measures to repress the "socialist millionaires."

Tito has certainly not been unmindful of these problems—contrary to the charge that he is reintroducing capitalism. In January 1972, responding to the fact that efforts to curb inequality had not succeeded, he introduced an "Action Program" whereby the League of Communists would function in a more disciplined manner. He evidently hoped that by coordinating efforts the party could dampen demands for privilege by the richer republics and take sterner measures against the "socialist millionaires." Later in the year the Tito group began a purge of men in top leaderships, such as Miko Tripalo of Croatia, whom it considered opportunists. Alvin Z. Rubinstein calls this the beginning of Tito's "mini-cultural revolution"[10]—a reference to the much more far-reaching cultural revolution of China. More correctly, it is one of a number of shifts back and forth to determine the ratio between centralism and decentralism needed to expand the economy while sustaining human rights.

With all its uncertainties Titoism has confirmed not only that socialism works but that it has an inner thrust toward humanism. Claude Bourdet, a non-Communist French leftist who has visited Yugoslavia often, writes in the *Nation* of September 20, 1971, "that Yugoslavia is now a country of freedom, of a creative, burgeoning freedom that one finds in the liveliness of the streets, in the nearly exaggerated disappearance of all police, . . . in artistic creation of every kind, in economic and political invention." In Bourdet's opinion—which I share—the lot of the common man in Yugoslavia is better, taken as a whole, than in any other socialist country, including the Soviet Union.

Critics from the capitalist side pounce on every crisis, every devaluation of the dinar, as an indication that socialism is doomed. But these difficulties lend themselves to another, more realistic interpretation—namely, that the problems of a socialist society in a backward country will not be resolved in a day or a decade, and that vigilance, protest, pressure, and even struggle are indispensable for a long time to come. But a socialism that can sextuple per-capita income in one decade from 1956 to 1967, and can do it while increasing the scope of freedom and popular participation, is marching in the path that was designated for it by Marx, Lenin, and other left-wing theorists. It would be brash to say, as Lincoln Steffens said of the Soviet Union in its first years, that "I have seen the future, and it works." Yet the Yugoslav experiment is the most methodical attempt to create a decentralized humanistic society of this century. With all its weaknesses it does point to the future, and it does shred to tatters the assumption in the West that socialism can only operate under dictatorship.

IV

No socialist country has as yet widened the process of decision-making or extended personal freedom as far as Yugoslavia. But that does not mean that nothing is happening along similar lines in the twelve other Communist states or in the many Third World countries, such as Algeria, Libya, Iraq, Guinea, and Tanzania, which are also on a leftist course. On the contrary, parallel developments are evident virtually everywhere, including the Soviet Union.

The propulsion toward what the U.S. press calls "liberalization" is not due to the caprice of individuals or a sudden burst of conscience but to more solid objective factors. One of them is that socialism has become easier to build. The Soviet Union, once poor and forlorn, now plays a role similar to what Lenin expected of a Communist Germany; it provides vitally needed nascent capital to weather the first storms of economic development. From 1945 to 1957 the Russians bestowed credits to East Europe of $7 billion. Another $2 billion was made available to China from 1950 to 1962, and $3.4 billion to 24 non-Communist countries from 1954 to 1963. North Korea received loans and grants of $690 million from 1945 to 1962, North Vietnam $369 million, Mongolia $658 million.[11] The sums later pledged to Cuba are unknown, but they certainly run into hundreds of millions. In addition the Soviets provided technicians and know-how on a vast scale. At the time of the Sino-Soviet break there were 1,390 Soviet technicians at work in China on hundreds of projects. The tens of thousands of technical and scientific documents sent to China cost a half million dollars just to copy. According to Russian sources: "If China had had to obtain these blueprints from the capitalists or to work them out with its own forces, it would have had to pay many billions of rubles and long years of hard work."[12] These benefits were offset to an extent by the reparations and other exactions of the 1945–50 period, but on balance they lightened the load for a host of countries, Communist and non-Communist, which thereby avoided some of the difficulties that Russia itself confronted in its years of isolation.

Three other factors have been nudging the socialist world in the humanist direction. One has been the insistent pressure of ordinary citizens, especially as material hardship eases, for a better life. Inevitably that pressure, though for the most part subterranean, has found spokesmen among writers, academicians, scientists, and political leaders. A second factor, as evidenced in the Stalin-Tito schism, has been the demand by lesser partners of the socialist coalition for autonomy. Though Stalin and his successors were able to quash demands for more independence—for instance, in East Germany (1953), Hungary (1956), and Czechoslovakia (1968)— that pressure has not been entirely sidetracked. Witness the offbeat behavior of Romania. Comecon originally assigned this country, rich in natural resources, the function of raw material producer in the "international division of labor," but Romania demurred and successfully pressed its point to develop a basic industry. Romania today enjoys good relations—and trade—with Israel, whereas the rest of the Soviet bloc are on frigid terms with the Zionist state. It maintains close ties with China, again in contrast to the rest of the bloc. We can be certain that the smaller Communist nations have all insisted behind the scenes on the right to minor apostases and in some instances have won their point.

Most important of all as a factor in the continuing transformation of socialism has been the exigencies of economics. Soviet planning, as previously noted, has been overcentralized, stringently controlled, wasteful, and relatively inefficient. According to Isaac Deutscher, "As late as the mid-sixties Russian output per man-hour was estimated at only 40 percent that of the American."[13] This was considerable progress from the 1920s, when it was only 10 percent, but it was still some distance from closing the gap. Up to a point the disparity was not particularly onerous, because the socialist countries (except for Czechoslovakia) could draw on a vast reserve of labor in the villages. Two men operating at 50 percent efficiency presumably can produce as much as one at 100 percent. But the surplus labor to be drawn from the village is not inexhaustible, and as it dwindles the socialist countries find they can improve matters only by producing or importing better machinery and computers and by liberating the initiative of managers and workers which has been dammed up for a long time.

A surly proletarian, tied to his job, living in fear of reprisal for taking up a grievance, is no boon to efficiency. Neither is a plant manager who must clear the most trivial decision with higher-ups in Moscow. At a certain stage of development—whether in a capitalist or socialist state—excessive state control becomes a hindrance to expansion. Without relaxing restraints and granting democratic prerogatives, it is therefore difficult to increase productivity.

Had the two steps—relaxing restraints and granting democratic rights—been taken together, the departure from the past would have been strikingly obvious. The Soviet leadership, however, while willing to moderate coercion, was unwilling to widen democratic horizons for fear it would lose control of the situation. Unwinding the reel after twenty-five years of Stalinism—particularly against the background of cold war—ran counter to their habit and experience. Even so, periodically in the last two decades, one can see the light peeking behind the shadows.

Immediately after the death of Stalin on March 5, 1953, the "collective leadership" that took his place began to free hundreds of thousands of people in the forced labor camps; and the camps as an institution, operated by the hated GULAG, were abolished. The arrest of secret police chief Lavrenti Beria in June 1953 and his execution on Christmas eve—the last time, incidentally, a leading opponent was shot for political differences—signaled the downgrading of the secret police and the return of a semblance of legality. Leaders who subsequently fell out of favor—including Malenkov, Molotov, and Khrushchev—were removed from office but not imprisoned or executed. The average citizen, too, found it possible to take up a grievance in the factory or press his case for a new apartment without looking over his shoulder to see if the NKVD was watching. This was not yet freedom—especially since the party and the state had ample means of enforcing conformity: a worker could be denied an apartment or a promotion; a student could be denied a scholarship; a writer could be expelled from the writers' union and his chance of publication reduced to zero. Moreover, in exceptional cases, dissenting writers and intellectuals were still jailed or thrown into mental institutions. On the whole, however, the average citizen lost his fear of capricious imprisonment or exile to the labor camps.

Within the party, too, there was a loosening of monolithicism, at least insofar as the higher bodies were concerned. Members of the Presidium and Central Committee, who in Stalin's day voted exactly and invariably in accordance with the dictator's wishes, now expressed their convictions more freely. In June 1957, for instance, the Presidium voted to remove Khrushchev from office by a majority of eight to three but was overruled by a hastily assembled Central Committee which voted the other way. Though we are not yet privy to the details, there has obviously been sharp division in the top Soviet ranks on such issues as the accession of Gomulka to power in Poland, the Hungarian Revolution of 1956, China, the Cuban missile crisis, the 1968 Czech invasion, and economic policy.

One of the interesting features of the post-Stalin era was the reappearance, in muted form, of old disputes—heavy industry versus light industry, producer goods as against consumer goods—that wracked the Soviet Union during the days of contention between Bukharin, Trotsky, and Stalin. On August 8, 1953, Premier Georgi Malenkov, appearing before the Supreme Soviet, defined what he said would be a "New Course." Heavy industry, Malenkov conceded, "is the foundation of foundations of our socialist economy," but there must also be a concurrent "sharp rise in production of consumer goods."[14] A large number of machinery plants, he announced, had been converted to such production and more would follow. For the collective farmers he pledged an end to the compulsory buy-up and an increase in income by two billion rubles. For the worker he held forth the prospect of lower prices and higher wages.

The New Course in Russia had parallels elsewhere. In East Germany, on the heels of the Berlin revolt of June 1953, the fifteenth plenum of the German Socialist Unity Party (SED) voted to cut investments in heavy industry by 1.7 billion marks, as well as reduce prices and taxes. Imre Nagy, just installed as premier of Hungary, also committed himself to a curtailment of investments for heavy industry and a simultaneous improvement of living standards. Among other things his program envisioned a controlled withdrawal of peasants from collectives, more religious tolerance, the closing of the internment camps, and a partial amnesty. The New Course, adopted in one form or another by the whole bloc, meant that socialism was ready to slow the mad pace of capital investment and to meet at least some of the needs of its people. Typically, the Polish plan slashed the capital accumulation budget from 25.1 percent of the national product in 1953 to 19.8 percent in 1955. In those two years it was expected that retail trade would rise by a fifth.

The New Course was aborted by Khrushchev after he arranged the ouster of Malenkov. Russia, Khrushchev felt, was not ready to cut the umbilical cord with the past so quickly. Nonetheless the tone of internal politics softened, relations with other socialist countries improved, and more consumer goods and housing did become available. Above all, the pathological terror of the Stalin days was ended. The states in the Soviet orbit remained at a sort of midpoint, neither Stalinist nor democratic.

V

After the quiet burial of Malenkov's New Course, the internal struggle within the socialist camp made its next appearance in Poland and Hungary during the fateful year 1956.

Even before Khrushchev's historic speech that year, there were ominous rumblings in Warsaw. As in Yugoslavia almost a decade before, national pride and the craving for autonomy were central factors of the upheaval. Students declaimed, more or less openly, against "Soviet imperialism." Polish writers penned irreverent articles on almost every phase of Polish life, doing little to conceal their feeling that conditions were as they were because of Soviet overlordship. Party papers here and there poked fun at the invarying unanimity in parliament, the Sejm. The ferment brought concessions. The hard-line leadership, under Edward Ochab, while damning the critics as "petty-bourgeois" opportunists and nationalists, nonetheless released 9,000 political prisoners from jail and reduced the secret police staff by 22 percent. In June popular fury spilled over from the intelligentsia to the working class, as the city of Poznan was shaken by a spate of strikes and riots, protesting factory conditions. It was a traumatic shock for the regime, which, true to institutionalized habit, castigated the participants as agents of a foreign counterrevolutionary plot and sent the army to suppress them. The very act of suppression, however, added fuel to the fire and caused fissure even in the army itself. Professor Brzezinski records:

> The use of the army had disastrous consequences on the morale of the military. This writer, visiting Poland one year after the Poznan events, had occasion to observe the deep sense of shame prevailing among the military that they had allowed themselves to be used against their own workers and countrymen.[15]

Four months after Poznan, in the midst of new strikes and student demonstrations, this time centering in Warsaw, Ochab was forced to yield his preeminence to Wladyslaw Gomulka. Poland by this time was a bedlam of well-defined factions, ranging from the reformers or "revisionists" to the "dogmatists" of the Natolin group. The youth paper *Po Prostu* (Speaking Frankly) was the focal point for all sorts of maverick ideas expressed by a disillusioned youth, and in effect a rival to the party's youth organizations; automobile workers at the Zeran plant raised the slogan for workers' councils and working-class autonomy. Against this background of agitation Gomulka's name rang like a clarion. He had spent years in jail for his opposition to forced collectivization and his generally reformist views. Only a miracle had saved him from execution. Now he was the rallying point for "socialist democracy" and his return to power the signal for popular jubilation.

A sign of the fiercenesss of the internecine war which the Poles dubbed their "October Revolution" was the frantic—though aborted—conspiracy by the Natolin group to execute a coup d'etat and the surprise appearance in Warsaw October 19 of a blue-ribbon delegation from Moscow: Khrushchev, Molotov, Kaganovich, Mikoyan. The obvious objective of the uninvited committee was to thwart Gomulka and put a lid on the popular agitation. At the peak of the crisis tanks and soldiers, under the command of a Russian general who had been born in Poland, Marshal Rokossovsky, stood in readiness outside the capital prepared for a miltary attack, waiting only for a signal. In the factories, meanwhile, workers were given arms and told to remain at their benches. When reports came of an imminent move by Rokossovsky's troops, Gomulka warned Khrushchev he would take to the radio to mobilize his nation to defend itself. In the eyeball-to-eyeball confrontation, the Russians backed down. For a few years thereafter Poland was transformed along humanistic lines, not far behind Yugoslavia. One of Gomulka's first acts was to strip the secret police of most of its power. Farmers were authorized to leave the collectives, and they did so in droves. Personal freedom and dissent became, for a time, normal features of Polish life.

In due course most of the gains of the Polish October were dissipated as Gomulka himself adopted many of the practices he had once opposed. Yet it is noteworthy that in late 1970 another wave of strikes in Gdansk and in the Baltic ports led to Gomulka's ouster and his replacement by a "softer" leadership under Edward Gierek.

Returning to 1956, concurrent with the upheaval in Warsaw a similar one broke out in Budapest, one which illustrates even more graphically the dimensions of inner socialist conflict. The economy of Hungary in mid-1953, in the words of Khrushchev, Malenkov, and Mikoyan, was "on the verge of catastrophe." At a conference in Moscow, therefore, it was agreed that Imre Nagy, an advocate of the "New Course," would replace the frostbitten Stalinist Matyas Rakosi as premier. Under Nagy's rule—for nearly two years— voluntarism replaced coercion in the villages and 51 percent of the collective farmers left their collectives to return to private farming. Nagy's program, like that of almost all the so-called "liberals," was a modification of Bukharin's in the twenties— reduce investments in heavy industry, increase them for agriculture and consumer industry, decentralize the administration, free local governments from control by the Minister of Interior.

All this, of course, was repugnant to Rakosi and his followers, who paid lip service to the New Course but sabotaged it in practice. "The Nagy-Rakosi semiparalysis," writes Brzezinski of this period, "meant that something vaguely reminiscent of pluralism began to emerge on the Hungarian political scene."[16] In the spring of 1955, following the fall of Malenkov in Moscow, Rakosi was able to recapture his seat at the peak of the pyramid in Hungary. Nagy was expelled from the Politbureau, the General Committee, and the premiership; forced collectivization was reinstituted; the secret police refortified and arrests accelerated. What followed was a tug of war in which neither side was able to pull the other down. Intellectuals of the Petofi Clubs persevered in their discussions and agitations; Rakosi was forced to release some political prisoners and to rehabilitate—posthumously—his old rival, Rajk. Subsequently, however, he closed down three literary publications sympathetic to the Petofi Clubs and arrested Nagy and 400 of his followers. The aging dictator interpreted the Khrushchev-Tito declaration of June 1956 that there were "many roads to socialism" as a license for reinvesting Stalinism. He clearly misjudged the depth of disenchantment.

In late October political controversy turned into insurrection on the streets of Budapest. It began with a demonstration of students at Bem Square to air their grievances and in support of the rebels in Poland. What followed is well-known: the outpouring of 150,000 demonstrators on October 23, the seizure of the radio station, the toppling of a statue of Stalin, young people throwing Molotov cocktails at Soviet tanks, troops at the Kilian Barracks under Major General Pal Maleter coming to the side of the revolution. Erno Gero, only recently installed as first secretary of the party to still the storms, gave up; Nagy returned to power with Janos Kadar as his second in command; and for ten days or thereabouts Hungary enjoyed more freedom of speech and press, as well as political and trade union independence, than at any other time in its history. It would have been a mammoth victory for "socialism with a human face" if the situation could have been stabilized.

Within a few days after a cease-fire, however, Russian troops encircled Budapest and initiated an assault which took 20,000 Hungarian lives. What had happened in the meantime was that Nagy broke two Soviet idols—the one-party system and the Warsaw Pact. He formed a coalition government which included the Smallholders Party, the Social Democrats, and the National Peasant Party, newly risen from the underground; and he announced his intention to withdraw Hungary from the Soviet military alliance. Khrushchev and his associates in the Kremlin might have tolerated most of the other reforms, as they grudgingly tolerated the reforms in Poland. But Nagy had gone too far: the contagious effect of one Communist state breaking its bonds so decisively would have resulted, at the least, in dissolution of the Soviet-East European bloc and at worst in the eclipse of the Soviet leadership as well. Morally, justice was with the Hungarian people, but Nagy made the mistake of moving too fast too soon, without due concern for the realities of power, like a trade unionist who calls a strike when only one third of the workers are ready to walk out.

Contrary to the conventional wisdom, however, the Soviet bloodbath in Hungary and the execution of Nagy and Maleter did not end the conflict between socialist reformers and socialist conservatives. The Hungarians, in fact, came out better eventually than the Poles. Kadar, who had spent time in prison, like Gomulka, during the Stalin days and was widely castigated in 1956 for presiding over the liquidation of the revolution, took the scepter when the Russians—according to word in Budapest—warned him that if he didn't they would bring back Rakosi. For a few years, as captive of the conservatives, Kadar imprisoned thousands of dissenting intellectuals, students, and workers active in the uprising. He reintroduced village compulsion and other distasteful measures. But by 1958, having asserted his supremacy in the party, Kadar reversed the tide. The arrests ended, to be followed within a couple of years by release of all those previously held. Reform economists spurned in Rakosi's day, such as Imre Vajda and Josef Bognar, became the intellectual architects—with Kadar's support —of far-reaching changes. Kadar, a man of low key whose picture is seldom seen on public display, quietly but methodically widened the scope of individual freedom and overhauled the economy so that by the mid-1960s Hungary was without doubt the most reform-conscious of any nation in the Soviet bloc.

In January 1968 the landlocked state southwest of the U.S.S.R. formulated a New Economic Mechanism which incorporated many aspects of Titoism. Profitability became the motif of economic activity, and decentralization the mode for implementing it. Under the New Mechanism Hungary shifted to "indicator" planning, except insofar as the infrastructure—roads, dams, electrification— and new investments were concerned. The price system was modified so that some items fluctuated freely (mostly luxury goods and nonessentials), some were fixed (basic articles, bread, sugar, milk, meat), others were limited to a certain maximum (e.g., washing machines), and still others were unrestricted though subject to guidelines (e.g., textiles). The plant manager and his staff no longer were required to be party members to hold their positions; within their own province they elaborated a plan, free of state intervention. They could produce what they saw fit, sell it anywhere, and at any price—within the prescribed limits. Depending on the profit they earned they were assured annual bonuses up to 50 and 75 percent of normal earnings.

Wages too were relieved of uniformity; they were set in every factory in collective bargaining agreements between the plant manager and the union, the only proviso being that they could not rise more than a certain percentage—much like the New Economic Policy introduced by Nixon in the United States in 1971. At the end of the year the laborers were also given a bonus, up to two months' pay, again depending on profits. Collective farming was retained, but overhauled to make it less harsh. Among the new rights won by the farmer was the right to receive rent from the collective based on the acreage he had contributed to it, as well as greater latitude in marketing the produce of his private plot. According to Henry Kamm of the *New York Times* (May 23, 1973), "satisfying the consumer appears to have been elevated to the principal goal of the movement. As a result, more Hungarians now appear content with their lot." Most of all, the state and the party have relaxed their control over the individual, as evidenced by increasingly open discussion and the fact that almost no one is ever denied a passport. "We no longer try to lead the country on every point," says Peter Renyi, associate editor of the largest newspaper in Budapest, and that seems to be an accurate description.

Hungary does not yet enjoy true independence; its leadership is still compelled by the unequal partnership with the Soviet Union to participate in actions, such as the 1968 invasion of Czechoslovakia, which go against its grain. Strikes remain illegal; the principle of self-management is in its infancy. But there is no question that in the struggle betwen reformers and conservatives the former are definitely in the ascendancy. As Kadar once put it to his intimates, "ours is an evolutionary revolution."

VI

An "evolutionary revolution" is under way in virtually all the socialist world, characterized on the one hand by the increasing trend toward nonconformity in intellectual and student circles and on the other hand by the exigencies of economics. Often the two interlink.

While Vajda and Bognar were fighting for their economic nostrums in Hungary, as were Ota Sik in Czechoslovakia and

Kalecki and Bobrowski in Poland, a Kharkov economist named Yevsei G. Liberman was promoting a similar campaign in the Soviet Union for competition, decentralization, profitability, and utilization of the market mechanism. His proposals sparked few fires from 1956 to 1962 but finally ignited a sharp debate. The debate culminated three years later in the decision by the party's Central Committee to eliminate "excessive control of individual enterprises" and reduce "the number of planned targets which the enterprises are assigned *from above*."[17]

That meant that in the targeted industries—three quarters of the whole by 1970—the factory manager was free to pick and choose his customers, to negotiate directly with retail outlets (and vice versa), to set employment quotas, and to charge what he could get—all functions that were previously performed in the rarefied atmosphere of government offices. With his staff, he was also authorized to set production targets, guided by the single principle of showing a profit. The goals, in other words, were no longer expressed in numbers or weight but in the difference between cost and price. Moreover, incentives were added: if the manager and his workers did well they received bonuses based on actual earnings.

The reform was modest by Yugoslav or Hungarian standards, a sort of halfway house which still concentrated vast powers in the central planners—control of heavy industry, the setting of national wage scales, continued fixed prices in many fields. But it was a thaw, a digression from old Stalinist economics. Inevitably it unleashed further intellectual ferment, since it is impossible for plant managers, scientists, and engineers to express their views freely on industrial matters without correlating them to social and political issues.

The result of that thaw was a spawning of dissent among the intelligentsia, most of it subterranean but not insignificant. In the summer 1970 issue of *New Politics*, Jacob S. Dreyer recited the chronology of that dissent. It began, he says, even before Khrushchev's revelations to the 20th Congress, with the publication of Ilya Ehrenburg's book, *The Thaw*, and Vera Panova's *The Seasons*. In the late 1950s a counterculture emerged among students, similar to the counterculture of youth in the West. Grouplets emerged around the issue of "universal disarmament," and young editors such as Alexander Ginzburg and Vladimir Osipov launched maverick literary publications. Among other dissident forces were General Piotr Grigorenko's Society for the Restoration of Leninism and the Leningrad Communards, both suppressed by the secret police in 1963 and 1965 respectively.

In September 1965 the government arrested two young authors, Andrei Sinyavsky and Yuli Daniel, for "agitation or propaganda carried out with the purpose of subverting or weakening the Soviet State." Their trial became a cause célèbre for Russian dissenters and marked the beginnings of the present dissent movement. Since then all kinds of secret underground leagues have come into being, new ones replacing those snuffed out by the KGB with surprising consistency. A minority of them are rightist forces, such as one headed by an economist named Fetisov, which espouses strong rule from above and anti-Semitism. The mainstream of dissent, however, is reformist (within the context of socialism). The groups, of necessity, are loose; they publish a few papers or leaflets until their leaders are arrested or otherwise repressed and then they re-form.

Some of the dissidents, however, are as yet untouchable, too valuable to the regime to be put in prison—for instance, the academician Andrei Sakharov, the world-famous nuclear scientist, Piotr Kapitza, and the novelist Alexander Solzhenitsyn. Sakharov, Roy Medvedev (whose book *Let History Judge* was published in the United States recently), and Valerii Turchin openly addressed a letter (referred to in chapter six) to Brezhnev, Kosygin, and Podgorny, which undoubtedly reflects a large body of public opinion in the Soviet Union. "What awaits our country," asked the letter,

> if the course is not set towards democracy? A growing lag in relations to the capitalist countries . . . increasing economic difficulties; a worsening relationship between the Party and the Government apparatus and the intelligentsia; the danger of lurches to the right and to the left. . . . A shift to the right, i.e. the victory of trends towards harsh administration, the tightening of the screws . . . will aggravate these problems and will lead the country into a tragic cul-de-sac.

Among the proposals they suggested was a loosening of state control and inauguration of a system to allow "several candidates to stand for one post in elections for party and governmental bodies at all levels."

Other forces have confined their protest to the issue of human rights. In April 1968 there appeared a little publication, *Chronicle of Current Events*, which has had a wide distribution in intellectual circles. The following year another secret organization, the Initiative Group for the Defense of Human Rights, came into existence. "Eight of the fifteen founders of the Initiative Group," reports Dreyer, "were arrested; five imprisoned or exiled, the other three confined to a mental asylum." The movement for humanism, nonetheless, cannot be entirely obliterated, nor is it entirely without small victories. In May 1970, when the biologist Zhores Medvedev was confined to a mental institution, Kapitza, Igor Tamm, and other leading scientists organized a protest action which led to Medvedev's release.

The hierarchy of the Soviet Union is impaled on a dilemma. You cannot run a modern society, capitalist or socialist, without physicists, social scientists, technicians, engineers, teachers, students, and managers in increasing number; and you cannot harness the brainpower of these men and women without giving them latitude to roam, experiment, improvise, theorize. Inevitably they spin off critiques showing that an emergency form of overcentralized planning is wasteful and inefficient. They prove by reference to life itself as well as theory that freedom is a factor not only in socialist morality but production. Ideas thereby clash with power and reveal the dilemma of the Kremlin leadership. If it enlarges the scope of freedom too rapidly it risks removal from power. If it postpones it too long it inhibits economic advance and falls behind in the contest with capitalism. No matter how many times they put Yuli Daniel in jail, this dilemma haunts them. The reality is so obvious that other Daniels must take the place of the ones imprisoned—manyfold—only making the dilemma more torturous. Brezhnev and Kosygin undoubtedly are aware of all this and have indeed given ground to the pressures. But they fear giving ground all at once—as was demanded by Nagy and in 1968 by the Czechs. They try therefore to yield an inch at a time, which only exacerbates their problem. As every social scientist knows, people resist most vigorously not when they are denied concessions but in cadence with winning them; not when times are bad but when they are beginning to get better. Note, for instance, how the

American unions spurted forward not in the depths of the great depression but when New Deal ministrations were beginning to roll the economy forward. So too in the Soviet bloc, as conditions improve, dissent too extends its boundaries, no matter how much the leadership tries to hold it in check.

VII

The ultimate question is whether "evolutionary revolution" will proceed until dissent coagulates into revolt or the hierarchs themselves permit enough change to avoid revolt. It is useless to speculate on this point, for the example of Czechoslovakia in 1968 shows how both a palace revolt and an actual revolt take place. The Czech "renaissance" was put down because it came too early and went too far ("being right too early," a French friend once told me, "is worse than being right too late.") And the Czechs currently are living under the worst tyranny in the Soviet Bloc. But all this is ephemeral, for the struggle for a "second" socialist revolution goes on, and the Czechoslovakia of 1968 is almost certainly an augury of tomorrow throughout the Communist world.

There were, at the outset, two points of difference between Czechoslovakia and the other East European states: first, that it had a tradition of liberal democracy; second, that before World War II it was the tenth most industrialized nation on earth, producing an excellent quality of engineering products, autos, shoes, and glassware, three fifths of which were sold to the advanced Western nations. After the war, President Eduard Benes and his associate Jan Masaryk accepted the country's status as part of the Soviet sphere of influence and as a "people's democracy," but their government was toppled in 1948. The next few years, as everywhere else in Eastern Europe except Yugoslavia, was punctuated by Stalinism—the extensive purges of 1950-52, the execution of deputy prime minister Rudolf Slansky (and others), the overemphasis on steel mills and heavy goods production, overcentralization, and all the other facets of administrative socialism. There were strikes and riots in 1952—put down by local police—but nothing on the order of East Berlin the following year.

Nonetheless, a few years later pockets of dissent began to crystalize within the intelligentsia. Not long after Khrushchev's 1956 speech, writers such as Antonin Liehm and Ludvik Vaculik renewed demands for basic freedoms and abolition of censorship. Economist Ota Sik pleaded for a new economic model to decentralize planning. By and large Czechoslovakia after 1956, though not embroiled in uprisings such as those in Hungary, was more relaxed than its neighbors; democratic elements found unique ways to survive and function. "Revisionist" writers, scientists, and economists clustered around particular publications and academies whose editors or chairmen tended in their direction. Frequently a man who had been expelled from the party or the Writers' Union for an alleged malfeasance was able to write for "revisionist" publications under a pseudonym or to stay on the payroll of an academy without doing any work. In due course the intellectual reformers won political allies and prevailed on the regime (in 1967) to introduce a few of Sik's economic measures.

If the intellectuals acted as a catalyst, however, the underlying cause of the 1967-68 tumult was an impasse in Czech economic development. It was bound to happen because Czechoslovakia, far and away the most advanced socialist state after the war, could no longer proceed under the strictures of administrative socialism. A Czech leader recalls:

> Already in 1956, we began to feel something was wrong. Countries in the West began buying high quality goods from other Western countries, instead of average quality goods from us. Our orientation on heavy industry, it became obvious, had been a mistake since we were poor in raw materials such as iron ore. Our strength in the past had been our skilled labor in glass, wood, ceramics, shoes, textiles, leather, and the Skoda Works. But after the war those fields were neglected. We operated along "extensive" lines, drawing in new people to the labor force from agriculture and women from the homes. But that supply of labor reached its peak in 1960 and after that we were in trouble. We needed "intensive" development through efficiency and automation; instead we thought we could solve our problems by adding more manpower. It didn't work.[18]

One of the reasons it didn't work was that only 18 percent of the Czech population lived on the farm, as against 40 to 60 percent in the other socialist countries.

The economists of the old regime, it is true, claimed "steady growth" far higher than in the nearby capitalist states—and offered statistics to prove it. But those statistics were grossly distorted. They did not reveal, for instance, the alarming increase of "input." Western nations estimate that they require an input of 2 percent in raw materials to assure a 1-percent rise in national income. But in Czechoslovakia each additional percent of income was paid for by a 6-percent input. Thus, even though the *national* income rose appreciably, *individual* income did not. Czechoslovakia was simply importing far more in raw materials and paying for them with exports of tomatoes or shoes that should have been going to its own working class but was not. When the day of reckoning came after 1960, living standards remained stationary for fully five years. "It was like running an economy on the 'cost-plus' principle," said one Czech economist. "No one cared about how much was put in or who benefitted from it, so long as the global figures came out higher." The institutionalized controls whereby the state and party had the final say on every wage, every price, every change of jobs, every managerial decision, and every allocation of materials and workers actually made it difficult to plan effectively. New factories were built, for instance, but remained inoperative because there was not enough skilled labor to man them; yet hundreds of thousands of people were employed at unneeded tasks, just to keep them at work.

The dilemma of Czechoslovakia can be expressed thus: to rationalize its industry the country needed machinery and computers of a more advanced type than could be had in the Soviet sphere of influence. To pay for such equipment from the West, Czechoslovakia had to sell more goods *in* the West. But since its product was of inferior quality, it could not compete sufficiently on the world market. In at least one instance Prague sold finished steel rails to Britain at scrap-metal prices, because the rails were far below foreign standards. To resolve its difficulties, therefore, Czechoslovakia needed credits for Western equipment and most of all a reorientation of its economy so as to stimulate the initiative of workers and managers. The economic problem, in other words, boiled down to a political dilemma: either grant a sizeable degree of freedom or stagnate.

This point eluded the Czech leadership for a long time, but when the economy reached near-collapse it was driven home to men like Alexander Dubcek and Cestmir Cisar, who eventually took political power. Thus economic exigency and popular agitation blended to direct Czechoslovakia into a short period of humanistic socialism. In the autumn of 1967 students in Prague demonstrated against poor lighting, bad sanitation, and lack of hot water in their dormitories. With lit candles in their hands, they marched toward Hradcany Castle, were intercepted by police at the bottom of a hill, and forced back. On returning to their quarters they were set upon and brutally mishandled. This was the tiny spark that lit a bonfire. At the central committee meetings of the party in October and December that year, the division between reformers and neo-Stalinists reached an open crisis; by the beginning of 1968 Dubcek had replaced Antonin Novotny as the general secretary of the party, and in the next seven months Czechoslovakia enjoyed a "renaissance." A leader of the Romanian Communist Party called it "the most significant event since the Russian Revolution." It was certainly the most hopeful development in the socialist camp in decades, even more than Yugoslavia because it came in a single spurt.

Freedom of assembly and speech were revived and censorship abolished. The unions expelled their old leaders (they refused to permit them to resign), reasserted the right to strike, and established a fund to pay strike benefits. Minority elements, such as the Slovaks, were granted a considerable degree of autonomy, and it was generally assumed that Czechoslovakia would become a federation of republics on the Yugoslav model. Most important of all, the party removed itself from day-to-day control of the government and day-to-day control of mass organizations, confining itself to policymaking and leaving the implementation to those in office or at the grass roots. Scores of new organizations suddenly blossomed to express divergent interests and views. Thirty new youth groups were formed in a couple of months to compete with the party-controlled Union of Youth. At Myslbek Square on any given day there were hundreds of people discussing a host of controversial subjects. Demonstrations were held in front of the Ministry of Foreign Affairs in support of Biafra or—against the official line—in support of Israel. Few people, however, spoke of withdrawing from the Warsaw pact or liquidating socialism. The mood of the rebels was to make socialism work, not abolish it.

The political changes, everyone admitted, were merely a prelude to an economic overhauling that was due to begin after the special congress of the party scheduled for September 9. Under the projected economic model, the handiwork of Sik and much like that of Yugoslavia, the government would confine itself to *indicator* planning—gathering statistics, setting targets—and using indirect means such as taxes, import licenses, and monetary controls to guide production into certain channels. In each enterprise a council would be established composed of the administration, worker delegates, and representatives of the government, with full authority to hire and fire the director, negotiate wage agreements with the unions, set prices (except for basic necessities which would remain controlled for some time), determine production schedules, and the like. Instead of targets expressed in numbers or tonnage, the new target was to be profits. If the enterprise made a profit, the manager and the workers would be rewarded with additional pay; if it showed a loss, the manager and his administrative staff would have their salaries cut. In service industries such as restaurants and taxis, some private enterprise was to be encouraged in order to stimulate initiative. This was not as far-reaching as the Yugoslav experiment, but it was clearly understood to be the first step toward social ownership and self-management.

The Soviet reaction to the Czech renaissance was similar to its reaction to Hungary twelve years before: not so much a fear of change as of *uncontrolled* and *un-guided* change. I was in Prague the day before the Russian tanks arrived to snuff out "socialism with a human face." There were East Germans, Bulgarians, Romanians, and others at the hotels, all discussing favorably the Czech events as an example their own countries might emulate. Doubtless this was the major concern of the Kremlin leaders as they ordered their army and that of the Eastern European countries to invade Czechoslovakia in August 1968. They feared the infection of changes, already made and those being planned, on their own people. They feared an economic rapprochement between Czechoslovakia and West Germany which might splinter Comecon. A less extensive and more controlled change probably would have been tolerated; this one was not.

The resulting occupation by Soviet tanks, and the removal of the Dubcek government at the point of a bayonet, was not as bloody as the attack on Hungary in 1956. Seventy-two people were reported killed, not thousands, as in the previous incident. But a grand experiment came to an end—at least for the moment. Since

1968, under the heavy hand of Gustav Husak, once a reformer himself, the pendulum has swung in the other direction. Hundreds of rebel intellectuals and youth have either been arrested or forced to take refuge abroad. Old leaders, like Dubcek, have been reassigned to insignificant jobs outside the government and the party apparatus. Conformity has been reestablished with the soldier's rifle and the policeman's knout.

VIII

The failure of the Czech renaissance, nonetheless, must be assessed at two levels: as an event in itself and as part of the broad conflict between socialist reformism and socialist conservatism Those who see socialism as inherently totalitarian—and doomed to extinction—offer the August 1968 intervention as proof of their thesis. It seems to me, however, to prove just the opposite, that there is a persisting conflict in the socialist camp, as there must be in every society in its formative decades, between divergent approaches to social and economic development. The important thing to note is not where the new society stands today but in which *direction* it is headed. In that sense it is clear that while conditions favored the antidemocratic elements in the internal struggle for a long time, they now favor the democratic ones. That the reformers do not win their point all at once is no more surprising than the fact that it took American labor, for instance, seven decades from the Civil War to the New Deal to win the right to bargain collectively, or that it took the French Revolution eighty-two years from 1789 to 1871 to win bourgeois democracy.

Establishment writers in the West judge socialist evolution by static criteria they do not apply to their own capitalism. By way of example, a *Newsweek* bureau chief, writing in the *New Leader* (Oct. 30, 1961), reports a series of catastrophes in China, including "block long queues" for food, men and women picking food from garbage piles, young people in revolt, intellectuals fighting a silent war against the government, corruption, and other "bad" news.

Let us assume part or all of this is true. What was the situation before the socialist regime came to power? It was also "bad"; there may have been no queues but there was much more hunger, including periodic famines that took hundreds of thousands, even millions, of lives. There was dissatisfaction among the youth; there was "major," not "minor," corruption. Whatever mistakes the Chinese have made, and there doubtless were many, they were not made to line the pockets of an upper class or to feather anyone's nest. They were mistakes in judgment or strategy by men who had fought long for social justice and truly wanted to see it put into practice.

The real question is where is China headed? An old United Nations report, as already noted, estimated the total gross national product of China in 1949 at $12 billion, or $25 per capita. Sixteen years later, according to Edwin F. Jones of the U.S. State Department, the Chinese GNP was $73.3 billion and per-capita income $101 annually.[19] A jump of 400 percent in living standards in sixteen years—and despite deliberate isolation by all foreign powers and misjudgments by the Chinese leadership such as the "great leap forward"—is nothing to be ashamed of. As indicated in chapter two, some years ago I asked Indira Gandhi, then a cabinet member in India, which revolution—Indian or Chinese—had done more for the common man. She answered, without hesitation, the Chinese. Surprisingly, I received the same answer from American experts in the U.S. consulate at Hong Kong. For the New Leader reporter, therefore, to deal with the "crisis" in China in a vacuum, apart from its past, and without comparison to other countries at the same level, is a distortion of the true situation. One could have made a similar assertion about the United States in 1972: "The news from America is bad. There is so much unemployment in Seattle that Japanese citizens are sending food packages for relief. Joblessness for the nation as a whole is at the highest peak in more than a decade. The number of people on welfare has almost doubled in the past five years. Scandals such as I.T.T., the grain sale to the Soviet Union, the milk price increase, the Watergate bugging are rampant. The youth are so dissatisfied over the war in Vietnam and the draft that there have been hundreds of riots on university campuses." All of this is true, but it does not prove that America is in imminent danger of dissolution. Yet the New Leader article concludes relative to China that if it "were either an individual or a corporation beset by comparable difficulties, it would already have been naturally or legally dissolved." A decade later, when President Nixon and the entourage of American correspondents visited China, they came away with reports of a backward but thriving society. When Joseph Alsop, a notorious conservative, revisited China, a country which he had known for a long time a generation before, he wrote glowing articles about its progress.

The successes and adversities of the socialist world, both insofar as development and democracy are concerned, are part of a deeper process, and the social scientist who deals with them must first of all delineate their central thrust. Which way is that part of the world heading? We do not know enough as yet—at least I don't—about the inner life of China, North Korea, North Vietnam, or Cuba. What is obvious, however, is that in those countries too there is a struggle between the humanistic and the conservative strains. How else explain, for instance, the short period in the mid-1950s when China proclaimed the policy of "let all flowers bloom" or the internal fights which resulted in the ouster of Kao Kang, Jao Shuh-shih, Liu Shao-chi, Lin Piao, Peng Teh-huai, Teng Hsiao-ping, Peng Chen, and many others? The Chinese are traveling their own road to socialism, trying to create a new socialist man and inculcate him with a sense of mission. Whether they are doing it well or poorly, and which group represents the more humanistic element, is not as significant as the fact that there is and has been a constant struggle.

That that struggle has now passed its critical period is evident from many circumstances. Cuba never underwent a period of Stalinism, and Castro has always permitted a measure of dissent within *fidelista* ranks. North Vietnam and the National Liberation Front of South Vietnam were able to fight an eight-year war against the United States because—as conceded by almost everyone but extreme hawks—they had the active loyalty of their people.

Individual defeats in the saga of socialist humanism may obfuscate the issue, but the *trend* is relentless. It will become more evident with each passing year.

CHAPTER EIGHT

Postponing a Debacle

I

The irony of this moment in history is that while socialism is shifting from totalitarian to humanist forms because of economic necessity, capitalism is shifting from democratic forms to totalitarianism because of another type of economic necessity. This is perhaps the major cause of confusion in evaluating the two social systems, for what we are witnessing is a twin development which is *in process* but far from completed. The final destination of each of the two systems is only dimly outlined as yet, and we tend therefore to see it for what it is at the moment, not what it is becoming. We overlook the dynamic element, that what seems on the surface to be undemocratic is fertilizing the seeds of democracy, while what seems to be democratic is fertilizing those of dictatorship. Indeed, so strong is the conventional wisdom about "socialist tyranny," most Americans are convinced that socialism is an ephemeral phenomenon, soon to pass on—like Nazism. "You still see communism as a historic bastard," Georgi Arbatov, director of the U.S.A. Institute in Moscow, told a *Newsweek* correspondent in 1971. "The United States hasn't recognized that we are here to stay."[1] On the other hand the average American, forgetting that his own house nearly toppled during the great depression, is certain not only that capitalism is here to stay but

175

that it will prosper into the indefinite future. Both these myths weaken realistic perspective, for we are in fact watching two patients, one thin and pale but recovering steadily from a non-fatal illness, the other still ruddy and hale but with a cancerous growth that has begun to metastasize.

Socialism is being transformed, among other reasons, because its economic advance is now becoming dependent on intensive rather than extensive forms of development. It cannot rely, as in the past, on its reservoir of redundant village labor. Instead it must concentrate on making each man-hour of labor of its present laborers more productive. That calls for better equipment and computers but, even more, for popular involvement in decision making.

Capitalism, on the other hand, is reaching a dead end because it can no longer reconcile democracy with the principle of maximizing profits. So long as economic expansion was unimpeded, profits and living standards could both rise simultaneously. If the pie grew bigger each year, everyone's share could also grow bigger. But the principle of maximizing private profits has now run aground on four shoals:

1. The limited profit potential afforded by the world economy is being contested for more fiercely as other capitalist nations, notably Germany and Japan, reach a competitive level equal to, or exceeding, that of the United States.

2. Productivity and productive capacity of the capitalist states are increasing more rapidly than population and therefore adding to the problem of surpluses that must be disposed of. Unless there is a basic redistribution of income—between classes and between nations—that overcapacity must lead to the kind of glut in goods and capital that spells trade wars and depressions.

3. The profit-maximization principle is at loggerheads with the aspirations of more than two billion people who are in the midst of revolution and who are unwilling to be exploited by the great powers as they were in the past.

4. The profit-maximization principle is also out of balance with the supply of natural resources. The anarchistic production and consumption of goods without regard to the delicate ecology of this small planet threatens by itself to topple the capitalist system in the not-too-distant future, if nothing else does.

What this adds up to is an impasse between profits and living standards. When the pie—the gross national product—stops growing sufficiently to increase profits *and* improve living standards, it is inevitable that the capitalist state will intervene to place curbs on the latter. We have seen the beginning of this process in America after August 1971, when the state placed controls over wages but none over profits, and in England more recently. We are sure to have still more government direction of the economy as the shoe pinches tighter. Thus, while socialism is moving toward decentralization, capitalism drifts steadily toward greater centralization, heading for the corporate state.

I am aware, of course, that this thesis flies in the face of three decades of experience during which capitalism has prospered *without* serious depressions and *with* political democracy. The Marxist prediction of periodic crises obviously failed to allow for the system's resiliency, its ability to improvise. Since the early 1930s capitalism has used ingenious techniques for *postponing* the debacle. Applying the twin devices of compensatory spending and deficit financing—first within national boundaries and later, under Pax Americana, internationally as well—it has staved off the anticipated catastrophe. What it has done, stripped to essentials, is mortgage the future—spend monies belonging to future generations—in order to stabilize conditions for the present. It has placed today's load on tomorrow's shoulders. But there is a limit to that too. After four decades of Keynesian economics and a quarter of a century of Pax Americana, that limit is at hand. Compensatory spending and the militarism that has become interlinked with it are no longer adequate to assure uninterrupted expansion. And though Marxism has been wrong in its *timetable* for the collapse of capitalism, it has not been wrong in analyzing the basic contradiction between the social character of production and private appropriation of the product. That contradiction is coming to the fore again, and very likely with an unexpectedly sharp impact.

In this and the next chapter, let's briefly trace the development by which the crisis was delayed and now reappears.

II

The central thesis of capitalism was that if people were free to operate their own enterprise they would devise organizational methods and initiate technological improvements to make both themselves and their nations richer. Out of the millions of individual greeds would come a collective good. In striving for his own gain the entrepreneur would open the door to affluence both for himself and for others, who in the process of competing with him would borrow on his talents to propel technological efficiency a step or two forward. According to Adam Smith in *The Wealth of Nations*, each individual under free enterprise is "led by an invisible hand to promote an end which was no part of his intention. . . . By pursuing his own interest he frequently promotes that of the society more effectually than when he really intends to promote it." Free enterprise, according to the classical economists, liberates human energies that were shackled by the political power of feudal lords. The peasant who was told what to grow, where to grow it, and what portion he might keep for himself lacked incentive to improve the methods of production. And the merchant or craftsman who was restricted as to price, quality, the hiring of labor, and other matters utilized only part of his genius in the process of production. Freedom of enterprise, it was said, was the road to progress, and competition its motor force, the means by which it would achieve fulfillment.

Freedom of enterprise, of course, was never assumed to be an unlimited right, for there is a point at which the self-interest of one person, class, or nation impinges on that of another. A man who works his own land, for instance, is not free to seize that of a neighbor. The state establishes certain elementary rules for guiding those relationships, such as laws sanctifying private property or procedures for registering titles. Beyond that, however, the state was expected to "leave alone," to let individuals work out their destiny according to the dictates of an impersonal free market.

The doctrines of laissez-faire and of free market were the twin religions of capitalism. Give them full play, said the economists, and they would guarantee orderly progress indefinitely. The market, they averred, was a self-regulating mechanism which brought labor and capital to bear in such a way as to avoid economic dislocations. If the supply of any commodity was less than the demand, buyers would bid up the price and capitalists, spurred by the prospect of higher profits, would invest capital to produce more of the scarce commodity. If the supply was greater than demand, buyers would hold out for lower prices, capitalists would temporarily retire some of their redundant facilities, as well as their redundant workers, until an equilibrium was reached and the upward spiral renewed. If there were too many workers, the price of labor—wages—would fall and workers would go elsewhere to seek jobs; if there was an undersupply of labor, wages would go up and workers would flood into the area until wages reached their normal levels. If there was an oversupply of savings in the banks or in company accounts, interest rates would go down, encouraging capitalists to borrow more for new facilities; if there was an undersupply, interest rates would go up and unnecessary expansion would be checked.

The free market supposedly was a perpetual motion machine which circulated commodities without interruption. Every sale, said one of Adam Smith's followers, Jean Baptiste Say, is followed by a purchase of equal sum. Since there is always someone to buy and someone to sell, according to Say's Law of Markets, there is no possibility of overproduction or a crisis.[2] The system should work like a well-oiled watch.

In fact, however, it didn't. Every decade or less there were periods in which sellers could *not* find purchasers and the economy backed into a painful depression. In the United States alone there were sixteen such depressions from 1819 to 1929, each one lasting two, three, five, or more years.[3] During those periods it could *not* be said that the millions of individual greeds playing themselves out on the free market performed a collective good. On the contrary, hundreds of thousands, even millions, of workers were tossed out of work and reduced to privation, hunger, and hopelessness.

For a long time establishment economists treated depressions as an aberration, something that wasn't supposed to happen but for "peculiar" or "special" reasons occasionally did. The boom-and-bust business cycle received only negligible attention by them until many years into the twentieth century, and the explanations, even then, were neither credible nor particularly useful in telling us what to expect. The slashing downturns were attributed to such esoteric phenomena as "sunspots," which supposedly affected weather and agricultural crops; to the lack of credit; to excessive savings by working people—hence "underconsumption"; or to cycles of optimism and pessimism. Invariably the economists concluded that these were episodic phenomena that could be avoided in the future. Their optimism, in retrospect, was anything but scientific, and so naïve as to border on the unreal.

Even so bitter a critic of Marxism as William J. Blake, an associate editor of the *Magazine of Wall Street,* is properly disdainful of the bourgeois economists for the cavalier manner in which they treated depressions. He writes:

> Every crash is the last, according to the philosphers in fashion during the succeeeding boom. After 1857, everyone said that the disturbances due to sudden gold discoveries could never recur. After 1873 it was said that the railroad developments of the American West that brought on the crisis were over with, that American industry was mature. When Baring's crashed in 1890, it was said that the development of the Argentine represented the end of the growing pains of capitalism, the economy of the world was developed and in reasonable balance thereafter. The panic of 1907 in America led to bank failures and a shortage of credit instruments. The Federal Reserve Bank was founded. Now all was well. In 1921 the commodity structure of the earth came tumbling. Then from 1924 to 1929 America made a startling recovery. . . . The theoreticians of prosperity buried Karl Marx, that exploded thinker, and pointed out that Ford's rationalization of industry had produced a permanent prosperity. The systematized inanities of Herbert Hoover gave countenance to this recurrent illusion. The crash of 1929 finished all that.[4]

Very little that has been written by establishment thinkers on the business cycle and crises has been convincing. The French economist Jean Lescure expressed the view in 1907 that economies such as the American "which are organized in trusts or trust associations are immune from crises." The United States, as we all know, became more trustified in subsequent years, but it did not on that account avoid the depressions of 1914, 1921, and 1929. Just two years before the worst depression of all a German economist, Gustav Cassell, wrote, "The old proposition that crises will become ever more devastating, is, at all events, already very obsolete."[5] America's most acclaimed economist, Irving Fisher, boasted that the United States would remain indefinitely at a "high plateau" of prosperity, and President Herbert Hoover, evidently intoxicated by the surveys of his economists, boldly noted, as mentioned earlier, that "we in America today are nearer to the final triumph over poverty than ever before in our land."

Hundreds of economists have written erudite critiques of Marx, but it is indisputable that he alone of the major thinkers showed that depressions were endemic to capitalism. The Marxist explanation of the workings of the system carried far more cogency than any other. Marx and his followers pointed out, to begin with, that the market wasn't quite as free as it was said to be. The impersonal interplay of supply and demand was hindered by monopolistic restrictions of a dozen kinds. Railroads entered into pooling arrangements to raise freight rates far higher than they would have been in a competitive market. Corporations merged into bigger corporations that dominated the sale of a particular commodity and virtually set prices as they pleased. In our day administered prices have become accepted practice in major industries such as automobiles, steel, aluminum, cereals, and rubber. In such industries it is not the market but collusion that plays the decisive role in determining what the buyer pays. Even on the other side of the equation—that of labor—wages are not entirely controlled by the laws of the market but by the ability of unions to exact a higher wage than the worker could secure by bargaining individually in a free market transaction.

On the world market as on the domestic one, free trade and competition are also subverted by innumerable devices. Though many nations pay fealty to such principles, in practice they rely far too often on restrictive measures. Weak countries, such as the United States in the last half of the nineteenth century, erect high tariff walls to protect nascent industries from foreign competition. They also exclude foreign goods through quotas and licensing provisions, and they invariably try to weaken competitors by other artificial means. By way of example, at the beginning of the century the British-ruled Malay States held a predominant position in the world tin ore market, since they produced 60 percent of the total, most of it smelted by British companies in Singapore. When an American firm, International Tin, announced plans for building a smelter near New York, the Malayans imposed a prohibitive tax on ore destined for any place other than Singapore. The New

York firm had to give up. Conversely, from 1902 to 1913 the United States levied a large tax on all manila hemp produced in its colony, the Philippines—except for hemp destined for the United States—in order to give American fabricators of binder twine an advantage. Such instances can be multiplied by the thousands, all tending to show that the free market, to a significant extent, is un-free. It is like an expensive watch with a beautiful face that lacks some vital parts.

But even if the market were operating perfectly, free and totally competitive, capitalism would still be prone to crises. It is true, Marx said, that "No one can sell unless someone else purchases," but it is equally true that "no one is forthwith bound to purchase because he has just sold."[6] Before capitalism, when barter was the means of exchange, one commodity, say shoes, was exchanged directly for another commodity, say a certain amount of wheat. The number of sales and purchases was equal; in effect one person exchanged the labor he put into fabricating a pair of shoes for an equivalent amount of labor in so many bushels of wheat. But in a capitalist economy, commodities are not exchanged directly for each other but for money; the man who sells wheat receives money, not shoes, and with that money he may or may not buy shoes. If he withholds that money from the market for an extended period, the economy is in trouble. There is an interruption in the circulation of commodities and a glut both of shoes and money.

Such gluts, according to Marx and the Marxists, not only have occurred with distressing regularity but *must* occur. There are factors built into the system which inevitably interrupt the buy-sell process, causing the economy to break down. Marx's explanation for this phenomenon was complicated, but boiled down and simplified it goes something like this: The value of every commodity is determined by the socially necessary labor time in its production. In other words, when you sell ten bushels of wheat for $20 and then buy a pair of shoes for $20, it is because the same amount of labor time went into growing the wheat as in fabricating animal hide into shoes. The price of wheat and shoes may vary somewhat depending on supply and demand, but in the long run those prices will fluctuate around their true value. On this there was no dispute between Marx and classical economists. The divergence started with the subject of profits. If you concede that a certain amount of labor embodied in one commodity is exchanged for an equal amount of labor embodied in another, where do profits come from? According to Marx they come from the unique character of one commodity—labor power—which is able to produce more values than its own value. The worker sells his labor power, like any other commodity, for a price (wage) "equal to the labor time required for the production of the means of subsistence necessary for the reproduction of the labor power."[7] He sells it, in other words, for the equivalent of the food, clothing, shelter, and other items necessary to keep himself and his family alive. Considered as a simple market transaction he is not cheated; he gets the true value of his labor power. But labor power, unlike other commodities, has the special quality that it creates new values. Apply $10 worth of labor power to certain raw materials, machinery, etc., and it increases their value by, let us say, $20. The value it *adds* is greater than its own *price* (wage). That surplus value—between $10 and $20—goes to the entrepreneurial class in the form of profit, rent, and interest.

This is where the problem begins. The worker obviously can only buy back part of what he produced (in our example, $10 of the $20). What then happens to the rest, the surplus? A small part of it, of course, is used for the capitalist's own needs. The remainder, the overwhelming share of the surplus, goes either to buy better machinery and new facilities so as to increase efficiency, volume, and profits or is exported to foreign countries in the form of capital or goods. Theoretically, the capitalist could convert his goods into money and leave it under the mattress in his bedroom. But that is not his style or purpose; maximizing profits is the philosophy that motivates him. His objective is to invest more in equipment, raw materials, and labor power, so as to realize an ever larger profit.

Here we run into the same problem as that in the circulation of commodities—namely, that there is no assurance that surpluses will be plowed back into business indefinitely. Just as it is not certain that for every seller there is a buyer, so there is no certainty that for every dollar of saving there is a favorable opportunity for investment. Laissez-faire capitalism is steeped in anarchy, each capitalist being driven by his desire for profit without regard to the overall needs of the economy. The more capital he puts to work the more efficient his operation becomes, so that the same amount of labor power provides larger amounts of commodities. A point is ultimately reached where the economy is expanding *faster than population* and the supply of laborers. "In the very nature of capitalist production," Marx observed in Volume II of *Capital,* "we have production without regard to the limits of the market."[8]

In such circumstances the demand for labor rises, wages go up apace, and hence the rate of surplus value—profit—goes down. The capitalist now becomes hesitant about investing his surpluses. If he is earning a $2,000 annual profit on a $20,000 investment, why should he pour another $10,000 into the business if his total profit can be expected to rise only to, let us say, $2,100? The additional small sum is not worth the risk. In Marx's view, therefore, the most important reason for depressions is the fall in the rate of profit that is inevitable under the anarchy of laissez-faire capitalism. As businessmen curtail their expenditures on capital goods, the cycle of money-commodities-more money ($M-C-M^V$) is interrupted, the economy slows down, workers are laid off, and there is a depression. In due course all this is corrected: the bigger and better-endowed businessmen and bankers buy out those who are bankrupt or near-bankrupt. Warehouses slowly empty of their glut. Interest rates fall, and it now becomes profitable to resume spending on capital goods, especially since existing equipment and facilities have greatly depreciated and can be bought for a song. The rate of profit returns to "normal." Unemployed workers are called back to work. The depression is over. What remains is a bitter memory—until the next crisis, which may or may not be the final one.

There is still another factor to the equation. The smooth movement of goods and capital domestically presupposes, on the one hand, that necessary raw materials can be acquired from faraway places and, on the other, that part of the surplus accruing to our capitalist can be shipped abroad, as commodities or capital, to relieve the glut at home. Here we run into other problems. There is much competition between the great powers for sources of raw materials. There are also barriers to foreign trade and investment —licensing provisions, outright exclusion, quotas, tariffs, high taxes. Moreover, the underdeveloped countries tend to resist penetration, since they would like to develop—and protect—their own industries. The end result is that powerful nations try to assure for themselves control of particular markets and sources of raw materials, by military conquest or other artificial means. Britain at one time occupied dozens of countries and its empire encompassed more than 13 million square miles—one fourth the land surface of the earth—and one fourth of the world's population. France occupied more than thirty countries extending over 4,693,107 square miles.

In any event, the train of circumstance leading from expanding needs for raw materials and markets to imperialism caused the world to be divided into colonies and spheres of influence belonging to the great powers. From the standpoint of these powers this was a sine qua non for continued prosperity. But since the territory of the world available for colonies is not endless, and since surpluses of goods and capital and the demand for primary materials grow incessantly, there comes a time when the competition between the great nations for colonies and spheres of influence reaches a point of no return. The have nations refuse to share their largesse with the have-nots, the capitalist states less endowed with colonies. Finally the dispute is resolved through military conflict and another redivision of the world. Thus the harvest of capitalism, according to Marx and Lenin, is depression on the one hand and war on the other.

III

This simplified exposition of Marxist political economy is a credible explanation for the crises and wars which punctuated the capitalist saga. It was particularly pertinent to the great depression that began in 1929, which in the words of Professor Lionel Robbins of London University "eclipsed all preceding movements of a similar nature both in magnitude and intensity."[9] Prior to the sudden collapse, capitalism displayed all the vices Marx had written about: a technology and productive capacity that outpaced the growth of population, the inability of workers to buy back what they produced as profits maximized, the great surpluses without outlet in the world's markets.

In the United States during the boom days of the 1920s—the era in which the assembly line came into its own—production rose sensationally, in pace with investment in laborsaving equipment. The physical output in manufacturing, for instance, jumped 49 percent from 1920 to 1929, though the number of workers at the factory bench remained the same; each worker was producing half as much again as he did a decade back. In mining, output rose by 43 percent but the labor force actually shrank 12 percent. The economy was primed for a much larger population, yet the census showed a gain of only 15 percent during that hectic decade. Theoretically the surpluses rolling off the assembly line could have been absorbed if wages had kept up with the boom or if prices had been lowered apace, but neither took place. What did happen was that profits pyramided to the point where they were three times as high in 1929 as in 1920. The result of this planless anarchy was the stock market crash of October-November 1929, when it became apparent that the high rate of profits could not be maintained in the face of inadequate purchasing power at the grass roots.

Establishment economists who did not anticipate the depression, who in fact predicted interminable prosperity, have a handy answer for their myopia; it may be called the accident theory of history. "Economists today," writes Robert L. Heilbroner, "no longer seek a single explanation of the phenomenon" of business cycles.[10] By attributing the slashing downturns to *many* causes, they imply that the system is basically healthy, subject only to this or that unanticipated—and perhaps unanticipatable—accident. So much presumably for Karl Marx. But it is worth noting that the same establishment economists have in the meantime jettisoned their central thesis—namely, that the free market is a self-regulating mechanism that precludes crisis—and have adopted, without attribution, Marx's, that it is not self-regulating and does not preclude crisis. Badly battered by the great depression, they retreated to a bastardized economic model in which the government, not the market, is the main regulator of the economy.

The great depression tore to shreds the theory that laissez-faire can keep the system afloat. "Leave alone," of course, was always a one-sided principle. Government has always helped the rich grow richer. From Alexander Hamilton's funding of the national debt and stimulation of manufacture to William Howard Taft's dollar diplomacy, which searched out foreign investment opportunities for American companies, to Herbert Hoover's prodding of corporations into 2,000 associations, which in the words of Eric F. Goldman "virtually ignored the anti-trust laws," the government has consistently intervened in economic matters—but intervened to help the upper classes. In the early nineteenth century it sold large patches of land to speculators when it could have sold smaller tracts to the poor; later, from 1850 to 1871, it gave away, free and unfettered, 180 million acres to the railroads. It helped big business and big bankers in a thousand ways, ranging from mail subsidies to military orders to breaking strikes. It was laissez-faire only in the sense that its restrictions on business were minimal, that almost any gambit was permitted on the vacuous theory that government had an obligation to help business make a profit. Laissez-faire, in other words, reinforced the anarchy of capitalism —everyone for himself, devil take the hindmost. In the condition of the great depression, however, when everything was falling apart, laissez-faire was no longer feasible. "In 1932," said Harry Truman with the hindsight of history, more than a decade later, "the private enterprise system was close to collapse. There was real danger that the American people might turn to some other system."[11]

Under these circumstances the government was forced to move from laissez-faire to discipline and control. There was not only the crisis itself to consider but the spinoff of revolutionary agitation that traced to the Russian Revolution twelve years earlier and the resurgence of leftist forces eager to spread that revolution. The open espousal of socialism by such eminent non-Marxist figures as Gov. Floyd B. Olson of Minnesota, who prayed that "the present system of government goes right down to hell,"[12] could not be taken lightly. The establishment, therefore, reluctantly accepted the obvious, that laissez-faire was no longer a viable doctrine. "This depression," commented Colonel Leonard Ayres in *The Economics of Recovery,* "has been far more severe than any of the 20 depressions that we have experienced in this country since 1790."[13]

The gross national product, yardstick of economic health, fell from $103 billion in 1929 to $56 billion in 1933. Unemployment enlarged from 1.5 million to 13 million. Industrial production fell by a half, construction by six sevenths. Nine million savings accounts were wiped out as thousands of banks went under. The Pennsylvania Department of Labor reported in 1932 wages of 5 cents an hour in sawmills, 6 cents in brick and tile manufacturing, 7.5 cents in general contracting. In Tennessee, women in mills earned as little as $2.39 for a fifty-hour week. In Kentucky, miners ate weeds ordinarily eaten by cows. Most important of all, from the focal point of confirming Marx's thesis about the relationship between investment and crisis, was the shattering drop in private spending for expansion from $15 billion in 1929 to a mere $886 million in 1932, a decline of 94 percent.

The great depression in the United States dragged down all the other capitalist economies, with the exception of Japan's, whose boiler was temporarily fired by a war in China. As of 1932 industrial production in Germany, France, and Canada had fallen by two fifths; in Britain by about a seventh. The slump in world trade was even more precipitous, to barely 44 percent of 1929 figures. The catastrophe was so encompassing—like a hopeless traffic jam—that nothing but some form of government direction could bring order out of the chaos. Other depressions had worked themselves out on their own, within the confines of laissez-faire; this one couldn't. President Herbert Hoover tried the magic of voluntarism for more than three years, but on the day he left office there were ten states, including New York, Michigan, and California, which had shut down their private banks, and the general situation was worse than ever. Not even the $3.5 billion made available to banks, insurance companies, and similar institutions under the January 1932 Reconstruction Finance Corporation bill could hold back the tide of disintegration. By the time Franklin Roosevelt assumed the Presidency in March 1933 it was clear that laissez-faire was headed for indecent burial.

It was replaced by a system of patchworks which is best described as controlled capitalism. The government regulated and manipulated major facets of the economy like a doctor administering adrenaline to a deathly sick patient, and took up the slack in spending and investment that private enterprise had failed to do. Short of accepting revolution there was just no other way out. Roosevelt later boasted he had in fact saved America from revolution, and he was probably right. He did it by throwing the government into the economic maelstrom as had never been done before.

The impulse for recovery in 1933—and since then—came not from private enterprise but the state. Though conservatives still argue that given a little more time Hoover's voluntarism would have worked, the fact is that no administration since Hoover's has ever returned to laissez-faire. From 1933 to the present the government has been the mother hen of the economy, the primary force shaping its destiny. It began in the 1930s with measures of an emergency nature. A Federal Emergency Relief Administration stimulated consumption by allocating monies for direct relief and, by undertaking 180,000 projects within four months, providing jobs for the jobless. The Works Progress Administration (WPA) and the Civilian Conservation Corps (CCC) subsequently gave work to millions of unemployed. The Public Works Administration (PWA) spent $4 billion on 34,000 projects, including the Tennessee Valley Authority, the Hoover Dam, the New York Triborough Bridge, schools, auditoriums, sewage systems, roads, and aircraft carriers, in order to revive the construction industry. The National Recovery Administration grouped businessmen in separate industries into associations which drew up codes of fair practices dealing with prices, wages, hours, exchange of information, and selling methods—subject to presidential approval. In effect the government pledged that if industry raised wages and reduced hours—thereby increasing the demand for goods—it would be allowed to collude in raising prices without antitrust prosecution. The Agricultural Adjustment Administration spurred the rise in agricultural prices by paying farmers hundreds of millions to kill 6 million pigs and plow under 10 million acres of cotton. What the free market could not do to encourage recovery, the government did by artificial measures. And what private enterprise would not do to provide new investment capital, the government did in its place. From expenditures of less than $4 billion a year in fiscal 1929, federal spending rose to almost $10 billion in 1940; the national debt from $17 billion to $43 billion.

To repeat: capitalism was revived by mortgaging the income of future generations in order to subsidize the present one. Whereas Stalinist Russia exacted great hardships from the present generation in hopes of making life easier for future ones, capitalist America did it the other way around. Except in wartime, maintaining a balanced budget had been an unshakable gospel for previous Presidents. Every year from 1920 to 1930, for instance, the federal account showed a surplus; every year under Roosevelt it showed a whopping deficit, added to the national debt that later generations would have to pay.

Two new terms entered the lexicon of Western nations, indicating the turnaround from laissez-faire to state-managed capitalism: compensatory spending and deficit financing. According to the theories of British economist John Maynard Keynes, foremost exponent of the new economics, the worst thing in the world was not a budget deficit but a sick economy. Economies become sick, Keynes said, when savings are not converted into capital, when capitalists, in other words, see little purpose in borrowing the money stocked in banks to use in new ventures. Theoretically this defect should be overcome when interest rates go down and entrepreneurs decide again to invest in new buildings, equipment, land. In fact, however—as Heilbroner paraphrases Keynes—"an economy in depression might well stay there; there was nothing inherent in the situation to pull it out."[14] The reason for this is that at the bottom of the business cycle savings dry up too; people and corporations that earn no money do not save. In 1929, for instance, individual Americans banked $3.7 billion of their earnings, and corporations showed surpluses on their books, after taxes and dividends, of $2.6 billion. But by 1932 and 1933 total individual savings were zero, and corporations were losing piles of money rather than stockpiling surpluses. "The practical results of that decline in saving was . . . a paralyzing situation where the economy was in perfect *economic* balance, even though it was in the throes of social agony. For if there were *no* surplus of savings, there would be *no* pressure on interest rates to encourage businessmen to borrow."[15] The depression therefore had no way of curing itself and had to be cured by government action.

The essential theme of compensatory spending was that in times of distress the government was duty-bound to compensate for the decrease in spending and investment by disbursing its own money—pump priming. In that way it would renew the interrupted circulation of commodities and capital. In one of his jauntier moments, Keynes went so far as to suggest that

> If the Treasury were to fill old bottles with bank notes, bury them at suitable depths in disused coal mines which are then filled up to the surface with town rubbish, and leave it to private enterprise on the well-tried principles of *laissez-faire* to dig the notes up again . . . there need be no more unemployment . . . [and] the real income of the community would probably become a good deal larger than it is.[16]

In fact the government eventually did something similar to filling old bottles when it poured billions into the military manhole. Generally, however, Keynesian economics called for more positive ways of priming the pump, such as building houses, roads, and bridges. The money supplied by government could not be inserted into the economy carelessly, for it might end up in a static bank account or under a mattress, doing no one any good. It had to be converted as quickly as possible into venture capital or individual spending. The government of course would have to borrow the money—deficit financing—but that was no great hardship since we "owed the money to ourselves." It was Americans who bought the bonds of the American government. And when times improved we could raise taxes to pay off part of the debt, as well as keep the economy from overheating.

One might ask at this point why it didn't occur to Keynes and his contemporaries that society should itself take over the operation of business. Private enterprise obviously was bankrupt in the 1930s. If government were the only force that could save it from its follies, why shouldn't government nationalize and run it? Why should it have given business a reward for anarchy and ineptness? Neither Keynes nor his followers ever answered that question. Instead they perpetuated the myth that private profit is the best motivation for economic development. They patched up the system so that the people as a whole paid, through taxes and inflation, the cost of encouraging the lust for profits. They primed the pump, with taxpayers' money, and socialized many capitalist losses, again with taxpayers' money, through such devices as state subsidies for airlines, tax benefits for business, depletion allowances, and absorption of research and development costs. With all that, the Keynesians did not do away with the problem, for capitalism is still saddled with a planless mode of production which continues to produce huge surpluses, much of which cannot be disposed of except by artificial means.

That the Keynesians themselves are not a little queasy about their ministrations is evident from a paragraph in a 1955 book by Nobel Prize winner Paul Samuelson.

To democratic nations the business cycle presents a challenge —almost an ultimatum. Either we learn to control depressions and inflationary booms better than we did before World War II, or the political structure of our society will hang in jeopardy. . . . If, as before the war, America marks time for another decade, the collectivized [socialist] nations of the world, who need have no fear of the business cycle as we know it, will forge that much nearer or beyond us. Worse than that, peace-loving people who do not pretend to know very much advanced economics will begin to wonder why it is that during two World Wars individuals were freed for the first time from the insecurity of losing their jobs and livelihoods.[17]

A good point—why is it that socialist economies do not have to worry about depressions and that capitalist economies avoid them only through war and militarism?

IV

In truth, even compensatory spending and deficit financing failed to deliver America (or the rest of the world) from the torture of depression. By 1939 the gross national product in the United States was almost as high as it had been in 1929; wages had risen, particularly after the birth of the CIO; and a few million people had found jobs. But there were still 9.5 million jobless in 1939 (17.2 percent of the labor force), down only 3.5 million from the depression peak. It was the World War, not the compensatory spending of the 1930s, that put America back to work; and the cold war and military expenditures thereafter that kept it at work. Almost $200 billion was spent on munitions during the war, another $50 billion for lend-lease to foreign allies, and more than $20 billion for new factories built by the government but operated by private industry. The expenditure on munitions in the single year 1944, $64 billion, was many times the monies appropriated for New Deal programs from 1933 through 1938. The cold war introduced even more monumental spending on militarism: from 1946 through 1967, according to Senate Foreign Relations Committee Chairman William Fulbright, the nation spent $904 billion "for military power," or more than 57 percent of the regular national budget in those years. Over the next five years, another $400 billion was pumped into the military veins, or a total of $1.3 trillion. How dependent we have become on the government for maintaining a "sound" economy is shown by statistics on federal government purchases. They have jumped from $1.25 billion in 1929, to $2 billion in 1933, $5.5 billion in 1938, and $100 billion in 1970, most of it in 1970 for the military. This was pump priming on a scale unmatched—or even remotely approximated—by any nation in history. It brought in its wake budget deficits as high as $54 billion (in fiscal 1943) and $25 billion (in fiscal 1968). Deficit financing has become so ingrained in the American system that since 1931 the federal accounts have shown black ink only seven times. The national debt jumped from $17 billion in 1931 to $285 billion in 1959 and is currently hovering around the $475 billion mark.

Given this vast amount of government injection, the American economy appears to be in ruddy health. There have been no depressions for three decades—only five "recessions," none of which brought a level of unemployment higher than 6 percent annually. The gross national product, in real terms, is more than five times what it was in 1933 and four times what it was in 1938. The product, of course, is ill distributed and the number of poor—by the government's own standards—is still one eighth of the population. Moreover, there were stern warning signs after Richard Nixon took office that the gilded age for America was coming to an end: of the twenty-two most developed countries, the 1969 and 1970 growth in GNP for the United States was the lowest, a mere 1.2 percent—only one tenth that of Japan, one fifth that of Germany, France, and Italy. In per capita terms the American achievement was even farther behind—just 0.2 percent as against 10.7 percent annually in Japan, 5.9 percent in France, 5.4 percent in Germany, 4.6 percent in Italy. Nonetheless, during the three decades since the outbreak of World War II the United States has attained a level of prosperity unknown in world history, far higher than its wildest dreams in the 1930s.

The question is: How durable is an economy whose mainspring is military? Leaving aside the moral issue, how much longer can an economy stimulated by such artificial means survive as a healthy organism? Richard P. Oliver of the Bureau of Labor Statistics estimated in September 1967 that employment generated by military spending, including military personnel, factory workers directly engaged in war production, and Department of Defense civilian employees, came to about 10 percent of the labor force, or 1.5 million people.[18] The total amount of employment created by pumping large sums into the economy for military purposes is much greater, since there is a multiplier effect for each dollar spent. The dollar changes hands once, twice, or three times as it is spent and respent by the grocers, butchers, and landlords who receive it, thereby producing still more jobs. Even allowing for the fact that if these monies were not allocated to the military, taxes would be lower and people might spend part of the saving on shoes and sailboats, the number of unemployed clearly would be reaching 1930-33 proportions—or higher—if the strange pump priming were reduced to the levels of the New Deal era.

As disturbing as is this realization—that the economic health of capitalism rests on the artificial stimulus of militarism—is the even more disturbing realization that this condition is permanent under the present social order. A military machine of unprecedented size, either concentrated in one superpower or dispersed among all the capitalist states, has become the sine qua non for the preservation of the old system. Militarism has been immensely costly and has finally whittled down even America's resources, but without it the capitalist economy could not have survived. Indeed, the role of militarism as a crutch to the domestic economy has been of far lesser importance than its function as the cement that held the system together—or at least tried to—on the international front. Put differently, capitalism would already have foundered if it had not used the military and corollary institutions, such as the CIA, to engage in a worldwide ongoing counterrevolution.

Permanent militarism, like compensatory spending in the 1930s, has emerged as a new factor in the present equation of history. The scenario of the past four decades, then, can be reduced to the following sequence:

1. After the "golden twenties" comes the great depression, which reveals the utter futility of laissez-faire capitalism.

2. The major capitalist nations all turn to government control and compensatory spending to save their domestic economies.

3. Keynesian measures applied internally, though effective to an extent, are incapable of staving off the trade and money wars between the great powers that lead ultimately to the worldwide military war.

4. In the postwar period the United States, as the fulcrum of capitalist power, devises two more artificial techniques for saving itself and its allies: a Keynesian economic plan applied on an

international scale and a military network that enforces discipline for Pax Americana.

5. The combination of international compensatory spending and international counterrevolution acts as adrenaline for the system for a quarter of a century, until a new set of imbalances is reached: the imbalance between a depleted America and a recovered Europe and Japan; the imbalance between productive capacity and markets; the imbalance between antirevolutionary and revolutionary nations; and the imbalance between private profit and natural resources.

Thus the crisis endemic to capitalism, long postponed by Keynesian ministrations and by militarism, is reappearing. And it portends for a system that has only recently made the retreat from laissez-faire to controlled capitalism, another shift—this time to a totally government-managed economy and a corporate state.

Let's look a little more closely at the whys and wherefores of this process.

CHAPTER NINE

Doors
Without
Exits

I

In a fanciful peek at the future, John Maynard Keynes wrote a book in 1930, *Economic Possibilities for Our Grandchildren,* in which he optimistically predicted that by the year 2030 humanity would no longer face an economic problem. Keynes came to that conclusion by extrapolating the figures for the rise of labor productivity in previous decades, to show that by 2030 every man and woman would be producing seven and a half times as much goods per man-hour of labor as in 1930. With endless consumer wares rolling off the assembly lines the era of scarcity would be over, and every man and woman could lavish on the bounties of abundance.

Keynes's excursion into tomorrow, alas, was based on at least two assumptions which science does not seem likely to confirm. One was that the supply of food and natural resources was inexhaustible. The other was that the flow of goods and capital would be indefinitely uninterrupted, so that production and productivity could spiral without hindrance. The first assumption we shall return to presently; the second is still at the core of capitalism's problems. Compensatory spending relieved some of the gluts on the home market, but foreign commerce and foreign investment were not amenable to the same rules. On the domestic front the government could enforce its will because it enjoyed power—police power, political power, judicial power. If it passed a law that bank deposits must be insured and a federal bank refused to insure them, the administration simply lifted the bank's charter. If it decided that the maximum wage increase allowable under control legislation was 5.5 percent, a union that chose to strike for 10 percent could be restrained through a court injunction and/or the arrest of its leaders. If government wanted to reduce the price of aluminum, as it did in 1966, it could dump part of its own stockpile on the market. Domestic life, it is evident, is governed by law, so that the rough edges of capitalist anarchy can be smoothed down—though not eliminated—by government action.

But there is no enforceable law *between* nations. "The relations among nations with each other today," writes Professor Paul A. Schilpp, "can, in truth, only be characterized as anarchial." John Dewey said it more picturesquely: "Disguise it as one may, the doctrine of national sovereignty . . . is a doctrine of international anarchy."[1] There are hundreds of books on something called international law, but there is no way that any sovereign nation can be made to do anything it doesn't feel is in its own interests. Within U.S. borders, California is prohibited from assessing a tariff on automobiles coming from Michigan. But there is nothing to stop Japan from placing a high or low tariff—or no tariff—on those same automobiles. What Japan does inevitably affects the prerogatives of America and American corporations. Thus in the grand anarchy of international relations the sovereignty of one nation actually impinges on the sovereignty of another, and there is little that can be done about it except, in extreme situations, through economic reprisal and military action.

In practice, of course, the nations arrive at modus vivendi with each other. Japan agrees, for instance, that if the United States adds no new levies on Toyota automobiles Japan will "voluntarily" restrict the export of its textiles; or the United States agrees that if Japan revalues its currency Uncle Sam will lift a surcharge on imports. But despite tens of thousands of such understandings and treaties, the arrangement is not always satisfactory, for it is subject, when the shoe begins to pinch, to unilateral modification and wholesale evasion. The self-interest of one country is not always adjustable to the self-interest of another, and where it is not, the tendency is for one "sovereign power" to find means of self-defense. In 1930 when America's economy was sick, Uncle Sam defended his position by placing enormously high tariffs on dutiable imports—53 percent of their value.[2] Those tariffs severely restricted other nations that wanted to sell on the American market. After World War II, however, when it was in the interests of the United States to make trade as free as possible, tariffs were lowered to the point where they are now about 10 percent of the value of dutiable imports. Even so, America does not shrink from using nontariff barriers for achieving some of the same exclusionary results. To give one example: Washington has permitted raw coffee to come in duty-free but placed a levy on instant coffee so that Brazil or Colombia find it impractical to process coffee. Other nations react in much the same fashion. The Common Market countries adopted something called variable levies (uncertain tariffs) against American feed grains, such as corn or soybeans, the effect of which was to whittle U.S. exports of those commodities from $533 million in 1966 to $247 million in 1970.[3]

In 1947 the "free world" established a body called the General Agreement on Tariffs and Trade (GATT), to lift restrictions on international commerce and investment. But GATT is circumvented by dozens of means, limited only by human ingenuity. Osaka, Japan, excludes U.S. automobiles through a local ordinance that prohibits cars more than two meters wide from using the streets 9 A.M. to 7 P.M., Monday through Saturday. By the provisions of GATT, the Common Market is prohibited from giving preferential treatment to any nation outside its ranks that it does not accord to the United States. But in practice it has given them to dozens of other nations, including eighteen in Africa, while denying them to Uncle Sam. Japan, though pledged by a 1953 treaty to grant American entrepreneurs rights to investment equal to those for its own citizens, still refuses to permit U.S. firms either to buy control of Japanese companies or establish wholly owned U.S. businesses on its soil. The United States, says Gaylord Freeman, Board Chairman of Chicago's First National Bank, is "guilty of similar violations. Our near exclusion of dairy products or our so-called voluntary limitation on imports of textiles and steel, are violations on our part."[4]

Another frequent manifestation of the anarchy of world capitalism has been the unilateral manipulation of money. At Bretton Woods in 1944 the "free world" agreed to certain fixed rates by which each of its currencies was convertible into the dollar—so many French francs for a dollar, so many Dutch guilder for a dollar, and so on. This was hailed as one of the most significant steps of our times to guarantee international stability. It was designed to check the nefarious practice by which one nation unilaterally lowers the price of its own exports and raises those of others, or vice versa, by the simple device of devaluing or revaluing its currency. If 600 Italian lire are equal in value to $1, and a pair of Italian shoes is worth 6,000 lire, by devaluing the lira so that it is 700 to the dollar, the cost of Italian shoes in the United States falls from $10 to $8.57. That is a big advantage for Italian shoe manufacturers and a big headache for Florsheim in Chicago. Bretton Woods was expected to prevent such practices. Yet despite that conclusive agreement thirty-nine of the forty-four countries who entered into it have devalued their money since then at least once; France has done it five times. Each of those devaluations hurt American (and other) exporters, while aiding exporters of the nations that devalued.

The evasion or violation of ratified agreements—not to mention the flouting of general principles on free trade—emphasizes the fact that there is no foolproof means of resolving disputes between nations. "Inasmuch as every existing nation state today lays claim to sovereignty," writes Schilpp,

> it follows that no national government today will accept any law as being above its own laws. Consequently the relations of nations with each other are not . . . lawful relations, that is to say, relations maintained in obedience to laws above the separate, individual nations. Consequently, all such relations can, in the nature of the case, only be anarchical. And there is no better seed bed for war than international anarchy.[5]

History indicates that what begins as a dispute over commerce or currency escalates, in the absence of restraint, into a trade war, a money war, a diplomatic war, and finally a military war. In "normal" times the process does not reach its ultimate conclusion because there are still opportunities for expansion; the conflicts do not become intense. War can also be evaded for a time when there is one nation strong enough, economically and militarily, to make the other nations dance its tune, as Britain was able to do under Pax Britannica and America, from 1945 to 1971, under Pax Americana. Cecil Rhodes, the adventurous gentleman who conquered much of Africa for the British, once proposed that the true road to peace was for Britain to conquer the whole world. Arrogant as that sounds, it is not far from the mark: so long as the guiding motif of capitalism is the maximization of profits, and so long as foreign markets are indispensable to siphon off the gluts of goods and capital at home, some means must be found to prevent conflict from erupting into confrontation. Rhodes believed that if Britain ruled the whole world such conflicts could be sidetracked. Less dramatic—and more realistic—leaders have tried to keep the world at peace through a balance of power or through international discipline imposed by one powerful nation strong enough to impose it.

Neither of these techniques, however, is foolproof. Britain's vaunted balance of power fell out of balance in the 1930s—and the road was paved for World War II. America's predominance since the end of that war has not eliminated militarism as the ultimate arbiter of international disputes but in fact has greatly enlarged its scope. Given the capitalist system—and its reliance on the private profit motive—the United States could not have remained a great power, and the "free world" could not have been stabilized, without the military stick on the one hand and the carrot of economic aid on the other. Even so, Pax Americana is currently breaking down because rampaging militarism, like Keynesianism, has been unable permanently to avoid the consequences of anarchy. The United States, the bastion of world capitalism, is caught in the ironic circumstance that in its present form it cannot survive without militarism—and it cannot survive with it.

II

The disciples of the established order who argue that depressions are accidental aberrations also leave the issue of war and militarism hanging in midair, as if it too were unrelated to any fundamental imbalance within the system. Why did World War II break out? The accepted answer in accepted circles is that there were many causes, including the fact, as historian Samuel Eliot Morison claims, that Hitler was an "uneducated paranoiac." The current militarism, these sources argue, was in response to the Russians, who made excellent allies during World War II but suddenly turned into power-hungry demons; they couldn't be trusted, they violated treaties, they threatened to overrun Europe, and they were, in addition, tyrants, murderers, and wardens of slave labor camps. Such explanations have the dubious virtue of placing all the blame on the "other side," but they obfuscate the true state of affairs. Would World War II have been averted if Hitler had been educated and perfectly sane? Would the world now be spending a trifling $20 billion on armaments instead of the $216 billion in 1971 if Stalin had been as cooperative as he was during the war itself? Neither of these hypotheses is very convincing.

The theorists who assert that there are many causes for war—including personality quirks, and cultural, ideological, administrative, and educational factors—are in effect saying that each war is an accident, due to someone's miscalculation. They are denying thereby that there is, in addition to the many factors, an *overriding* one, the economic. It may be true that in the day-to-day functioning of foreign offices and embassies, the consul who stamps visas in passports or the cultural attaché who arranges student exchanges is on occasion as important as the commercial attaché who watches for trade opportunities. But that is quite irrelevant, for not since the Napoleonic wars, and probably not then, has anyone heard of a capitalist nation going to war because of personality frictions or cultural or ideological disputes. Every war has had goals which directly or indirectly are tied to profit. Even the intervention in Russia, 1918–20, had economic overtones. The war in Vietnam had the twin purpose of warning irreverent revolutionaries elsewhere that they would suffer terrible consequences if they withdrew their nations from the "free world" and of securing Southeast Asia as an ultimate source for commerce and investment. In both purposes there was the long-term expectation of profit.

In frank and unguarded moments, leaders of the West have conceded that their preponderant concern has been economic—and specifically markets and raw materials. Consider some typical expressions by American leaders. "We desire," wrote James G. (Jingo Jim) Blaine, Secretary of State in 1881 and 1889–92, "to extend commerce, and in an especial degree with our friends and neighbors on this continent." The spirit of the United States, he averred in a confidential memo, was one "which seeks its outlet in the mines of South America and the railroads of Mexico," a spirit which "would not be slow to avail itself of openings of assured and profitable enterprise even in midocean."[6] Henry Cabot Lodge, at the turn of the century, expressed this principle more succinctly: "commerce follows the flag," a thesis joyously embraced by Teddy Roosevelt. Before the age of Madison Avenue circumspection, President William Howard Taft called his diplomacy "dollar diplomacy." The future chief executive, Woodrow Wilson, wrote in 1907 that

> since trade ignores national boundaries and the manufacturer insists on having the world as a market, the flag of his nation must follow him, and the doors of the nations which are closed against him must be battered down [and] concessions obtained or planted, in order that no useful corner of the world may be overlooked or left unused.[7]

Calvin Coolidge stated prosaically that "the business of America is business."[8] On the axiom that the international dealings of a country reflect its domestic preoccupations, that is as forthright a statement on foreign policy as one can hope for. Herbert Hoover's Secretary of State, Henry L. Stimson, asserted that "our foreign trade has now become an indispensable cog in the economic machinery of our country."[9] His successor, Cordell Hull, believed that "ever increasing surpluses" were America's major problem. "All past experience," he said, "teaches us that the power and influence of a nation are judged more by the extent and character of its commerce than by any other standard."[10]

The Marxists were wrong, as they frequently have been, in the schedule they set for the incapacitation of capitalism. Lenin called imperialism the last stage of the system, but it lived considerably beyond its last stage and fashioned a new imperialism to replace the old one Lenin referred to. But with all that, the Marxists were eminently right in their analysis—in showing the link between "ever increasing surpluses" and trade wars, money wars, diplomatic wars, militarism. There is no other way to explain World War II or the astounding expenditures on armaments since then.

Compensatory spending revived the slumbering *internal* market during the 1930s, but it could not of itself revive the *world* market. If capitalism had taken the advice of historian Charles Beard and philosopher John Dewey to adopt a planned economy, the sluggish world market would have caused little difficulty. The Beard-Dewey proposal called on government to fix a desired national standard of living and plan production and imports so that this standard could be met. By controlling both production and the distribution of domestic income, the United States (or any other country) could adjust to whatever resources were available, thereby reducing its reliance on world markets. If the plan showed there might be $20 billion of goods difficult to sell abroad, the planning commission would designate them for home consumption, or reassign production schedules from the goods-in-surplus to other industries —say, prefabricated housing or public services such as day-care centers.

The Beard-Dewey prescription was, and still is, an intelligent proposal, but Franklin Roosevelt was not about to jettison the capitalist system. "Foreign markets must be regained," he proclaimed. "There is no other way if we would avoid painful economic dislocation, social readjustments and unemployment."[11] Secretary of Agriculture Henry Wallace was more specific: without expansion into foreign markets, he said, the United States would lapse either into fascism or socialism, two alternatives he rejected. The trouble with the Roosevelt-Wallace formula, however, was that all the great nations, except for the Soviet Union, had the same compelling need—export or die. Each therefore intensified the economic war—by means most advantageous to itself—until the world was enmeshed in a military confrontation.

The United States devalued the dollar to 59 cents, which of course was a boon to American sales overseas and a catastrophe for foreigners who hoped to sell more on the U.S. market. Another device to secure what Roosevelt called "a lowering of foreign trade walls [so] that a larger measure of our surplus may be admitted abroad" was the reciprocal trade agreement. Such agreements were formerly subject to Senate approval, a long and arduous process, but under the Reciprocal Trade Agreements Act of 1934 FDR was empowered to raise or lower tariffs by as much as 50 percent by presidential fiat alone. Any nation willing to make the required concessions to allow penetration by U.S. goods and capital was assured a similar benefit here. A reciprocal trade agreement with Brazil, for instance, required the United States to keep coffee and cacao on the free list, while reducing tariffs on manganese, nuts, and castor beans. In return Brazil cut levies on U.S. autos, radios, electric batteries, cement, paints, fruit, and fish. The pact prohibited either government from introducing import quotas or a licensing system against each other, and contained a most-favored-nation clause, so that if greater concessions were made by Brazil to a third country they would automatically apply to the United States as well. On occasion the United States sweetened the trade agreement with a loan, such as the $60 million credit given the same Brazil to end its flirtation with Germany for a large barter deal. As of 1939 the Roosevelt administration had concluded reciprocal trade agreements with twenty-one nations, accounting for two-thirds of America's foreign business. It was a policy based on the belief that given "equality of opportunity" the superior American technology could sweep aside all competitors.

Needless to say, other nations designed methods of economic warfare to suit *their* purposes. England too went off the gold standard and entered into a preferential system with its British Commonwealth "partners" which favored commonwealth trade against that of outsiders. The most extreme measures, of course, were taken by the nations hardest pressed. One of them was Germany—with 6 million unemployed, gold reserves down to a meager 77 million reichsmarks as of June 1934, and exports reduced by almost two thirds. Under a complicated system worked out by a financial wizard named Hjalmar Schacht, Germany retreated to "autarchy" or "self-sufficiency." Schacht, like Roosevelt, revived the economy with pump-priming, except that his priming was a rearmament program that soon cost the staggering sum—at that time—of $4 billion a year. Since there was no money in the treasury to pay for this work creation, Germany floated short-term bonds and printed "Mefo" bills which had nothing behind them but a government prayer. Normally this increase of credit and the money supply would have pushed both prices and wages sky high. But the Nazis took care of the wage problem by outlawing trade unions and setting pay scales at the lowest possible level to keep body and soul together. Prices too were controlled by decree, and taxes were boosted from 6.5 billion reichsmarks in 1932–33 to 17 billion in 1938–39. so as to drain off excess money. The free market was replaced by state guidance much more severe than in the United States. but for exactly the same reasons.

Such a system obviously required equally stringent international measures. In order to husband meager foreign exchange, the Nazis cut imports to the bone and encouraged substitute (ersatz) industries. Large firms were given subsidies to manufacture synthetic rubber, textiles, fuel, and saltpeter (from nitrogen)—instead of importing them. The huge Hermann Goering Works was built to fabricate steel from low-grade ore, locally supplied, rather than higher grade imports. All this raised costs, but the state shifted the burden onto the backs of workers, who were forced to labor ten and twelve hours a day for real wages below those of 1932.

Schacht's most noteworthy achievement on the foreign front was the negotiation of a large number of barter deals. Under this cumbersome arrangement the Reich exchanged a certain number of locomotives, say, for an equal value in Brazilian coffee, or German drilling equipment for Mexican oil, German typewriters for Turkish tobacco. No money changed hands. Often the coffee, oil, or tobacco never arrived in Germany but was reexported to other European nations, such as Holland, for hard currency. With this foreign exchange Schacht was then able to buy goods from those countries that refused to barter, such as the United States. Admittedly it was a bizarre system, a throwback to precapitalist times, but it was made necessary by circumstances, and it worked —to an extent. Schacht was able to increase exports to Latin America by 178 percent from 1932 to 1937 and dramatically to improve Germany's trade with nearby countries such as Romania, Turkey, and Greece. On the whole, however, the Nazis increased exports from their low point in 1934 by only a third. Economic war by itself was clearly indecisive.[12]

The Nazi, Fascist, and militarist regimes of Germany, Italy, and Japan were of course loathesome, but they were more the effect of an unhealed crisis than its cause. The Axis nations did not have the flexibility to deal with their problems of investment, spending, and surpluses that the wealthy nations had. If they wanted to save capitalism within their borders, they were forced to take dire measures against their workers and dire measures on the international scene as well. Their lack of access to raw materials and markets drove them ultimately from economic warfare to diplomatic and military warfare. As one right-wing publicist, Hashimoto Kingoro, put it relative to his own country, there were only three ways for "Japan to escape from the pressure of surplus population . . . namely emigration, advance into world markets, and expansion of territory."[13] Emigration was foreclosed by "the anti-

Japanese immigration policies of other countries," including the United States. Penetration of world markets was hampered "by tariff barriers and the abrogation of commercial treaties." The only alternative was territorial expansion. "In fairness to Japan," writes Robert Leckie in his classic work *The Wars of America,* "it is not easy to see how she could have followed anything other than an imperialist course."[14]

To salvage its home economy Japan expanded outward. We have seen that from 1931 to 1937 the Nipponese captured Manchuria, Jehol, Inner Mongolia, and the provinces of northern China—an area larger than Britain, France, Italy, Spain, and Germany combined, with a population of 100 million—and provoked a little incident at the Marco Polo Bridge near Peking as a pretext for a total campaign against China. "To have not and want to have," wrote political analyst Hu Shih in 1938, "the only way is by the use of military force."[15] Italy established a sphere of influence over Hungary and Austria and warred against Haile Selassie to conquer Abyssinia. Germany rearmed to the teeth in preparation for its *Drang nach Osten* and successively regained the Saar (in 1935), reoccupied the demilitarized Rhineland (in 1936), and then took the Sudetenland and all of Czechoslovakia in the ensuing months. Neville Chamberlain and Edouard Daladier appeased Hitler at Munich, and in April 1939 Roosevelt pleaded with Hitler and Mussolini to refrain from any action against thirty specific nations for ten years—in return for which an international conference would be held to adjust problems of armaments and trade. But the needs and appetites of the Axis were too great to be thus appeased. World War II, fought to effect still another division of the earth, began in September 1939 with the invasion of Poland.

III

Weighing these developments of the 1930s, it is evident that the Keynesian medicine was not potent enough to terminate the crisis of capitalism; the crisis was simply transferred to the military front. Keynesianism ameliorated the pain of cancer but not the cancer itself. In effect, the capitalist nations traded off the danger of revolution at home for the reality of war abroad—and in the end confronted a wave of postwar revolutions anyway. If the core of capitalism, the advanced nations, was saved because of the unique circumstance that the United States still had the resources to nurse those nations back to health, the periphery of the system was overrun by nationalism and socialism. That part of the world dominated by the great powers shrank appreciably. And if capitalism somehow survived as a result of more patchwork and more improvisation, one can only wonder whether it has eliminated the cause of its difficulties or built up the pressures—like an overheated boiler—for a future, and worse, explosion.

At the end of hostilities the United States was in much the same situation vis-à-vis the world market as it had been vis-à-vis the domestic market during the great depression. Cranking up the economy during the war had given it an immense overage of industrial capacity. According to the National Planning Association the capital equipment industry by now was "nearly twice the size which would be needed domestically under the most fortuitous circumstances."[16] There was plenty of capital and goods crying for an outlet but for the moment few profitable prospects for either investment or trade. American exports during the war had averaged about $10 billion a year (more than three times the prewar figures) and imports $3.5 billion, leaving the rest of the world with a disheartening dollar deficit running into many billions. The balance of payments was so heavily weighted in favor of Uncle Sam that America accumulated a stockpile of $29 billion in gold, 77 percent of the world's reserves. Summarizing the American position early in the postwar era, James McMillan and Bernard Harris in *The American Take-over of Britain* estimated:

> On the production side the US with six and a half per cent of the world's population, harvested one-third of the world's grain; half its cotton; [s]melted 55 per cent of its steel and other basic metals; pumped 70 per cent of the world's oil; used 50 per cent of its rubber; generated 45 per cent of its mechanical energy; produced 60 per cent of its manufactured goods and enjoyed 45 per cent of the entire annual income of humanity.[17]

It owned an awesome economic mechanism that needed foreign markets more desperately than ever.

American leaders were well aware of this problem. "My contention is that we cannot have full employment and prosperity in the United States," said Assistant Secretary of State Dean Acheson in November 1944, "without the foreign markets." He conceded that under another system, e.g., socialism, "you could use the entire production of the country in the United States." But under free enterprise, the government "must look to foreign markets."[18] Echoing such sentiments Franklin Roosevelt observed that every worker, farmer, and businessman "has a stake in the production and flow of manufactured goods, agricultural products, and other supplies to all other countries of the world."[19] Without that flow the economy would have become constipated just as in the early 1930s, perhaps worse.

The difficulty was that both America's allies and its former enemies were too impoverished to recharge their economic batteries so as to buy Uncle Sam's wares. The world was prostrate. According to a Communist source the war had cost the nations of the globe more than $1 trillion in military expenditures, almost four times that much in destroyed property, not to mention 54 million civilian and military dead and 90 million wounded. Parenthetically, one may ask if a system so destructive of people and wealth deserves to be revived. Leaving that aside, however, it is obvious that except for the United States every other capitalist nation was in a near-terminal stage. Britain, better off than most of the belligerents, had had its wealth reduced by almost a third. She had been forced to sell much of her investments in the United States, South America, and Asia to amass dollars to aid her allies and finance wartime imports. Her exports, on which she depended to survive, had fallen by half; her gold had drained away to the point where in 1945 the reserve was only $12 *million.* Instead of being a $16-billion creditor nation, as before the war, she was now a $12-billion debtor. "The war has left us poor," lamented a big, jovial businessman, Lord Woolton, in the House of Lords. "It has left us the largest debtor nation in history. America, on the other hand, has been left by the war rich beyond her dreams."[20]

Despite its good fortune, the United States was in the same fix as the gold miner with a ton of gold in the desert but no means of transporting it. Uncle Sam had warehouses full of goods and banks full of savings, but to filter them into the world's economy he first had to revive a bankrupt system at the brink of dissolution. The flow of commodities and money had been interrupted and could not be renewed without vast amounts of compensatory spending —this time on an international scale.

In the folklore of America it is said that the scores of billions given or loaned to foreign nations was an act of unparalleled generosity. If so, it was the same kind of generosity as that of the citizen who pays taxes so that police and firemen will protect his property. During the war Washington loaned or leased to its allies $49.1 billion worth of munitions, food, goods, and services without which they could not have continued the war. From the end of the war to 1971 it doled out another $149 billion—$41.6 billion in arms, $19.7 billion in "food for peace," $88 billion in economic aid—all of which not only helped the rest of the "free world" recover but nourished the American economy as well. Abstractly it seems ludicrous for one capitalist nation to support its rivals, and on so lavish a scale; the whole idea of competition, after all, is to lay your competitor low, not help him. But the United States had to save its rivals to save itself; if it hadn't engaged in this international pump priming, a wave of revolution unquestionably would have engulfed most of Western Europe.

American aid, moreover, was far from eleemosynary; every penny had conditions attached to it, some of it very specific, some of it general. The $3.75-billion loan to Britain in 1946 was predicated on her curtailing the empire preference system by which members of the British Commonwealth had been granting each other lower tariff rates than outsiders; and on her agreeing to spend at least $1 billion in the United States. The $380 million given to the Philippines at the time of independence was conditioned on an agreement that U.S. citizens—but no other foreigners —enjoy the same legal rights as native entrepreneurs and that Philippine currency be tied to the dollar. In return for aid, Taiwan opened its doors to 500 American manufacturers. Thailand granted tax holidays to such firms as Caltex, Esso, Firestone, Chase Manhattan, and IBM and abolished quotas, licenses, and other restrictions. One of the provisos agreed to by Britain in 1948, according to Senator Arthur Vandenberg, "was that the United States be given a bigger share in the uranium development in the Congo."[21] In line with this understanding a group of American companies associated with the Rockefeller interests were permitted to buy 600,000 shares of Tanganyika Concessions, the largest financial holding company in sub-Saharan Africa. A loan of $24 million to improve railways in Northern and Southern Rhodesia (then under British control) carried the proviso that the loan be repaid in strategic raw materials such as chrome, cobalt, tungsten, and copper.

Generally, however, the aid had conditions that were broad in scope. In return for resuscitating the economies of its allies and former enemies, the United States exacted a pledge that they would accept the two principles that favored American industry most: the open door and convertibility of currency. Open door meant removal of restrictions on trade, investment, and access to raw materials. Convertibility meant, in effect, accepting the dollar as the international means of exchange, with all the advantages that accrue to a world banker—namely, the right to flood the planet with dollars. Under the $12.3 billion of Marshall Plan grants, the recipients had to agree to open their borders and that of their colonies to American entrepreneurs on an equal basis with their own nationals. They had to agree to lift most of their quotas on foreign imports. They had to certify each month that they were not shipping arms or strategic materials to the Soviet Union and its allies. The Alliance for Progress imposed even stiffer conditions. Latin-American countries were required to import from the United States an equivalent amount of goods to the money they received under the Alliance, to earmark half the loans for purchase of equipment from North America, to ship a large part of these purchases in American bottoms, to supply certain raw materials to the United States, and to agree not to nationalize U.S. firms without "fair" payment.

There is some question whether U.S. aid programs helped foreign economies in all instances—in many it only helped the entrenched oligarchies. But there is no doubt that it was a boon to the United States. As of 1965 almost a quarter of the iron and steel exports of Uncle Sam, 30 percent of the fertilizers, 30 percent of the railroad equipment, and about the same percentage of agricultural products were generated through foreign aid. According to Eugene Black, former president of the World Bank, foreign aid provided "a substantial and immediate market for U.S. goods and services," stimulated "the development of new overseas markets for U.S. companies," and oriented "national economies towards a free enterprise system in which U.S. firms can prosper."[22]

Thus, international pump priming not only rescued Western Europe from revolution but greatly augmented America's own foreign trade and investment, without which postwar prosperity would have been impossible. From 1950 to 1971 America's direct investment abroad skyrocketed from $11.8 billion to $86 billion. Investments by U.S. firms in Latin America jumped from $4.5 billion in 1950 to $10.3 billion in 1965 and were so lucrative that in the same period the corporations transferred more profits home than their original investments, $11.3 billion. According to a 1968 summary by Amaury de Riencourt,

> one-third of all automobiles manufactured in Europe are built in American-owned or -controlled plants; American firms control between a quarter and a third of the oil industry's market in Britain and the Common Market. In tires, earth-moving equipment, razor blades, sewing machines, and countless other industries, their share is even larger. By 1967, American firms had a stake of almost $6 billion in Britain alone, produced 10 percent of its manufacturing output, 17 percent of its exports, employed already one out of sixteen British workers, controlled about 7 percent of the country's total industrial assets—and at the present rate of growth, would control one quarter of Britain's entire economy by 1980.[23]

Direct private investments in Japan grew as a result of occupation from a negligible $19 million in 1950 to $676 million a decade and a half later—not a large sum, considering Japan's economy, but greater than in the past. In Australia it grew from $201 million to $1.7 billion. Following a similar pattern, U.S. exports climbed from $4 billion in 1940 to $10.5 billion in 1945 and $42 billion in 1970. Even more sensational were the production figures of American companies abroad. Judd Polk of the U.S. Council of the International Chamber of Commerce reported in December 1970 that "the output of goods and services by U.S. business abroad is well over $200 billion annually now."[24]

In elevating its own fortunes, however, the United States also helped elevate those of its major partners. Canada's national income grew from 14 billion dollars in 1950 to 39 billion in 1965; France from 78 billion new francs to 347 billion; West Germany from 75 billion marks to 342 billion; Italy from 6,911 billion lire to 28,468 billion; Japan from 3,382 billion yen to 23,877 billion; Britain from 10.8 billion pounds to 28.3 billion. Though poverty is far from eliminated in the capitalist world and the maldistribution of income is chronic, workers and others today enjoy living standards and amenities such as automobiles, refrigerators, washing machines, and television sets beyond anything known before.

IV

If this idyllic situation could have continued indefinitely, the establishment-oriented scholars would have proven their point about the enduring character of capitalist prosperity. The prosperity, however, carried the seed of its own undoing, for it rested not only on compensatory spending financed worldwide by the United States but, even more, on a military machine so wideranging it eclipsed by far anything humankind had ever seen before—in peace *or* war.

Here again, as with the aid programs, there was no a priori design, no blueprint worked out by generals and colonels in advance to get themselves promoted or by big corporations to win multimillion defense contracts. It was simply inherent in the situation, just as it is inherent in the situation of the commercial attaché in Bangkok or Madrid to ferret out opportunities for trade. The "American system" that evolved logically from America's new industrial capacity, and from the needs of its allies, called for access to raw materials and to a world market of certain dimensions, considerably larger than in the past. Some of that market had already been cut off—Eastern Europe, North Korea, later China, North Vietnam, Cuba. What remained had to be defended at all costs from secession—from nations that chose to leave the "free world" orbit because of revolution or because they refused to accept the discipline of Pax Americana. The consortium of states in which America was the senior partner was far from a harmonious community; indeed, most of its peoples not only felt no kinship for Washington's goals but had antagonistic interests. They could be held together in part with loans and grants; if Washington did not provide such aid, said Undersecretary of State William L. Clayton in December 1947, "the Iron Curtain would then move westward at least to the English Channel," which in turn would mean "a blackout of the European market" and compel changes in the United States "which could hardly be made under our democratic free-enterprise system."[25] Aid in itself, however, was not enough, for there were centrifugal tendencies in the American alliance that could be held in check only through force and conspiracy, the tools of the Pentagon and the Central Intelligence Agency.

The militarization of America and the "free world," then, began as a response to the danger of secession and grew with each act of revolution and defiance of Pax Americana into its present awesome dimensions. Assessing its own needs and that of capitalism generally, the United States was intent at war's end on building a world based on the open door in economic relationships and the status quo in social relationships. The first obstacle to that purpose was the Soviet Union, not because it represented a military threat —"it was perfectly clear to anyone with even a rudimentary knowledge of the Russia of that day," wrote George F. Kennan years later, "that the Soviet leaders had no intention of attempting to advance their cause by launching military attacks with their own armed forces across frontiers"[26]—but because Russia opposed the "open door" and might give material and moral support to nations-in-revolution. There is much evidence today that President Truman ordered the atom bomb dropped on Hiroshima and Nagasaki as a warning to the Soviet Union as much as a means of defeating Japan. According to atomic scientist Leo Szilard, Secretary of State James Byrnes "did not argue that it was necessary to use the bomb against the cities of Japan in order to win the war . . . [but] that our possessing and demonstrating the bomb would make Russia more manageable in Europe."[27] After the war, the nuclear shield was flaunted at the Soviets as a warning to stay "manageable"—not to trespass, through revolution or otherwise, beyond a certain line. It was made clear to the Russians that if they invaded or subverted any country on "our" side of the line the bombers carrying nuclear payloads that roared constantly over Europe, and bombers at bases in Iran, Turkey, Pakistan, and elsewhere, would be ordered into action.

Holding the line against the Soviets, however, was only one aspect of the problem, for on this side of the line there was a great ferment that was autonomous of Russia. Many peoples of the budding "free world" were waiting in the wings to establish independent societies different from those of prewar days; left to their own devices they would have chosen governments or conducted revolutions at cross purposes with Pax Americana. To undercut this danger the United States applied its military power, along with the economic carrot. Japan and Germany were "saved" from an impending drift to the left by military occupation: Washington did not remove its troops from either country until political manipulation had weakened the Socialists and Communists and assured a return to power of big business. Greece—concurrently—was "saved" from revolution by military aid and training given the rightist Greek army. Britain had already spent $760 million in a vain effort to suppress the Communist-tinged EAM guerrillas, once the backbone of resistance to Hitler, who were now fighting the Greek monarchist dictatorship. But as of February 1947 Britain was no longer able to bear this burden. President Truman took over the obligation by supplying Greece (and nearby Turkey) with $400 million in arms and economic aid, without which the rebels could not have been defeated. Another $1.5 billion was supplied to that little country in armaments alone from 1950 to 1968 to guarantee right-of-center Greek governments protection from their own people. Similar aid and training, though on a smaller scale, was provided Philippine governments to help them overcome the Hukbalahap guerrillas.

From episodic beginnings the militarist response to crisis grew steadily until it became a Pavlovian reflex. The danger of revolution in Western Europe was met in part by Marshall Plan aid and in part by the formation of the North Atlantic Treaty Organization (NATO), one of whose major functions, according to a U.S. interdepartmental committee, was "to protect the North Atlantic Countries against *internal* aggression."[28] Western Europe, it turned out, was less amenable to social upheaval than the pessimists feared, but no one could have anticipated that in advance. The turning point for the militarization of America (and its allies) came with the civil war that broke out in Korea June 25, 1950. Regardless of who was the aggressor and who the victim, this was an internal affair between two factions in one severed nation. But Truman was determined that the "free world" domain be held at all costs and intervened at a cost of 34,000 Americans killed and 103,000 wounded. Before the conflict was over almost 6 million American troops had filtered in and out of that ravaged country. The Korean War was a sort of watershed for America. During and after it there was a quantum jump in military spending; the

7th Fleet was dispatched to defend Taiwan, and militarism generally enlarged its operations unrestrained.

In subsequent years the sword was unsheathed in many places in many ways. The CIA and the Pentagon teamed up to supply, advise, and finance the counterrevolution of rightists against the neutralist governments of Jacobo Arbenz Guzmán in Guatemala and Mohammed Mossadegh in Iran. American-subsidized rearmament helped France combat the Indochinese and Algerian revolutions, and Britain to combat the Malayan and Kenyan revolutions. America itself landed troops in Lebanon, as a warning to revolutionaries in that country and in Iraq in 1958, and sent the marines headlong into the Dominican Republic in 1965 to prevent another neutralist, Juan Bosch, from returning to the presidential post to which he had been elected in the first honest poll of that country in decades. Uncle Sam recruited, trained, armed, transported, and paid all the expenses for a counterrevolutionary contingent that vainly attempted to invade Cuba in 1961 and, in October 1962, came within a hairsbreadth of sending a nuclear armada against that island during the Cuban missile crisis. The United States gave military and other aid to moderate elements in the Congo and Ethiopia and transported their troops to fight left-wing rebels. American arms, training, and support helped military dictators overthrow legitimate governments in Brazil, Argentina, Bolivia, and many other places. Finally, in the most flagrant of all interventions, the United States injected itself into civil wars in Vietnam, Laos, and Cambodia, at a cost of $150 billion, 55,000 Americans dead, and hundreds of thousands wounded.

The scope of intervention and planned intervention on behalf of the status quo is punctuated by the dozens of secret agreements, called contingency agreements, entered into by the Department of Defense and occasionally the State Department, without the U.S. Senate approval required by the Constitution. No one outside the cloistered official family knows how many such understandings exist or what they encompass. But *U.S. News and World Report* asserted on July 21, 1969, that there were at least twenty-four such arrangements with such countries as Spain, Iran, Jordan, the Congo Republic (Leopoldville), Ethiopia, Tunisia, and Thailand. Another barometer of intervention was the fact that under the Military Assistance Program of 1950 some $35 billion in weaponry was given to seventy-eight countries from 1950 through 1969. In the same period the Pentagon trained 297,087 officers of sixty-nine nations in the gentle art of counterinsurgency—fighting their own people. And to back up this program the U.S. Navy, now "second to none," as well as the Air Force and Army, ensconced themselves in 429 major and 2,972 minor bases, camps, and installations around the world, including 400 around the Soviet Union and 120 around China, from which to transport troops and launch offensives in case of "contingency."

Rank-and-file Americans may delude themselves that there is a moral objective to all this, such as preserving freedom, but the generals and admirals suffer no such misconceptions. General Robert Porter, Jr., in underscoring the importance of his work as commander of American military forces in the Panama Canal Zone, pointed out that "Latin America is one of our largest trading partners—$7 billion in 1967—and after Canada and Western Europe, the largest area for United States private investments now totalling almost $13 billion. During and since World War II Latin America has been a major supplier of approximately 30 strategic materials, including copper, tin, and petroleum." The Latin-American counterinsurgents being trained in the Canal Zone, he said, are therefore needed to "act in conjunction with the police and other security forces . . . to control disorders and riots" and to discourage "those elements which are tempted to resort to violence and overthrow the government."[29] No present-day Lenin could have stated the militarist purpose more forthrightly: it defends the established order from any upheaval that might limit U.S. access to investment or commerce.

V

The cost of this defense has been staggering, yet it has been indispensable. Even if we assume that Western Europe and Japan could have been held against the tide of revolution—a debatable assumption—there is no doubt that South Korea, South Vietnam, Laos, Cambodia, Taiwan, Brazil, Bolivia, Guatemala, Panama, the Dominican Republic, Greece, Ethiopia, Iran, and Jordan, among others, would long ago have succumbed to socialist or neutralist rule. What the domino effect might have been of such a wholesale secession from Pax Americana we can only surmise. President Eisenhower underscored this point—probably unwittingly—

when he asked the rhetorical question in 1953 "If we lost Vietnam and Malaya, how would we, of the free world, hold the rich empire of Indonesia?" The same question might be asked if we "lost" Brazil or the Middle East, or any other major spheres of influence. Clearly, however, the capitalist-dominated area of the world would be far more compressed than it is—and far less prosperous. It is more than likely that it would have been caught in the web of disintegration.

But if militarism, combined with compensatory spending, has given succor to the old system in this last quarter of a century, it has also pushed it into a revolving door from which there is no exit. Three glaring weaknesses are now apparent in Pax Americana: first, that its cost is too prohibitive to be borne indefinitely; second, that it cannot appease the aspirations of peoples in underdeveloped countries; and third, that it can no longer retain the high degree of discipline within the bloc that it did when America was all-powerful.

Consider the money costs. World exports grew from $58 billion in 1948 to $270 billion in 1969, but in the latter year the world was spending $200 billion on armaments, $112 billion of it by the NATO countries. The American outlay on this function since World War II, $1.3 trillion, is more than twice what American corporations received from export sales in that period and many times what American firms earned in profits from overseas activities. From 1921 through 1939 there was never a year in which the United States spent as much as $1 billion on defense—in some years it was only a couple of hundred million—whereas appropriations today are on an order of magnitude 80 to 320 times higher. The military establishment prewar was minute compared to today, when it owns $202.5 billion worth of property, including $100 billion in weaponry and 39 million acres of land, thousands of bases abroad and even more at home. It is far and away the largest business on earth, responsible on its own for balance-of-payments deficits with foreign nations of $2 to $3 billion a year—$17.6 billion from 1961 through 1968 alone, or almost twice as much as the present U.S. gold hoard.

By its own criteria capitalism has gone insane, out of control. I am not referring to such phenomena as alienation, pollution, or waste of resources—which also indicate that the system has failed to respond to reality—but simply to its economic trauma. The whole idea of capitalism was that efficiency and growth are spurred by competition, that one entrepreneur or one country thrives by seeking to gain advantage against another. Who, then, would have thought that the only way America could protect its own skin would be by giving away scores of billions to rival nations? And who would have thought that the only way to achieve affluence was to waste a couple of trillion dollars on military institutions that produce nothing of a useful nature?

The West in general and the United States in particular are now in the position of a businessman who spends $10 in advertising to lure an additional $1 of sales. So long as the businessman has money left in the bank he can continue this exercise in futility, but when his funds run short he is bankrupt. The rise of postwar militarism has that same illogical trait. In another day it was relatively simple to subdue the peoples of underdeveloped nations. Britain was able, in the nineteenth century, to pacify the subcontinent of India with 50,000 soldiers. The French seized large parts of Indochina with only 2,000 troops. China's Boxer Rebellion was suppressed with 20,000 Western fighting men. But after World War II, when seventy-four countries gained national independence, the amount of military force needed for "stability" rose by geometric progression. In Malaya, Britain had to use 40,000 of its own troops, 100,000 police, and 200,000 home guards to hold in check a nationalist and Communist guerrilla force varying from 1,800 to 12,000 men—and it took twelve long years to complete the job. Britain deployed 50,000 soldiers, police, and home guards against a ragged group of 14,000 Mau Mau in Kenya and was able to bring them to brook only after five years of fighting. France commanded 500,000 troops against a mere 45,000 Algerian guerrillas but was incapable of subduing the revolutionaries after seven years; in 1962 it was forced to grant independence. A French force of 116,000 was ignominiously defeated by the Vietminh in Indochina. And an American force that reached a peak of 540,000, supplemented by 1 million puppet troops—armed and trained by the Pentagon—as well as South Koreans, Australians, and New Zealanders was unable to thwart 250,000 Vietcong and North Vietnamese, despite an expenditure of upwards of $150 billion.

America's armed forces before the 1846-48 Mexican War numbered a mere 9,000, some 53,000 in 1904, and only 139,000 not long before World War II. But the war machine of the 1960s had a permanent contingent of 2.5 to 3 million men; its "strategic forces" were ready to fight an all-out nuclear war at a few minutes' notice; and its "general purpose" forces were prepared to wage "two and a half wars" simultaneously—a NATO war in Europe, a war against China in Asia, and a minor war in Latin America. Directly linked to the war machine, in addition, was a Central Intelligence Agency which had tens of thousands—perhaps as many as 200,000—men at its disposal and spent billions each year on covert activities against the sovereignty of other nations.

Yet with all the expenditures in money and men, the basic goal of militarism—to forge a disciplined alliance under American tutelage—remains unachievable. It is subject to too many strains. On the one hand it is beset by the widening gulf between America, Europe, and Japan, as the latter become more competitive with the United States and more independent. On the other it has been unable to mitigate the basic clash of interests between the advanced capitalist nations and the underdeveloped ones. No matter how many successes militarism records, it becomes more difficult with each passing year, as the cry for true independence grows stronger, for the West to hold the line against former spheres of influence and colonies—a fact attested to by Vietnam, Laos, Peru, Argentina, and others only recently. It is in the interests of the great powers that the weak ones remain suppliers of raw materials and underindustrialized; or, if the latter do acquire an industry, that it be foreign-owned, its profits going into the coffers of the rich nations rather than for the development of the poor. For the advanced states the backward ones are their poaching ground and the open door their means of access. For the weak ones, on the other hand, the open door is a disaster, for it not only turns over vital resources to foreign exploitation but precludes orderly, planned economic development and subordinates the local economy to the needs of foreigners rather than their own people. When Kenya or Colombia open their doors for the manufactures of Britain, America, or Japan they thereby stunt the growth of their own native industry. What such countries need is exactly the reverse of the open door, a closed door to protect nascent manufacture. America itself followed the closed door policy in the last half of the nineteenth century by legislating high tariffs to support its tenuous industry.

The uneven relation between rich and poor nations not only

impedes industrialization and balanced progress for the latter but has side effects that mire them in debt and poverty. One such side effect is the unfavorable terms of trade between the weak and the strong nations. Raw materials sold by the underdeveloped states either go down in price or rise much more slowly than the price of finished goods supplied by the highly developed states. While the price of Colombian coffee, for instance, was dropping from 85 cents a pound to 40 cents in the mid-1950s and early 1960s, the price of American Chevrolets was rising. Colombia had to export three or four times as much coffee in 1963 to earn the exchange for the same number of American automobiles as in the 1950s. A tractor made by Ford, the Major, could be bought in 1954 for the equivalent of twenty-two Uruguayan young bulls but cost the equivalent of forty-two bulls in 1963. To compensate for these "unfavorable terms of trade" weak nations must borrow from the strong and pay ever larger sums in interest and principal. In 1956 only 6 percent of the money Latin America earned from exports (overwhelmingly in raw materials) went to service the foreign debt; by 1965 it had jumped to 16 percent. The only solution to this problem is native industrialization, protected by high tariffs and other devices. But that is exactly what Pax Americana tried to forbid.

The result has been that the gap in income between the rich nations and the poor ones has widened, not narrowed. Robert S. McNamara, president of the World Bank and former U.S. Secretary of Defense, noted in an article published late in 1972 that of the ninety-five nations who are affiliated with the World Bank two thirds subsist on a yearly gross product of less than $200 per capita. In the last decade the GNP of these nations has grown by an average of 3.9 percent a year or less than $8 per person.[30] By contrast, Western Europe, which enjoys a gross per-capita product of $2,070 a year, is growing at a 5-percent clip or more than $100 annually. Not only is the disparity growing greater but that indefinable something called rising expectations is being stretched beyond the safety mark. People who are currently living on $1, $2, and $3 a week cannot be expected to wait 100 years to earn half of what Europeans earn now. They are not going to. Whatever the initial hardship, the "soft" states, as Gunnar Myrdal calls them, will strike out, one after another, on an independent course— perhaps along the Marxist road that Cuba is traveling, the non-

Marxist but revolutionary path adopted by Peru, or along some other trail. But in any event they are bound to sever ties with the American system, to reject satellite status and the open door.

VI

Here we have a clue as to why the United States and its major allies are loath to disarm. Three decades after World War II and many years after Khrushchev put forth his plan for total disarmament in four years, there is not even a hint of reversing the arms race. The best that has been achieved thus far was an agreement in 1972, in the Strategic Arms Limitation Talks, to slow down the *rate of increase* in nuclear weaponry. General-purpose armaments have not yet been touched, even though a reduction of the U.S. troops in Europe and the Mid-East, which now drain $9.4 billion from Uncle Sam's exchequer annually, would significantly ameliorate the balance-of-payments problem.[31]

Washington, however, is impaled on the horns of a dilemma: if it disarms it will lose its position as a world power; if it continues to arm it will drain away its resources and lose its position as a world power. Consider the question so to speak, from the bottom up. On April 28, 1965, President Johnson dispatched the marines to the Dominican Republic, where young officers were conducting a revolt to restore democratically elected Juan Bosch to the presidency from which he had been ousted by a military coup two years earlier. By May 2 there were 22,000 U.S. soldiers on the scene, and they did not leave until Ambassador Ellsworth Bunker was able to install, through terror and fraudulent elections, a puppet named Joaquin Balaguer as president. Under Balaguer, writes the Ecumenical Program for Inter-American Communication & Action (EPICA), a U.S. religious group,

> U.S. investors are deepening their historic control over the Dominican economy. The vast conglomerate, Gulf and Western Industries . . . owns two percent of the national territory and produces over one-third of the island's sugar output, the country's most important commodity. A virtual island within an island, Gulf & Western also owns a tax-free industrial zone and port, tourist facilities . . . , extensive cattle herds, food processing plants, a cement plant and finance company. It also turns

out that of all its holdings in the world, Gulf & Western's Dominican properties yield the greatest returns. . . . . A more recent arrival, the Falconbridge Nickel Company, "invested" $200 million in the construction of a mine and plant that will employ only 1000 workers. . . . In the next ten years the Dominican government expects to earn about $43 million in this venture while Falconbridge is projecting a whopping $336 million.[32]

If Bosch or other radical elements should ever return to power, these bonanzas would be terminated. Left to their own devices the Dominican people would undoubtedly bring Bosch back, for they are living under conditions that defy description: 35 percent unemployment in Santo Domingo, concentration of land in a few hundred hands, wages of $1 a day. "Only 11 percent of the people," reports EPICA, "drink milk, four percent eat meat, two percent consume eggs." The Dominicans are ripe for revolution and would take that road if given a chance. But the Balaguer regime checkmates them by conducting a reign of terror, through its official police and through terrorist groups such as Los Incontrolables or La Mano, that has resulted in the killing or "disappearance" of many hundreds of revolutionaries. As of 1970 there was one death or "disappearance" every thirty-four hours, not unlike the deaths and disappearances arranged under the Phoenix program in Vietnam or a similar program in Guatemala. The United States, though protesting innocence, is directly involved in this mini-massacre, for it has trained thousands of Dominican police, supplied them with mountains of weapons, built a police academy, and given 2,600 military personnel special instruction in counterinsurgency.

The sums involved, a few tens of millions, are small by comparison with what the United States spent in Vietnam, but they have a lineal connection with the sort of thing the United States did in Indochina. The first line of defense, as the Pentagon and State Department see it, is the creation of a puppet army and a puppet police. If that fails to hold the fort, as it did in 1965, America's own troops are dispatched to establish "order." For that the Pentagon needs a navy, military bases throughout the world, and an army and air force ready to spring into action—as they did in Vietnam —on a day's notice. The few millions spent for creating a puppet force are incomplete and perhaps ineffective unless supplemented by the billions that go for a round-the-clock worldwide alert.

Multiply the Dominican situation by dozens of similar ones (Brazil, Thailand, Taiwan, Bolivia) and one gets an idea of the dimensions of the problem. Everything fits as in a jigsaw puzzle; to retain and expand world markets, Uncle Sam needs "safe" governments responsive to its "needs." Those governments are retained in power through military aid and compensatory spending—more of the former and less of the latter in the developing countries, and vice versa in the advanced countries. But military aid is inadequate if there is no machinery for *intervention in an emergency.* A Pentagon lecturer at one of its national security seminars put the U.S. options in insurgency situations in this order:

1. Military advice and assistance to the country's military establishment.
2. Training by American officers and enlisted men.
3. Adequate and suitable material for this kind of war.
4. If necessary, direct support by U.S. forces of combat missions launched by government troops, and *unilateral U.S. operations against the insurgents.*[33]

Theoretically, as many liberals believe, Washington could cut its military budget by 10, 20, 30, or 50 percent. It could close most or all of its foreign bases and end all aid to dictators, diverting the monies saved to useful projects at home. Yes, it could—but not without giving up its position as the world's leading capitalist power. If the United States refused to give weapons or train the military personnel of Brazil, Japan or Germany or France might, thereby easing Uncle Sam out of a position of dominance in the economy of that country as well. If the United States were to contract its navy and close its foreign bases, Japan would take up the slack in Asia, the Common Market countries elsewhere. Socialist countries, though they have also spent billions on arms and have also used their troops for a few interventions (Hungary, Czechoslovakia), do not have the same inherent compulsions. Militarism is not necessary for them to keep *economic* wheels turning. With or without foreign markets, they can adjust their economies to work moderately well. They *want* more foreign trade so they can buy many items they do not themselves produce or produce inefficiently. But they can survive without large foreign markets—excess goods and capital can be redirected to domestic use by the stroke of a pen. The capitalist countries, however, are in an entirely different position; for them there is a causal connection between the maximization of profits, the mad drive for markets, and the equally mad reliance on militarism.

Without militarism the United States could not have risen so high; with it, it can only fall from grace. There, as the bard said, is the rub. For a quarter of a century the price of a rollicking prosperity based on militarism was deemed tolerable. The prosperity itself acted as a soporific. Who cared about paying the piper at some time in the hereafter when the majority of Americans (and Japanese and Frenchmen and Germans and Englishmen and Italians) were receiving a little bigger slice of a bigger pie every year? Few economists pointed out, and few rank-and-file citizens realized, that the prosperity was predicated on mortgaging the future. It wasn't considered critical that, from 1948 through 1969 in the United States, government debt rose from $274 billion to $548 billion, corporate debt from $138.8 billion to $858 billion, consumer debt from $14.4 billion to $122.5 billion, home-mortgage debt from $32 billion to $262.4 billion.[34] All told the gross liability quadrupled—jumped by almost $1.5 trillion. At what point it will become untenable I don't know, but it is evident from the dollar crisis that began in 1968 that the pyramiding of debts cannot continue endlessly.

America has become so inured to the military way of life, its citizens—and especially its economists—have long forgotten that there was a price tag on it. One of the effects was inflation, the corruption of money as a means of exchange, threatening new interruptions in the flow of goods and investment, such as those that harried the world during the 1920s and 1930s. The value of the dollar in 1971 was less than half what it was in 1945. Measured in 1967 consumer prices it was worth $1.86 in the former year and a mere $.82 in the latter. The currency of other countries has been corrupted too, of course, each to a different extent. But while this uneven corruption of money disturbed the pattern of fixed currency rates arrived at in Bretton Woods, it was not a world-shaking problem so long as the *dollar* was "as good as gold." The dollar stood as a bastion against instability, seemingly immune to inflationary follies.

But after a quarter of a century there was a day of reckoning: so many dollars had been injected into the monetary bloodstream that the dollar was no longer "as good as gold." In fact it was soft currency. The reason for that was that the United States had financed much of its military ventures, military aid, and foreign investments by foisting paper dollars on the rest of the "free world." Had it not done so its economy would have been glutted at home, but in forcing its allies to accept tens of billions of dollars for which there was no adequate backing, it undermined the dollar anyway. In the last two decades, except for two years (1957 and 1968), the United States has had a deficit in its balance of payments every year. More dollars flowed out annually to pay for military bases and wars, imports, foreign investments, and tourism than flowed in. The deficit reached an all-time high of $6 billion in 1969, only to be far outstripped in 1971 and 1972. To make matters worse, in 1971 and 1972, for the first time since 1893, the United States showed red ink not only in its payments account but in its balance of *trade*. Imports exceeded exports by $2.7 billion and $6.4 billion respectively. To make matters still worse, the payments and trade deficits came at a time when the Nixon administration, in an effort to shore up the home economy, was committing itself to budget deficits totaling $80 to $90 billion.

Taken together, what all this meant was that the world was stuck with billions of dollars that were little better than counterfeit. The dollar, after all, is only a piece of paper with a picture on it, or a notation in a bank account. Until 1968, it had behind it Washington's promise that each piece of paper—in effect, each IOU—would be redeemed for one thirty-fifth of an ounce of gold. But the ounces of gold in Fort Knox kept shrinking, from $24.6 billion worth in 1949 to $10.1 billion in 1971; whereas the IOUs held by foreigners in the form of dollars grew from $16 billion in 1957 to $38 billion in 1968, $63 billion in November 1971, and approximately $82 billion at the end of 1972.[35] Not only was there no gold behind those dollars anymore, there was little else than a nebulous promise to accept them for U.S. goods and services. Understandably, businessmen overseas, including American businessmen, became edgy about the redeemability of the dollar and rushed to convert it into harder currencies with more promise—the German mark, the Japanese yen, the Swiss franc.

"Unless other nations greatly stimulate their own inflation," warned Gaylord A. Freeman of Chicago's First National Bank on November 24, 1970,

> within a year or so we will become increasingly less competitive in world markets—our exports will suffer. And, feeling rich in our easy, expansionary economic policies, we will import more, and our trade balance will decline. We will have an increased balance of payments deficit, and some day—some day, uncomfortably soon—the foreign central bankers may want to cash in their chips. They will present their dollar claims and ask for gold—and we don't have it.[36]

That uncomfortable day came with the monetary crisis of 1971, when President Nixon in effect devalued the dollar 8.57 percent by raising the price of gold. More ominous than the devaluation itself was what accompanied it. In violation of innumerable agreements and its own avowed allegiance to free trade, the Nixon regime imposed a 10 percent surcharge on foreign imports. This was a temporary measure and was lifted after a few months, but it nonetheless indicated that America would not shrink from protectionism and a trade war if it became necessary. The burden of Uncle Sam's crisis had to be borne by someone. It could have been borne by the American upper classes: President Nixon might have frozen or cut back profits, reduced prices by fiat so as to make American goods more competitive, prohibited further export of capital, redistributed income, and instituted a planned economy to free the system from the vicissitudes of the world market—as Charles Beard and John Dewey had suggested in the 1930s. But Nixon, like Roosevelt, was not ready to entomb "free enterprise." Instead he tried to pass part of the burden onto foreign nations and part onto the American working class. In his own gruff way Secretary of the Treasury John Connally demanded that other capitalist nations revalue their currency and make trade concessions that would bring Uncle Sam $13 billion a year in additional revenue. Connally got part of his wish, but even that didn't help: the balance of payments deficit remained approximately as high in 1972 as in 1971.

The other victim chosen by Nixon to carry the load was the American working class. The administration froze wages and prices for three months and then imposed wage controls limiting raises to 5.5 percent a year. As it turned out, the controls redistributed income in favor of big business. But that is not really as important as the fact that the government was forced to *regiment* the economy to save it from deterioration. Back in 1947 President Truman had warned that unless the United States checked the trend toward regimented economies elsewhere, it would succumb to regimentation itself. Free enterprise and free trade, he said, were the only barriers against regimentation and the only guarantors of democratic rights. The significance of President Nixon's New Economic Policy of 1971 was that it showed, on the contrary, that the ultimate product of free enterprise is regimentation—no matter how long delayed. The state *must* manage what the market fails to manage and must do it, if necessary, not merely by indirect means, such as compensatory spending, but by direct control of the market itself, as well as of the citizens who function in that market.

Despite the monetary agreement of December 1972, which Nixon hailed as the greatest monetary pact in the history of the world, a new 10-percent devaluation was decreed in February 1973, when the dollar again refused to respond to artificial respiration. Once more, the incident itself was not as consequential in the short run as its portent for the future. Clearly, the American government is stating to the world and its own people that it is prepared to risk money and trade wars, as well as regimentation of its own citizens, to defend its position. That regimentation is only in its infancy at the moment, but its logic is ineluctable. Wages cannot be held in line indefinitely without limiting or abolishing the right to strike—as Americans learned during World War II. And strikes cannot be limited or abolished without eventually curtailing free speech, free assembly, and the unfettered right of movement from one job to another. Nixon himself recognized this when he said, on the day after Phase II was inaugurated, that Phase II must include "enough control to control the inflation, [but] not so much to destroy freedom." One can be sure that he sincerely believes this and wants to avoid a remaking of the American system, if only because a regimented economy will pose greater problems than it solves. But one can also be sure that the decision does not rest with Nixon. If the game is played to the end, the ultimate result of militarism will be a corporate state at home and a vicious trade war on the international front.

The *New York Times* of February 7, 1973, correctly observed that "the money crisis, dangerous in itself, is a symptom of an even greater political danger: the possibility of a dissolution of the partnership between the United States, Europe and Japan." In effect the maneuvering for position on the monetary front represents nothing less than a contest between the great powers as to which one will have a depression first. It tells us that the world market is pinched, that the growth in productivity and capacity—especially in the linchpin of capitalism, the United States—has outstripped the market potential. Who will be hurt most by that circumstance depends on who resists most fiercely. The money crisis tells us too that the jockeying for spheres of influence, which has been an orderly process for a quarter of a century, will soon become heated and disorderly. The artificial stability sustained by American aid and American arms is being demolished as the system blends back to its inherent anarchy.

A barometer of the impending decline of capitalism was the 1972 visits by President Nixon to Peking and Moscow, which at least for the time being signaled the end of the policy of containment. Washington now seeks the coexistence it rejected a generation ago—not because it has suddenly become aware of the moral virtues of coexistence or because the Soviet Union or China have made a volte-face, but because the bastion of world capitalism *needs* the aid of the two Communist countries. It looks to them, as Roosevelt did in the 1930s, as a source for sizable commercial benefits, and it hopes they will be allies in promoting "stability" in the Third World. The latter certainly is a vain hope, for no outside force can turn on and off the spigot of revolution. Whatever the influence of the Soviets or China in the developing lands, they cannot barter away the aspirations of a world-in-revolution quite that easily, assuming they want to. The commercial aspect of coexistence does have potential. It will help America for a time (and help the Soviets and China even more). But the reprieve cannot be long-lasting, if only because America's détente opens the door not only for itself but for Japan and the Common Market countries, which are also rushing into the formerly closed arena to sell their wares and invest their capital.

Capitalism was rescued from disaster after World War II by the single fortunate circumstance that the United States still had vast reserves to fashion a war machine and give economic succor to its junior partners. Had the two belligerent camps been more equal, and had the United States suffered damage on the scale, say, of Britain, this outcome would have been impossible. The system would have collapsed years ago.

But who has the reserves today to meet a new crisis? The United States is asking its allies for aid (in the form of revaluation of currency, lifting of restrictions on U.S. goods, voluntary agreement to curtail some exports to the United States), that is different in form but not in essence from the help that the United States supplied not too long ago. Can the allies meet those requests? It is not very likely, for they too have similar needs. Who has the military power today to weld the weakened alliance and keep the developing countries quiescent? Japan? Hardly, except in Asia. The Common Market countries? They are still some distance from uniting into a single sovereignty, and they have wide fissures of their own. There is no one to heal the wounds and exact the discipline, as America did in the glorious quarter of a century of Pax Americana.

There is still hope in establishment circles of patching the rent fabric. Banker Gaylord Freeman is convinced that through international negotiations the capitalist nations can arrive at a modus vivendi to "return to the principles of GATT"—i.e., freer trade and less restrictions—and to preserve "the dollar as the international currency." This is hardly a prescription for change nor very realistic. Freeman doesn't tell us where Japan or France will find substitute markets if they must yield some to Uncle Sam, or what will happen to the American economy if it redeems the tens of billions of dollars abroad, or how U.S. industry will fare if there is to be more austerity at home, or what will happen in the Third World if America curtails its military stick in order to balance its budget.

Inexorable laws must soon demand a reckoning. Militarism cannot continue unto eternity without plunging the world into war. The White House and the Pentagon hope that the wars can remain "little." Henry Kissinger hopes to avoid even "small wars" by a new balance of world power. But "little wars"—counterrevolutions—are and must be endemic to a system whose motivation is the maximization of profits. So too with economic regimentation. Anarchy was contained during the 1930s through compensatory spending and deficit financing—but only domestically, not internationally; we were plunged into the worst war in history. Anarchy was contained after the war by the various devices of Pax Americana. But those devices have only delayed the debacle; they have not turned it aside. The specter of anarchy still hangs like the Damoclean sword over capitalism's head, and the choice still comes down to the two alternatives that Henry Wallace rejected a generation ago: fascism or socialism. Should the great powers opt for war, the choice, in its aftermath, will still be—if anyone survives —fascism or socialism.

VII

The contradictions of capitalism, it is apparent, are heading America and its allies toward economic, political, and military breakdown, much as predicted by Marx and Lenin—though some decades later than they predicted. What Marx and Lenin did not foresee was that the principle of maximization of profits would also lead to a second cul de sac, an ecological crisis as grave as the economic-political crisis. When they spoke of capitalism creating its own gravediggers they were referring to animate people, the exploited workers who would rise up to overthrow the system. In their wildest speculation they did not envision the day when those gravediggers would be inanimate phenomena such as the dissipation of natural resources, pollution, and military technology. Perhaps it was because they expected capitalism to be long dead by now, but in any event the ecological problem must rank with the political-economic one as a potent reason for revolution and socialism.

Perhaps the ingenuity of men and women can meet this challenge, can find sources of food and raw materials in the air, oceans, and space far beyond anything we can currently imagine. But no one has yet shown how this can be accomplished without international planning and a single international sovereignty to direct it. "I do not wish to seem overdramatic," said former United Nations Secretary-General U Thant in 1969,

> but I can only conclude . . . that the Members of the United Nations have perhaps ten years left in which to subordinate their ancient quarrels and launch a global partnership to curb the

arms race, to improve the human environment, to defuse the population explosion, and to supply the required momentum to development efforts. If such a global partnership is not forged within the next decade, then I very much fear that the problems I have mentioned will have reached such staggering proportions that they will be beyond our capacity to control.[37]

The population of the world in 1970 was 3.56 billion. If the present rate of increase continues, the number of people on earth will double to 7 billion by the year 2006 and a hundred years from now will reach the astounding figure of 28 billion. If the recent rate of economic growth continues, the per-capita product of the Soviet Union will jump from $1,100 (in constant 1968 dollars) to $6,300, that of the United States from $3,980 to $11,000, that of Germany from $1,970 to $5,850, and that of Japan from $1,190 to $23,000. (On the other hand, India's will rise only from $100 in 1968 to $140, and Nigeria's will fall from $70 to $60.)[38]

Where will the food and natural resources come from to accommodate such large numbers of people and their generally higher standard of living? A group of thirty scientists and scholars from ten countries, who formed themselves into the Club of Rome in April 1968 to study environmental problems, concluded that while "there has been an overwhelming excess of potentially arable land for all of history," the prospect for the end of the century "may be a serious shortage."[39] The reason is that much of the 3.2 billion hectares of arable land now available will be removed for urban-industrial use, thereby reducing the supply to less than 3 billion hectares by 2000 and less than 2 billion by 2050, only three generations from now. No one today has a clear idea as to how to increase protein production from 70 million tons currently consumed annually to the 140 million tons needed by the year 2000 and the 560 million tons a century from now. No one in fact is certain that we can avoid famines in the *immediate* future. The predictions by William and Paul Paddock and Gunnar Myrdal, back in 1965, that such famines were imminent in this decade may have been short-circuited by the discovery of miracle grains and rice, called the Green Revolution. But the Green Revolution seems to have reached its limits, and according to the head of the International Food and Agriculture Organization "the outbreak of famines within the next five to ten years cannot be excluded." "History teaches us," says Addeke Boerma, director of the FAO, "that situations of this kind"—the disparity between food supply and population—"leads sooner or later to violence and political upheaval."[40] But even if there is no upheaval, the problem of food for additional billions is not easily solved. "To achieve a 34 percent increase in world food production from 1951 to 1966," wrote the Club of Rome scholars, "agriculturalists increased yearly expenditures on tractors by 63 percent, annual investment in nitrate fertilizers by 146 percent, and annual use of pesticides by 300 percent. The next 34 percent increase will require even greater inputs of capital and resources."[41] Where the money and resources will come from no one has as yet said.

In addition there is the problem of nonrenewable resources. Based on present-known supplies in the United States, all but one of the eleven most needed minerals—coal—will be exhausted a few decades hence, according to the U.S. Bureau of Mines. If the resources are quintupled, the supply of aluminum, copper, lead, natural gas, petroleum, and silver will run out within sixty-five years, and tin and tungsten a few years later.[42] Perhaps there are synthetic substitutes to be developed by human skills. Perhaps the supplies can be increased by a factor of ten or twenty. But that poses a host of derivative problems: how will the ersatz industries be subsidized, what will happen to the underdeveloped nations whose natural resources are depleted, how will the conflict between nations that still have national resources and those that must rely on costly ersatz be resolved? None of this is amenable to solution without U Thant's global partnership and global planning.

Another result of planlessness is the poisoning of the planet's air and water. Even if one discounts the dire predictions of Paul Ehrlich about "the end of the ocean" by late 1979, there is no doubt that the delicate balance of nature, say between carbon dioxide and oxygen, is being harmfully and decisively altered. There are rivers in America that are so polluted they sometimes catch fire at the touch of a match. Lake Erie is so contaminated that, according to Lester R. Brown in his *World Without Borders,* it would take $40 billion to restore it to life.[43] Waterways are turning red with the blood of billions of fish killed off by human waste materials. As for the air we breathe, it is being defiled by scores of thousands of tons of pollutants every day; in Los Angeles alone 14,000 tons enter the air stream daily, 87.4 percent from the fuels burned by automobiles.[44] The number of people who die or whose life span is reduced by the poisoned air, as well as the crops destroyed, is already sizeable. One day not too far off the problem will become untenable.

We are rapidly learning that technological miracles can be both a boon and a menace. Consider the revolution in military technology. A generation ago, back in World War II, all the weaponry available to the great nations was capable of killing 10 to 15 percent of humanity. The 20-kiloton bomb that fell on Hiroshima, equivalent to 20,000 tons of dynamite, however, opened a new dimension in mass killing. The atom bomb, whose explosive power was measured in thousands of tons of dynamite-equivalent, was followed just a few years later by the hydrogen bomb, whose explosive power was measured in megatons, *millions* of tons of dynamite-equivalent. Within a single decade the Soviet Union, which had no nuclear bombs at war's end, was able to test a 57-megaton bomb, almost 3,000 times as powerful as the Hiroshima bomb.

In 1959, the Joint Committee on Atomic Energy of the U.S. Congress estimated that if the Soviets were to drop 1,446 megatons of bombs on American soil, most of them in nonurban areas, there would be 50 million dead and 20 million injured immediately.[45] Three years later, President Kennedy stated that had the crisis over Cuba escalated to nuclear war, it would have resulted in 300 million deaths—100 million each in Europe, the Soviet Union, and the United States. No matter who pushed the first button, said Kennedy, in such a war "all we have built up, all we have worked for, would be destroyed in the first 24 hours." Today it is generally agreed that both the Soviets and the United States have a sufficient nuclear arsenal to kill off all of humanity—and do it a number of times over. Every nuclear nation, of course, disclaims that it will use nuclear bombs first but history teaches us that arms races tend to fulfill themselves in wars. According to a study by the *Canadian Army Journal* for fall 1960 "there have been 1,656 arms races" since 650 B.C., "only 16 of which have not ended in war."[46] And while it is possible that scientists may be wrong in forecasting that nuclear or chemical war will kill all life, it certainly will kill enough human beings to make social organization impossible. Hanson Baldwin, military affairs editor of the *New York Times*, estimated "if about thirty percent of the population of any country is killed, wounded or put out of action, that country will no longer function as a rational and coherent social organization."[47] If we make the wish father to the thought and assume that no nuclear bomb is ever dropped again, the danger of fallout from nuclear waste is just as frightening. The 140 fifty-foot tanks containing 50 million gallons of nuclear waste which are buried at Hanford, Washington, for instance, are capable, according to scientists, of killing all of humanity should the tanks spring leaks from corrosion (as a few have) or should they be cracked open by an earthquake, such as the one that occurred in Hanford in 1918.[48]

Nor is the menace from military technology confined to hydrogen bombs. The late Bertrand Russell, writing in the *Minority of One* for February 1964, reported that

> the United States has, at the moment, a stockpile of 130,000 aerosol nerve gas bombs. This non-nuclear stockpile is as deadly as its nuclear counterpart. Each nerve gas bomb is capable of extinguishing life in an area of 3,500 square miles. The total stockpile is capable of eliminating life in an area of 455 million square miles. This is eight times the total land area of the globe and 151 times that of the United States of America.

There are other chemical weapons and other biological weapons equally awesome; and in this case too the problem of disposal in the event the world agrees to disarmament is by no means solved.

It would be wrong to suggest that pollution, overpopulation, and death-dealing military technology are restricted to the capitalist world. Such problems exist in the socialist countries as well, and it is not yet known whether they are being dealt with satisfactorily. But there is a difference: ecological insanity is inherent in the capitalist system and is incurable so long as profit maximization is our guiding motive. There would have been no ecological crisis to begin with if the advanced nations had *planned* their economic development so as to maintain a permanent balance between natural resources, technology, and population. But planning requires a collectivist élan, and capitalism, even in its latter stages, caters to individualism. Within its own confines the automobile industry may collectively collude to administer prices, but within the framework of society as a whole it runs rampant, seizing as large a share of the consumer dollar as possible, without government restraints. Thus the nation has developed a configuration of industries that bears no relationship to actual material or ecological needs.

If society had planned economic development, it certainly would not have planned it so that the automobile would dominate the economy. There are now almost 100 million vehicles on the road in the United States and 10 to 12 million more being sold annually. There are almost 4 million miles of highway, and as everyone knows it is far easier to get government money for a new road than a new school. The automobile and all its satellite industries—petroleum, rubber tire, glass, repair shops—has a low order of priorities on the scale of human needs and in addition is the worst polluter of the air that is our collective heritage. But it is too entrenched to be shunted aside in favor of a new industrial configuration. Can anyone really envision General Motors agreeing to reduce its annual production of automobiles from 3 or 4 million to, say, 250,000, or to produce vehicles that last twenty or twenty-five years rather than five or ten? In the Soviet Union the manufacture of automobiles has been deliberately held down to less than one twentieth that of the United States. But it is inconceivable that the pattern in America will be modified to accord with ecological requirements. Nor is it conceivable that the millions of tons of resources that are wasted on frills such as disposable bottles, packaging, knickknacks, and surplus TV sets will be salvaged by planned efforts to retire these products. We can expect much advertising by big business about the recycling of glass, or the installation of antipollution devices on vehicles, but no effort will be made to deal with the problem in toto.

When you add the ecological impasse to the political-economic impasse it becomes evident that the capitalist system is beyond reform. It is a train moving in the wrong direction on the wrong track, powered by the wrong fuel—*private* property, *private* profit—and headed for the precipice. It is a set of institutions sustained by an individualist élan at a time when the interdependency of humankind has become total, when no single individual, class, or government can effectively control its own fate. Capitalism exacerbates the tension between the one nation with 5 or 6 percent of the world's population, that diverts one half of the world's resources for its use, and the rest of the planet; between the one fourth of humanity that lives in relatively affluent countries and the three quarters that live in incredibly poor ones; and between the rich and the poor within each "free enterprise" nation. Those tensions were created by the profit motive, and they cannot be abolished by retaining that motive as the generator of human progress—no matter how many reforms are instituted, welcome as each may be in itself.

The history of reform itself is convincing proof of this thesis. In America, for instance, the Sherman Antitrust Act was passed in July 1890 to curb monopoly—then and now believed by liberals to be the central vice of our society. Since 1890 there have been other antitrust laws to close the loopholes of the first one, but monopolies have grown by leaps and bounds. In 1950 the 100 biggest corporations held 38.6 percent of the industrial assets of the nation; by 1965 it was 45.4 percent. From 1929 to 1968 the share of the 200 largest corporations in manufacturing assets grew from 46.1 percent to 60 percent.[49] The income tax, once hailed as the means of narrowing the gap between rich and poor, has been shot so full of loopholes it often widens the gap. Radicals welcome reforms because they ameliorate the plight of the underprivileged, even if only temporarily. But they realize that reforms do not and cannot get at the root of the problem.

The promise of revolution, then, is not that it is mathematically certain to solve humankind's problems—a misconception held by too many radicals—but that it is necessary, urgent, vital, and indispensable if there is to be any *hope* of solving them. History is crowding the human race toward self-destruction or fulfillment, leaving it no choice but to structure a new society.

CHAPTER TEN

Revolution in Stages

I

We have tried in these pages to demolish two myths which bedevil the radical movement—that socialism is inherently totalitarian and that capitalism, with all its faults, is the guarantor of enduring prosperity and democracy. Both myths, it seems to me, are dispelled when we look at the world in macrocosm to note the interaction between capitalism and socialism. What we see then is a socialism extending its orbit, and slowly reviving—both because of economic necessity and the subjective design of some of its leaders—its intrinsic humanism; and, on the other side, a capitalism that, despite unparalleled prosperity, is contracting, exhausting the options it gained through artificial measures such as compensatory spending, and drifting toward depression, totalitarianism, and the attenuated international strife that is a coefficient of its basic anarchy.

Flowing from these judgments of the world in macrocosm are strategical conclusions of considerable importance. What is suggested by our survey is that the present revolution, though it is a conglomerate of thousands of separate incidents in many separate places, is in fact a single global conflict between international capitalism and international socialism. No individual act in this unitary drama occurs in a vacuum; each is dependent for its success or failure on other events that either preceded it or are going on concurrently. The resistance of the National Liberation Front to American intervention in Vietnam, for instance, probably would have aborted if the Chinese Communists had not come to power a decade before the NLF was formed; if the Soviet Union, economically powerful by this time, had not supplied the NLF with great amounts of matériel; and if the antiwar movement in the United States had not restricted Lyndon Johnson's and Richard Nixon's options. Similarly, it is doubtful that the Marxist coalition around Salvador Allende in Chile would have been permitted to remain in power even briefly if the United States had not been preoccupied in Vietnam; Uncle Sam's intervention, covert and overt, would have been far more vigorous. On the other hand, the success of the CIA in sponsoring rightist coups in Guatemala, Brazil, the Dominican Republic, and Bolivia has without question slowed—though not stopped—the tide of social change in this hemisphere.

Viewed as a process unfolding in stages, at varying tempos in different places, the revolution—despite setbacks—is already far advanced, much more so than the bourgeois revolution at a comparable time. A half century after the Bolshevik Revolution, a greater portion of the world has been transformed than a half century after the Puritan Revolution or even a half century after the French Revolution. The formulation of strategy for social change in America, therefore, must begin with the status of the global conflict at this moment in history, because in a sense part of the American Revolution is already completed. Though that may seem like stressing the obvious, it is actually of pivotal importance.

II

What Marx legated to his followers was not a foolproof strategy, applicable at all times in all places, but a *method*, a *framework*, for determining that strategy. Contrary to those who insisted that there were many separate factors—such as economics, religion, nature, and human consciousness—that account for historical development, Marx held that there was a unity of these factors "subject," as Plekhanov put it, "to reciprocal action" on each other.[1] "My investigations," wrote Marx in "A Contribution to the Critique of Political Economy," led to the conclusion that legal relations as well as forms of State could not be understood from themselves, nor from the so-called general development of the human mind, but, on the contrary, are rooted in the material conditions of life. . . . In the social production of their means of existence men enter into definite, necessary relations which are independent of their will, productive relations which correspond to a definite stage of development of their material productive forces. The aggregate of these productive relationships constitutes the economic structure of society, the real basis on which a juridical and political superstructure arises, and to which definite forms of social consciousness correspond. . . . At a certain stage of their development the material productive forces of society come into contradiction with the existing productive relationships, or, what is but a legal expression for these, with the property relations within which they had moved before. From forms of development of the productive forces these relationships are transformed into their fetters. Then an epoch of social revolution opens.[2]

In brief this is the "framework" for historical development, and by using that framework as a guide it is possible to explain complicated social phenomena. The war in Vietnam, for instance, was not an outgrowth of "wrong" decisions by "bad" men, or of many accidental factors none of which was decisive by itself, but of the "productive forces and social relations" in the United States and the "productive forces and social relations" in Indochina, which put the two nations on a collision course. The wage and price controls instituted by Richard Nixon in August 1971 were not the result of whim—although whim may have played a part—but reflect instead the "contradiction" between America's "material productive forces" and its "productive relationships" at that moment. Had it not been for the specific "productive relationship" of capitalist and worker, and the profit maximization principle linked to it, there would have been no balance-of-payments crisis, no intensified struggle for world markets, and no need to introduce controls to ameliorate the crisis.

By applying the materialist conception of history to today's circumstances, we arrive at the general conclusion that the contradictions of capitalism are now beyond resolution except through a planned economy, social ownership of the means of production, and worldwide integration. We can foretell that depressions, the corporate state, trade wars, money wars, and military wars impend —unless new social relations are established.

This point is worth illustrating if only because the disaster building up on our planet is *in process,* neither concluded nor totally visible. To use a Heraclitean image, it is a being that is becoming but has not yet become. But let us assume that overnight the United States were to meet with a great calamity—its weather, from Maine to Florida and from New York to California, turns subfreezing year round. The tasks we would face in such a situation would be titanic: food would have to be grown in tens of thousands of hothouses instead of open fields, or produced from chemicals, or reclaimed from the oceans. Heating units would have to be installed in millions of homes in the South and West and additional electricity, natural gas, and fuel oil found to service them. The textile industry would have to double or quadruple its capacity in accord with the need for overcoats, heavy underwear, and hats, and some means found to grow more cotton, and produce more wool. The nation obviously would have to elaborate a plan—a crash program —simply to live.

In such a circumstance the government, clearly, could not be guided by the principle of profit maximization. If the steel for automobiles were needed to build hothouses, the giant auto industry would have to be closed down. Indeed the whole industrial machine would probably have to be placed under state management, without regard to anyone's profits. To prevent a black market in food, clothing, or heating units the government would have to institute rationing, and to secure the cooperation of its people it would have to assure fair distribution of necessities based on the requirements of each family, not wealth. Society could not tolerate "business as usual." Sharing, equality, collective concern—these would replace profit maximization as the guiding motifs of society. It would be impossible to survive on any other basis.

Let us assume further that the same catastrophe befell the whole planet—subfreezing temperatures year round. Every nation on earth would have to convert its economy to meet the emergency. Trade patterns would go by the boards; no country would ship anything to any other unless guaranteed in advance that it would be provided with items of the highest priority for itself. Venezuela would hardly permit its oil or iron ore to be exported to the United

States, since those items would be vital for its own subsistence, and if Washington chose to take them by military force it would confront endless guerrilla wars, there and in dozens of other places. If Washington chose to seize the vast natural gas resources of the Soviet Union through invasion, America itself (and Russia) would be incinerated within a few hours in the nuclear war that followed. All nations would be forced by the exigency of events to conclude agreements for global cooperation, global planning, global sharing. In those circumstances the United States could not expect less advantaged states to accept a situation whereby the colossus of the Western Hemisphere continued to enjoy half the world's income. Simple survival would demand national and class equality—and inevitably amalgamation into a single sovereignty.

Though it may be a few decades away, the world is currently approaching a catastrophe of these dimensions—either in the form of stagnation and depression, world war, famine, or exhaustion of resources—and requiring a crash program similar to that in our hypothetical calamity. The capitalist nations in fact are in much the same situation as the South in America before the Civil War. The owners of 4 million slaves below the Mason-Dixon line would have been far better off if they had collectively freed their chattels in one grand action and rehired them as wage workers. They could then have developed a viable industry and a more wholesome economy. But their investment in slaves was so great that they lacked the flexibility to do what was in their own long-term interests. The "free enterprise" nations of the 1970s also lack flexibility, also are mired in short-term self-interest which makes it difficult for them to see the approaching disaster or to adjust to it.

By applying the Marxist method to the dynamics of capitalism generally and to the artificial techniques such as compensatory spending and militarism that have delayed retribution specifically, it is possible to forecast where history is going. But the Marxist method does not tell us everything automatically; it is not a religion that predicts an afterlife with absolute certainty. On the contrary it can be related to concrete situations either intelligently or schematically, depending on who is doing the analysis, and above all it requires constant updating. What Marx wrote in 1848 or Lenin in 1921 is not necessarily pertinent to 1974; or what Mao said of China in 1935 or Castro of Cuba in 1955 is not necessarily relevant to the United States in the 1970s. There are new scientific discoveries that must be incorporated into the science of revolution periodically, and there are experiences which have not been anticipated which must be added to the historical equations. Moreover, there are subjects for which science as yet has not formulated answers. We do not know, for instance, whether humankind can live without hate, or whether it can contain hate within the boundaries of nonviolence so that it does not explode into new forms of violent conflict. We do not know whether the concept of mankind—a single international sovereignty—is feasible psychologically. Can any society exist, in other words, without "ins" and "outs"? Though the Maoists are experimenting with the problem of fashioning a new kind of human being, we do not know for certain how a truly free and creative person, unsaddled by alienation and the predilection—as Erich Fromm puts it—to escape from freedom, will evolve.

The Marxist method *opens the door* to answers but does not guarantee them. Were Marx alive today he would be the first to make that point, for he never conceived of his doctrines as hallowed theology. As a matter of fact the very terms Marxism or Marxism-Leninism were alien to his method, since no science, including the science of revolution, should be known by the name of its leading theorist, anymore than physics should be known as Newtonism or Einsteinism. Unfortunately, much of the Left is crippled by the disease of imitationism: instead of utilizing the scientific method to analyze the given circumstances of the present and the particular condition of a particular country, it regurgitates precepts expounded by successful revolutionaries in other places and other times, as if they were the ultimate verities. It extrapolates from the experience of Russia or China or Cuba or Korea a strategical approach for America, and from the condition of the planet fifty or a hundred years ago a blueprint for social change today.

Marx, using the method he had elaborated, foresaw as the main thrust of history the proletarian revolution in advanced countries rather than the twin revolution of peoples in underdeveloped countries. Marx's miscalculation is understandable, for he lived at a time before imperialism had ridden roughshod over the earth. Lenin, with the same method, writing at a time when capitalism was enervated by war and when class antagonisms were exacerbated almost everywhere, was convinced that the imperialism he dealt with was the last stage of capitalism, and its death throes imminent. He did not expect the old system to generate the resiliency that it eventually did. In both Marx's and Lenin's schema of revolution the heart—the advanced capitalist states—would die first, and the arteries, the colonial nations, would thereafter perish automatically.

Had the German revolutions succeeded in 1919, 1920, 1921, 1923–24, or 1930–32, Marx's or Lenin's scenario might have been played out as predicted. But for reasons we have discussed, the sequence of revolution was exactly the reverse of that expected; the revolution is now pinching off imperialism's arteries in the underdeveloped countries, but the heart, though enfeebled, continues to function. The import of this turnaround in sequence is momentous, for it means that we must look at the revolution in an entirely different manner, as a phenomenon proceeding in stages from the arteries to the heart, rather than as a single grand eruption. If the shocks that are weakening the network of advanced capitalist powers come primarily from the outside (the arteries), and if each shock is relatively minor in itself, it is likely that the heartland of capitalism will expire in spasms, in stages, rather than in one terminal heart attack. American (West European and Japanese) radicals, therefore, must formulate a strategy much different from those formulated by Lenin, Mao, Tito, or Castro for *their* situations.

III

There are three other reasons why the American Left would be well advised to construct a strategy for a revolution-in-stages:

1. The world revolution has now reached a point comparable to that of the last half of the nineteenth century when a number of bourgeois revolutions took place in stages—Germany, Italy—without the single, all-encompassing violent upheaval that characterized the French Revolution. The same dynamic may ensue in the United States or Japan or France today.

2. The lack of class consciousness in the advanced countries, let alone revolutionary consciousness, is so pronounced that even if there is ultimately to be a violent revolution on the English, French, American, or Russian model, the Left must *try* the strategy of revolution-in-stages in order to instill a sense of purpose to its potential constituency. If it doesn't, it begins too far away from where the

populace stands today to have any great impact on it; it is like a magnet too removed from the metal to draw it.

3. The class character of the advanced countries, unlike that confronted by Marx, Lenin, Mao, Tito, or Castro, is not one of fixed rigidity but of considerable fluidity.

This latter point is of the utmost significance, for we must prepare for the future based on that which is, not on that which we spin out of our heads or carry over schematically from other thinkers who lived in other milieus.

Writing in the mid-nineteenth century Marx adjudged the two major classes in our society as rigid entities with a gulf between them that grows ever wider. In the *Communist Manifesto* he observed that "Our epoch, the epoch of the bourgeoisie, possesses, however, this distinctive feature; it has simplified the class antagonisms. Society as a whole is more and more splitting up into two great hostile camps, into two great classes directly facing each other—bourgeoisie and proletariat."[3] The middle class of small producers, artisans, small farmers, and self-employed professionals was slowly disappearing, according to Marx, its members being driven out of business and absorbed into the working class. Thus the polarization between the two principal classes was almost total—especially with the emergence of impersonal large-scale industry—and the working class could be expected to develop a strong class and revolutionary consciousness.

Marx's theory that classes and class conflict were, as T. B. Bottomore paraphrases it, "bound up with particular historical phases in the development of production," was no different from that of bourgeois writers who preceded him, a fact he freely admitted in a letter to J. Weydemeyer, March 5, 1852. What was unique was his postulation that the gap between opposing classes would insistently widen.

The concept of simple, rigid confrontation does not stand the test of two historical developments: the emergence of power elites that are not, strictly speaking, capitalist, though they serve capitalism; and the *embourgeoisement* of considerable numbers of workers. Consider the status of generals and admirals, who obviously enjoy immense power but cannot comfortably be classified as capitalists. Their interests mesh with and are intertwined with that of the capitalists, yet they have a separate identity. There was a time when such men were recruited from the upper class, as they still are in many Latin-American countries, but that is no longer true. The military elite is imperialist not because it comes from propertied families but for other reasons, which we need not dwell on here. On the other side, the gulf between different segments of the working class has become so wide that there is a tenuous unity, if that, between, say, an airline pilot and a cotton picker. What the Left used to call the aristocracy of labor—highly paid craftsmen such as those in the building trades—is now a sizable segment of the working class. It includes not only yesterday's aristocracy but many in the mass production industries or trucking who earn five or six times as much as agricultural or service employees at the bottom of the ladder. Millions of proletarians today own tenement buildings or stocks and, as far as consciousness is concerned, consider themselves middle class, closer to the bourgeoisie than the proletariat.

The working class covers a wide range of incomes and attitudes. Below the $15,000-, $20,000-, and $25,000-a-year proletarians are many millions with more modest incomes but who nonetheless own their own homes and can afford to send their children to college. What we have are gradations going down finally to the very large numbers who have neither capital, property, nor sufficient earnings to keep body and soul together. And somewhat apart from this working class is a declassed element in the United States of 15 million people who live on welfare, many of whom have subsisted on such payments for generations. All these workers, from the airline pilot to the field hand and welfare recipient, may have a certain historic community of interest, but for the here and now they are a heterogeneous lot that feels little sense of affinity for each other and has not been mobilized for any common effort in a long time.

Realistically, the class structure of a country such as the United States is not stable but in flux. Men and women cross the boundary line from one class to another constantly. To be sure, the number who arrive from Scotland impoverished to become Andrew Carnegies is pitifully small, but the number of sons and daughters of destitute immigrants who have become doctors, lawyers, engineers, and capitalists is sizable, and the possibility of making that transition is sufficiently poignant to dampen whatever class consciousness may have existed within the working class in the past. In almost all of nineteenth-century Europe and in some advanced countries until recently, there was a fixed confrontational aspect to class relationships—two grim armies arrayed against each other, waiting only for the propitious moment to meet in the final combat of revolution. But for whatever reasons, this is no longer the case in the highly developed countries; for many years now the laboring class has been more disposed to accommodation with the capitalist class than eyeball-to-eyeball confrontation. I do not suggest that the class struggle has disappeared or that it may not again become as bitter as it once was. But for the moment it is muted. The injured and oppressed have won a measure of reforms and countervailing power which give them the impression—false though it may be—that they can make it within the system.

This fluidity of class relationships in America, Britain, et al. is also reflected in the nature of the state. "The State," Lenin once wrote, "is an organ of class *domination,* an organ of *oppression* of one class by another."[4] With its monopoly of the means of violence—troops, police—and "special bodies of men who have at their disposal prisons, etc.," the state serves the ruling class, and whatever benefits the lower classes gain are episodic or due to special circumstances. Lenin's thesis was generally true and certainly applicable to countries like Russia in his day or to Brazil, Spain, Taiwan, and Portugal today. It was proper for Lenin to emphasize this one-sided aspect of state power in the times in which he lived. The term class domination, however, is elastic, for there is obviously a difference between the class domination in Spain, where workers and peasants have virtually no rights, and the class domination in Denmark, where they have considerable rights. The degree of polarization in a capitalist society is determined by the outcome of class struggles, past and present, and the amount of countervailing power the underclasses have been able to seize. Marx's collaborator Friedrich Engels underscored this point when he noted that "by way of exception . . . there are periods when the warring classes so nearly attain equilibrium that the State power, ostensibly appearing as a mediator, assumed for the moment a certain independence in relation to both."[5] In other words, there are times of near-equilibrium when the lower classes can win real concessions. That suggests the state is subject to pressures that leave the capitalist class less than predominant, that force it to yield to some demands by the oppressed and pay obeisance to *countervailing* power. Otherwise we cannot account for the fact that the capitalist state in America permits the right to strike while the capitalist state in Portugal does not, or that there is free speech in Switzerland but not in today's Greece.

It is true, as socialist theorists have emphasized frequently, that reforms under capitalism tend to be of tenuous value. The inheritance tax is supposed to limit wealth, but capitalists find a means of avoiding the tax by establishing nonprofit foundations. An income tax law is supposed to narrow the gaps in earnings, but as said before, in the course of time enough loopholes are written into the law so that in many instances the gap between poor and rich is widened. The right of free speech, sanctified by the Bill of Rights, turns out to be empty when the voice of the majority is disregarded by the men of power, e.g., during the Vietnam war. What this signifies, however, is that there is a struggle between contending forces before a reform is won, while it is being passed, and afterward. The single victory in itself does not terminate the battle.

Consider U.S. regulation of railroads. Toward the end of the nineteenth century the carriers and the populists engaged in a strident little war over the right of the government to set freight rates. Congress was finally prevailed on to pass the Interstate Commerce Act of 1887, which made unreasonable rates, pooling, and other practices illegal. But the railroads were able to stymie this law by using their influence in the courts; the little war therefore continued until additional bills enacted during the Progressive Era, such as the Hepburn Act and the Mann-Elkins Act, as well as more favorable judicial decisions, permanently established the regulatory principle. It was a reform of some substance for hard-pressed farmers and others. What happened, however, was that in subsequent years the railroads used their political influence with the administration to win appointment of pro-management people to the Interstate Commerce Commission, thereby converting the law into an instrument of the carriers. What this indicates is that the capitalist class is sufficiently entrenched in the government to partly or fully eviscerate almost every reform, and that it will probably continue to do so until its power begins to wane. The struggle of itself, however, is of some value since it mobilizes countervailing power, wins partial gains, and prepares the way for a more decisive contest. The right of free speech may be very much circumscribed, yet it creates a climate of discord in which, for instance, antiwar activists such as Benjamin Spock and the Chicago Conspiracy Eight are able to secure reversal of their convictions. To say that countervailing power has a limited utility under present circumstances is one thing; to imply that it has none is false. And one day it will doubtless bring us to the position Engels describes as "near-equilibrium"—and beyond.

If we chart a line between total capitalist control of the state and Engels' "near-equilibrium," the ratio at one end of the chart will read 100 for the capitalists, zero for the working class, but go down thereafter to 90-10, 80-20, 70-30, 60-40. If it is possible to reach "near-equilibrium" it is also possible to reach shares of power less than "near-equilibrium" or more than "near-equilibrium." The ratio will differ from country to country, from time to time. Capitalists, and elites allied with them, certainly have carried the day on major issues but not necessarily on all. There are enough fissures within the ruling class for the lower classes to gain a few of their objectives; and in times of stress, when the state must tread warily, such as during war or depression, the lower classes can win substantial, even if temporary or clipped, benefits. The accretion or diminution of power within the state apparatus is, like the class struggle itself, a fluid process.

The capitalists, it should be recalled, were a middle class when they came to power, and they made their revolution only in conjunction with the lower classes. Those lower classes, represented by the Diggers in England, Babeuf in France, Jefferson, Paine, and Benjamin Rush in the United States, were unable to deny the middle class its fundamental goals, e.g., the right to free enterprise and profit. But they did gain certain rights, such as free speech and freedom of assembly, which to an extent limited the power of the new upper class. In subsequent years they won the right to buy land from the state in small plots or to secure 160-acre grants under the Homestead Act, free public school education, the right to form unions, abolition of child labor, unemployment compensation, social security, and welfare, none of which changed the *fundamental* relationship between classes but all of which *modified* those relationships. It is true that the upper classes have held the major share of economic and political power—and in some places at some times all the power—but it is also true that the lower classes have exercised a certain amount of *countervailing* power. Bourgeois democracy, in fact, is a barometer of the successes of that countervailing power. It is certainly inadequate, especially in terms of economic democracy, but it is not, as many radicals contend, irrelevant. Indeed, it is a down payment on the future socialist revolution, part of the long process by which the new society will be hatched.

IV

Why is this point important for revolutionary strategy? Because there is a narrow band of circumstances under which oppressed classes ordinarily take to armed revolt. They do not rebel when the odds are totally against them—as in present-day South Africa or in colonial countries of the past when the imperialist powers were too formidable. Nor do they rebel, on the other hand, when there is still some possibility of rectifying their grievances, at least partially, within the old system—when there is still some possibility, in other words, of exercising countervailing power. Men and women do not lightly put their lives on the line when there is still hope for ameliorating their plight through measures other than armed resistance. This is evident not only in the advanced countries but in some of the smaller and weaker ones as well.

Consider Puerto Rico. It is in fact a colony of the United States, exploited like a colony. In 1971 Uncle Sam earned $1,318 million from Puerto Rico—$561 million in profits of U.S. firms, $623 million in balance of trade surplus, and $133 million because of higher shipping rates Puerto Rico had to pay to American carriers. More than four fifths of the island's food and other wares were imported from the United States, $2.2 billion in all, making Puerto Rico the fifth largest trading partner of Uncle Sam, second in the Western Hemisphere. In addition Puerto Rico was required to house a number of large military bases; its men were subject to the U.S. military draft and its people generally to U.S. law. There is no doubt that a majority of the island's inhabitants would like to be independent of the colossus of the North. Yet in recent decades the independence movement has been unable to lead a mass revolution, organize guerrilla warfare, or procure more than a negligible vote in elections.

What happened was that an old socialist, Luis Muñoz Marin, succeeded, by threatening a struggle for independence, in gaining commonwealth status for the island. As an alleged commonwealth—not a true one—Puerto Rico receives benefits which tend to undercut the revolutionary thrust. Each year the United States doles out $500 million or thereabouts to provide food for 650,000 poor, pay welfare, and give other forms of assistance. Puerto Ricans are covered by unemployment compensation and social security; they can move freely to the American mainland in search of jobs; and while their wages at home may be only half that of American workers, they are much higher than that of the rest of Latin America. Under these circumstances the average Puerto Rican eschews revolution; he wants independence for cultural and historical reasons, but he is hesitant about giving up economic and political advantages he has wrung from Washington for the uncertainty of revolt.

Social upheavals are stirred by desperate people, but countervailing power takes the edge off the sense of desperation. The probability of armed uprising, therefore, is greater in countries where there is little or no countervailing power and where class antagonisms are as rigid as Marx described them in the *Communist Manifesto*. Conversely, the probability of armed uprising is smaller in countries where the class structure is fluid and popular pressure can still exact reforms. In the former instance a revolution may reach its climax in one big flash, one grand moment, such as 1917 in Russia or 1789 in France. In the latter case it may proceed over a long period of time, as in Denmark, described in a previous chapter, or in Germany, Italy, and other countries where the bourgeois revolution came in stages.

For all the reasons given, then, it seems to me that what the Left must plan for in America and similarly situated countries is a revolution-in-stages. If we go back to the heart-arteries analogy, the law of probability is that the heart will not die before many more arteries are cut away from it. The existence of countervailing power and the obverse lack of class consciousness give capitalism in the advanced countries a pliancy which the Left ought not to disregard. Of course, if there should be a nuclear war the survivors will be faced with the stark choice of either seizing state power immediately, for a socialist reconstruction of society, or succumbing to military dictatorship. Similarly, if the trend toward a corporate state is unchecked, at a certain point radicals will also be faced with an all-or-nothing choice; it will signify that capitalism no longer has any elasticity. But these contingencies aside, there is no possibility in the near future of a revolution in the United States on the model of 1917 or 1789, let alone on the model of Maoism in China or *Fidelismo* in Cuba—nor is it desirable.

A revolutionary situation occurs, Lenin wrote in 1915, "when it is impossible for the ruling classes to maintain their rule in an unchanged form," when the divisions in their ranks are so great and the wrath of the masses so intense that there is an outburst of "discontent and indignation of the oppressed classes."[6] Such a thorough breakdown of the capitalist system in the United States is not in the immediate offing. The ruling elites may suffer grave difficulties in the face of various international and domestic crises, but they are not likely to crumble all at once or to find themselves so disoriented as to be *entirely* unable to rule. Power will be taken from them piecemeal, in cadence with their decline and the growing willingness of the American people to challenge them.

In the meantime the revolution, so to speak, "waits." It waits for more and more arteries to be pinched off—for the revolution, in other words, to take root in countries where it has not yet begun, such as Brazil. It waits for the already established socialist countries to deepen their revolution in the direction of humanism and thereby give encouragement to people who have doubts about socialism. It waits for Third Camp countries to move into the socialist phase of their national revolution. And it waits for the inevitable crisis that is the backwash of imperialism, militarism, and economic anarchy to produce a radical consciousness at home.

That period of waiting need not be an empty hiatus in which the Left slumbers Rip Van Winkle style; it can and should be one of transformation. The radical forces either regroup into a new political party or restructure old parties to suit their purpose. They aid with all their might the revolution abroad. They continue to work for traditional reforms within the system, such as higher minimum wages or higher social security payments. But above all they put forth a transitional program which is simultaneously reformist and revolutionary—what the Communist Party calls radical reform. Without for a moment forgetting their ultimate objective of a single global order based on planning, participation, and egalitarianism, they fight for objectives which, while ameliorating present conditions, substantively undermine those *institutions which are rooted in the profit maximization principle.* Put differently, they make a revolution-in-stages, much as the Danes made their bourgeois revolution in the eighteenth and nineteenth centuries.

It is not our purpose here to present a full program but simply to indicate guiding principles for the revolution-in-stages. The focus of radicals in countries where there is no possibility of exercising countervailing power, and where an all-or-nothing confrontation impends, is power—the seizure of state power. All strategy is molded to that purpose. Leftists in such instances build a political party which is strictly centralized in order to match the centralized authority of the adversary—in the final showdown. And they recruit most heavily from that constituency which has the greatest possibility of immobilizing the established power structure. In Russia in 1917 it was the workers and soldiers. Lenin's democratic-centralist party and Marx's emphasis on the working class as the gravediggers of capitalism were both predicated on the strategy of a *single* lunge for power.

The strategy for a revolution-in-stages begins, however, with the recognition that there probably won't be a single lunge for power but a protracted struggle to change the *ratio* of power. Like the all-or-nothing strategists, those who orient on a phased transformation do whatever is possible "within" the system, such as lobbying, but concentrate their main energies "outside" the system, on strikes, demonstrations, civil disobedience, vigils— acts of resistance and defiance. They also function within the trade union movement as a left wing, seeking to reshape it and make it more militant. But the orientation of strategy is toward gaining *institutional* changes, one at a time and under the old order—until it is transformed. Thus the party that radicals build need not be so close-knit, nor does it have to be primarily an instrument for working-class goals. It can be, and probably will be in America, an amalgam of antiwar coalitions, left-wing unionists, black, Chicano, Puerto Rican, and Indian organizations, radicalized consumer movements that will emerge from Ralph Nader's crusade or from such forces as the Citizens Action Program in Chicago, and others not yet existing. If the purpose is to win institutional changes over a period of time rather than prepare for a single lunge, the radical party can be broader and looser than the Leninist parties of the past.

Admittedly there is little to go on in planning the revolution-in-stages, for the only such revolutions that have succeeded have been bourgeois revolutions that have not been studied in any detail. But all revolutions, in a sense, take place in stages, since it takes time to jettison old institutions and fashion new ones. Some of it begins before the seizure of state power by revolutionary classes, most of it afterward. What distinguishes the revolution-in-stages is that the transformation of institutions is more even-paced and goes on intensely even while the old classes are in the saddle. It is an ongoing process to eradicate the private profit factor in the political economy and to eviscerate those institutions (such as the military, the judicial system, the government structure) which enhance it.

No comprehensive program of this sort exists today, and I have none to offer here. Such a transitional platform requires concrete study of the specific circumstances of America in the 1970s; it cannot be spun out of thin air. But it is possible to give some indication of programmatic demands that, if implemented, pinch off the profit-maximization principle and disembowel the military-industrial complex.

By way of example, a radical platform for economic transformation might include:

1. A 100-percent inheritance tax above a certain level (say $50,000 or $100,000), combined with the liquidation and proscription of foundations that are designed to circumvent the inheritance tax.

2. A progressive income tax, without loopholes such as capital gains, interest payments, and depletion allowances, that establishes a confiscatory 100-percent tax above a specified amount.

3. The purchase of corporate stock by the government over a period of years—say 10 percent each year, as is currently contemplated in one of the Scandinavian countries—and their assignment to workers employed by that corporation, to consumer

groups, and to the public at large in an agreed-upon ratio, until the corporation is socially owned and socially managed.

4. A program for progressive redistribution of income through (a) cradle-to-the-grave social insurance, paid for entirely from income and inheritance taxes, and (b) a guaranteed annual income approximately equivalent to trade union wages.

5. A vastly expanded program of social construction—schools, low-cost housing, playgrounds, mental institutions, hospitals, and the like—under the supervision of community groups made up of professional experts and ordinary citizens with interest in each project.

6. National indicator planning that uses monetary, import, resource-allocation, and other controls to direct production into more useful channels and is charged particularly with redistributing income and wealth in favor of the lower classes.

7. Nationalization of banks, credit institutions, and utilities as a necessary supplement to planning.

8. A national (and hopefully international) ecological plan to mesh with the overall economic plan.

That Americans are ready for most of these planks—properly studied and modified—is attested to by the enormous popularity of George Wallace's tirades against the tax structure, the plaints of liberals for a reordering of priorities, Ralph Nader's consumerism, and the ongoing discussion of ecology. In the malaise that envelops America the ordinary citizen is groping in his own way toward the correct medicine chest. It remains for the Left merely to prove that these goals are incompatible with the principle of profit maximization. Americans do not yet see the connection. They are still bewitched by the notion that the economic motor can be fueled by material greed. They still luxuriate in subliminal dreams of becoming great magnates or movie stars. But they can be convinced in the course of struggle that the profit motive and survival are mutually exclusive.

On the social and political front the new radical crusade will focus on creating dual institutions that allow for popular participation in decision-making—from the precinct and factory to Washington. Such a program might include:

1. Some form of neighborhood control of police and schools.

2. Elected bodies of ordinary citizens to consult with city, state, and federal representatives regularly and to exercise a veto

over their votes. A few forward-looking legislators have already formed such countervailing institutions.

3. The addition of worker and consumer delegates to the boards of directors of non-nationalized companies, until they constitute a majority. (Germany, after the war, promulgated a program of "co-determination" with the goal of one-third to one-half labor representation on the boards of its major companies.)

4. The formation of shadow legislatures made up of experts and interested parties from the grass roots, to sanction or withhold sanction for legislation in their designated fields—much like the Yugoslav system. This is not as radical as it sounds, for even Congress admits today that it lacks the proficiency to study such matters as defense expenditures, the budget, economics, and many other problems on which it legislates. Bodies of experts and concerned citizens, functioning parallel to elected legislatures, would pump vitality into them and make it possible for them to ward off encroachments by the executive branch of government.

5. A government-financed program to convert privately owned apartment buildings, supermarkets, and department stores into self-managed cooperatives.

Other proposals would include judicial and penal reform, self-management of educational systems, autonomous operation of Indian reservations by native Americans, and many similar planks. The importance of proposals for popular participation is not merely that they whittle away at the power of ruling elites but that they replace the individualist elan with community concern and community responsibility. In our society we have taken for granted that the individual must provide for himself; it has not yet occurred to us how completely our fates are interlinked, how dependent individuals and businesses are on what society as a whole does for them. The vaunted American standard of living is dependent on the billions of dollars expended by the government on militarism and compensatory spending. General Motors could certainly not have grown so affluent unless the government built highways for its cars, winked at the automobile's pollution of the collectively owned atmosphere, and gave management tax breaks to modernize itself. On the one side we take it for granted that government has no obligation to provide free bus and trolley service, but on the other we accept as "normal" that it provide free research and development subsidies and free reports on commerce, shipping, and a thousand other items for entrepreneurs. Participation and community concern, along with a reform of the educational system, are some of the tools that will help reorient this thinking and help forge a new human being, without which no revolution can be complete.

Finally, a revolution-in-stages will work for such international goals as:

1. The closing of all military bases and withdrawal of all U.S. troops and equipment from overseas.

2. Multilateral negotiations for total disarmament; if that fails, unilateral initiatives by the United States to disarm itself. As of 1970 some 120 countries surveyed by the U.S. Arms Control and Disarmament Agency were spending the fabulous sum of $207 billion on arms, as against $168 billion for public education and $80 billion for health care. Apart from the fact that weapons no longer afford security for nuclear powers, this is immoral lunacy. America would be no less safe and doubtless much happier with a vanishing stockpile of weapons than with $100 billion in its arsenal and new expenditures of $80 billion a year.

3. Active support to popular revolutions by making available economic aid to developing countries in proportion as their governments institute social reforms.

4. A tax policy that would discourage private investment by U.S. corporations overseas and stringent measures to curb, then liquidate, the great multinational corporations. This is not isolationism, for it would be replaced by nation-to-nation economic aid. Furthermore, the power of the multinational firms is a threat not only to foreign nations, especially the weaker ones, but to America itself.

5. Termination of all military aid, both because it is inherently immoral and because it buttresses dictatorships.

6. Economic aid to encourage nations to coalesce into common markets and common sovereignties. Most of the countries of the world are small and unviable; unless they are amalgamated into *inter*nations they cannot be modernized. Internations, moreover, are a necessary intermediary step toward the single global nation. But unity can be costly, because in its wake inefficient industries of the least productive country are driven to the wall. Some type of subsidy is therefore needed to sustain these industries and

their workers in the period of transition, while they retool for other types of production.

In the foreign program, as in the domestic one, the revolution-in-stages strives not merely for reforms but for reforms that have revolutionary implications. They are designed to weaken the military-industrial complex at home while chipping away at its influence overseas. Is it possible to do this without totally dismembering the present system? History has shown that the middle classes and peasants in the past were able to force a number of institutional changes on feudal regimes—such as partial land reforms—before they were dismembered. It also showed that basic modification became progressively easier as the balance of world power shifted against the old system. There is no reason why the same thing can't happen in the present period of capitalism, as world socialism grows stronger.

V

Another indicated revision of radical strategy for the advanced countries, and in particular the United States, has to do with the national sense of identity. Nationalism is outmoded as a form of state rule—humanity must move beyond it to the global community—but it is very much alive as a culture, a tradition, and a unifying force. Some segments of the American society—notably the black, brown, and red—are sufficiently alienated from it to constitute true national minorities. They will doubtless form separate blocs within what is called the United States and within the radical coalition as well, and they will pursue a course, in each instance, peculiarly their own. But, like it or not, the majority—the white populace—is imbued with an implacable *sense of identity* as Americans that is almost religious. What Herbert Croly, the Progressive theorist, wrote in 1909 on this subject is still applicable:

> The faith of Americans in their own country is religious, if not in its intensity, at any rate in its almost absolute and universal authority. . . . We may distrust and dislike much that is done in the name of our country by our fellow-countrymen; but our country itself, its democratic system, and its prosperous future are above suspicion.[7]

In colonial or undeveloped nations, where the class relations are rigid, there is a feeling of antagonism not only to the regime but society itself. Mahatma Gandhi had little difficulty in uniting all classes in India against British rule; the anti-British sentiment was overwhelming. Nor did the revolutionaries of Russia find much allegiance left for Czarism by 1917. But there is a sense of pride by Americans in American history and culture that is not easily circumvented.

Nor should it be circumvented. There has always been, to be sure, a conservative and reactionary strain in American life, but there has also been a radical one worth emulating. America and Americans deserve kudos for the revolution of 1776; the brilliant strategical leadership of Sam Adams; the Declaration of Independence; the political preachings of Benjamin Franklin, Tom Paine, and Benjamin Rush; the militancy of the Jeffersonians in defending the French Revolution during the 1790s; the labor parties of the 1820s; the utopian socialist experiments of Robert Owen, Greeley, Brisbane, and Brook Farm; the crusade for black liberation initiated by William Lloyd Garrison, Nat Turner, Wendell Phillips, and John Brown; the Union Leagues and Negro militias of reconstruction days; the militant strikes of 1875 in the Pennsylvania coal fields; the railroad strikes of 1877 and 1894; the eight-hour-day struggle and Haymarket; the many labor wars in the Rockies; the nobility of men like Eugene V. Debs; the I.W.W. campaigns for free speech; the 1912 Lawrence strike; the Anti-Imperialist League during the Spanish-American War; the antiwar movements during World War I and Vietnam; the sitdowns of the 1930s; and the grandeur of pacifists like A. J. Muste.

The Old Left, for all practical purposes, turned its back on this heritage. It is understandable that Leftists should have been so enthralled by the first working-class revolution—in Russia— that they identified totally with its aims, strategy, even tactics. It is understandable, but it was a mistake nonetheless; first, because the revolution here was not destined to follow the Soviet path, and second, because it isolated the Left from millions who might have listened to it if they were not required to give up their sense of national identity to do so. The Old Left extolled other revolutionaries and other revolutions to such an extent as to make everything in the American experience seem irrelevant, even reactionary. All the wisdom of revolution was encapsuled in the head of Lenin (or Stalin or Trotsky), little or none in the heads of Samuel Adams, Tom Paine, Fanny Wright, Albert Parsons, Debs, Big Bill Haywood. Yet any reflection would have shown that Adams, for instance, was the equal of Lenin—considering the gap in time and place—as a revolutionary strategist. Indeed, their techniques were uniquely similar. Lenin worked inside the system on occasions—Bolsheviks ran for the Duma—and outside it, through his party and the soviets. Adams worked inside the system, by running for and serving in the Massachusetts House of Burgesses, but also outside, by forming Committees of Correspondence, Committees of Safety, the Continental Congress. Lenin forged a dual army; so did Adams with his Minutemen.

In the nomenclature of the Old Left, however, Adams was a bourgeois revolutionary who had nothing to teach socialist revolutionaries. Old leftists knew far more about the 1905 revolution in Russia than the 1776 revolution in America, more about the revolt of the sailors of the *Potemkin* than the 1894 Pullman strike. In factional disputes they invariably referred to the writings of Lenin, Stalin, Trotsky, and occasionally Rosa Luxemburg as the ultimate justification for their positions. No wonder that the majority of the members of the Communist Party in the 1920s were foreign born—men and women, in other words, who had not yet developed their sense of identity with the United States. For a half century or more the average American has considered radicalism a foreign import because it was not related to the American experience.

The problem, then, is how to put forth a radical program which calls for the disbanding of the present institutions without requiring the average citizen to give up his psychological link to the American past. Since the process of radicalization will probably take place over a considerable period of time, it is folly to expect sizable numbers of people to adhere to the revolutionary cause if they must give up their feeling of national identity. It would be a mistake in any case, but it would be doubly futile in a revolution that unfolds in stages.

Radicals must make it possible for potential recruits to continue believing in America, its people, and some or most of its heritage, while accepting the need to jettison the existing institutions. That is not really as difficult as it sounds; there are few progressive issues that cannot be related to American annals. The rationale for nationalizing the railroads and telegraphs was put forth just as cogently by the Populists as the Bolsheviks—in more colorful phrases. The limited liability company, the corporation, was damned by our forefathers with just as much emotional fervor as it is damned today by foreign or native Marxists. For more than fifty years during the nineteenth century American "hotheads" sought to restrict the corporation to a single type of business, such as flour milling, and for a specific period of time, say twenty or thirty years, after which it was to be dissolved. Both Herbert Croly and Walter Weyl, another Progressive theoretician, called for socializing *monopolistic* corporations—a position which under today's circumstances would make the biggest part of the American economy socialist. The point is not that these thinkers or activists were as lucid as some foreign writers on the evils of capitalism, but they were lucid enough to be points of reference for an American radicalism that intends to build on what they postulated. I cannot imagine a more ringing call to unite against injustice than the preamble of the program of the Populists, written in 1892:

> We meet in the midst of a nation brought to the verge of moral, political and material ruin. Corruption dominates the ballot-box, the legislatures, the Congress, and touches even the ermine of the bench. . . . The fruits of the toil of millions are boldly stolen to build up colossal fortunes for a few, unprecedented in the history of mankind; and the possessors of these, in turn, despise the republic and endanger liberty. From the same prolific womb of governmental injustice we breed the two great classes—tramps and millionaires. . . . We have witnessed for more than a quarter of a century the struggle of the two great political parties for power and plunder, while grievous wrongs have been inflicted upon the suffering people. . . . Wealth belongs to him who creates it, and every dollar taken from industry without an equivalent is robbery.[8]

It is not necessary to pigeonhole the writings of Marx, Lenin, Trotsky, Mao, and Castro, but they must be correlated, where possible, with the writing and struggles of Americans. And they must be correlated not in the synthetic way that Earl Browder's Communists did in the mid-1930s when they called communism "20th-Century Americanism" but out of actual recognition that the American revolution will have a distinctly American flavor, based on its own culture, history, and ethnic character. In the Russian Revolution it was necessary to *tear down* the old order and forge a totally new one, because there was little of countervailing power on which to build. In the coming American revolution it will be necessary to tear down part and transform other parts of the old order, because there are some things we must and should carry forward—such as the Bill of Rights—even if they are modified. Socialism may not be a 20th-century Americanism, but Americanism is not so entirely alien to socialism as Leftists insist. By referring to those elements of the American heritage that are compatible with socialism, the Left can make it possible for millions to retain a sense of identity with their own culture and still be radicals.

This does not mean that the radical will meekly confine himself to the four walls of "legality." He will lobby for certain reforms *within* the august halls of Congress, but he will—like our radical forebears—attempt to develop a climate of "creative discord" outside Congress, through strikes and demonstrations. Where the liberal insists that change must come about exclusively through "legal" action, the radical argues that legality itself, under capitalism, is a means of sustaining immorality—and in many instances, such as the flaunting of the Constitution by Presidents Johnson and Nixon during the Indochina war, of illegality itself. He—the radical—points out that virtually no major reform has ever been won through schematic adherence to "legality"; indeed, decent people have always had to violate immoral laws to redress their legitimate grievances. There would have been no large labor movement today and no body of labor laws protecting the working person if there had been no violation of injunctions in hundreds of strikes from 1894 through 1938. There would have been no change in the plight of Blacks if Martin Luther King had slavishly adhered to "legalism," and probably no truce in the Indochina war if it hadn't been for the willingness of young people to "illegally" burn their draft cards and commit a dozen types of civil disobedience. Violation of the law, the radical contends, is no crime when the law is stacked in favor of property rights against human rights; it is, in fact, a social duty. This too, however, is part of the American tradition. It can be fostered and sustained without forcing the would-be radical to give up his feeling of association with the American past.

The revolution-in-stages, then, is not merely a reform movement but a reform movement outside and against the system that seeks revolutionary transformation. It is not as sensational a social phenomenon as the all-or-nothing struggle for power in 1917, but it conforms to the reality in America (and much of the world) in the 1970s.

VI

Every generation of radicals has been required to attune its strategy to the experiences of its day. Almost no one believed at the outset of World War I that a socialist revolution was immediately possible in a country such as Russia, but the experience of 1917 proved that it was, and it was thereafter incorporated into Leftist doctrine as a feasible strategy. The radical's overview of history is generally valid, but there are specific nuances to each period that few, if any, anticipate in advance. History proceeds in its own way, heedless of a priori pronunciamentos. In our generation, living experience has taught us, among other things, that:

1. Socialist revolutions do not necessarily proceed in a straight course toward humanism but can be sidetracked and derailed for considerable periods.

2. Capitalism, though terminally ill, is able to catch a second (and third) wind through the application of Keynesian and militarist nostrums.

3. The sequence of revolution is not as orderly as proclaimed in *The Communist Manifesto* and is decisively affected by the nonexistence or existence of countervailing power.

4. There are limits to nature's bounty, as Parson Thomas Robert Malthus told us in 1798.

5. The march toward an egalitarian society is dependent not only on the outcome of the class struggle but of the struggle between nations as well.

This last point needs a few words of elaboration. If we back up a little and move forward a little from Marx's doctrine of historical materialism, the world appears as a crucible of conflicts that is less than and more than the class struggle. The class struggle is only one of the manifestations of inequality. Below it is the natural inequality of individuals who are unequal by nature—unequal in size, strength, mental agility, age, health. And beyond it is the inequality of nations, even nations that are socialist. If every country in the world were to complete its socialist revolution tomorrow, we would still be some distance away from a global egalitarian community. Socialist or not, it is in the very nature of nation-states to seek advantage over others. Radicals have always assumed that once the socialist revolution had gained momentum this aspect of human antagonism would be smoothed out automatically. The experience of the Soviet bloc since World War II, however, bids us to rethink this problem too. The Soviet invasions of Hungary in 1956 and Czechoslovakia in 1968 are testament to the fact that weak nations need protection from the strong, whatever their social system. This is an area of experience affecting radical strategy that is little explored and needs further study.

Silviu Brucan, a perceptive Romanian sociologist who once served as ambassador to the United States, includes the national struggle as adjunct to the class struggle in defining the goal of today's revolution.

> Whereas all revolutions up to the present have meant the passing of power from one class to another, a new type of revolution will mark the end of this century: supranational, and eventually, world integration. This will not mean the passing of power from one class to another, but the *dissolution of power* itself. . . . Instead of a power based on *domination,* originating in class and national inequality, [there will be] a power based rather on the *cohesion of integration,* originating in the common interest of society's members in the orderly organization of their new existence.[9]

Put differently, if power is the embodiment of privilege, then what humanity aspires to is the dissolution of two types of power, national and class, both of which will proceed side by side.

What the Left gropes for is a worldwide community in which

everyone has power and therefore no one has it. The New Left calls this participatory democracy. The Titoists call it self-management. But Brucan's vision of a dissolution of power is more apt, for it hints at the total need for a supranational revolution.

American radicalism will become credible only as it looks toward this broader objective and as it studies the problems that experience has dredged up for it to deal with in this epoch. It cannot be meaningful—or even Marxist—if it continues to languish in the mire of imitation.

Notes

Chapter One   The Incomplete Ideology

1. Gil Green, *The New Radicalism, Anarchist or Marxist?* (New York: International Publishers, 1971), p. 12.

2. David A. Shannon, ed., *The Great Depression* (Englewood Cliffs, N.J.: Prentice-Hall, 1960), p. 111.

3. The membership of left-wing parties was certainly smaller in the 1960s than in the 1930s, but the number of unaffiliated radicals on the periphery of the New Left was probably greater.

4. For similar expressions of optimism see Samuel Eliot Morison, *The Oxford History of the American People* (New York: Oxford University Press, 1965), pp. 939-40, or my *Radicalism in America* (New York: Thomas Y. Crowell Co., 1966), p. 297.

5. Karl Marx and Frederick Engels, *The Communist Manifesto* (New York: The New York Labor News Co., 1934), p. 23.

6. In a preface written in 1888, Engels notes that the *Manifesto* was written in German in January 1848, published in French a few weeks later, in English in 1850, and subsequently in Danish, Polish, and other languages.

7. Karl Marx, "India," reprint of articles in the *New York Tribune,* published in *A Handbook of Marxism* (New York: International Publishers, 1935), p. 187.

8. Eugene Dennis, "Report to Plenary Meeting of National Committee of the Communist Party, December 3-5, 1946," published in *Political Affairs,* January 1947.

9. V. I. Lenin, "Theses and Report on Bourgeois Democracy and the Dictatorship of the Proletariat," submitted to the First Congress of the Communist International, March 4, 1919, and published in *Selected Works* (New York: International Publishers), p. 231.

10. Clifton Brock, *Americans for Democratic Action* (New York: Public Affairs Press, 1962), p. 20.

11. Max Eastman, *Reflections on the Failure of Socialism* (New York: Devin-Adair, 1955), p. 31.

12. Martin Oppenheimer, in *On Revolution,* ed. William Lutz and Harry Brent (Cambridge, Mass.: Winthrop Publishers, 1971), p. 84.

13. Robert L. Heilbroner, *The Limits of American Capitalism* (New York: Harper & Row, 1966), p. 4. Used by permission.

14. Ibid., pp. 67-68.

15. Cited in Adam Smith, *Supercurrency* (New York: Random House, 1972), p. 286.

Chapter Two   The Double Revolution

1. H. G. Wells, *Outline of History* (New York: Macmillan, 1922), p. 607.

2. Marion Gibbs, *Feudal Order* (New York: Henry Schuman, 1953), pp. 5-7.

3. Cited in one of my earlier books, *A World in Revolution* (New York: Praeger Publishers, Inc., 1956), p. 42.

4. Quoted in Kumar Goshal, *People in Colonies* (New York: Sheridan House, 1948), p. 151.

5. *The Evening Standard*, London, May 28, 1930. Quoted in Goshal, op. cit., p. 152.

6. For more details, see Jawaharlal Nehru, *Autobiography* (London: John Lane, 1948).

7. For extensive treatment of this subject see United Nations document E/1910/Add. 2, *Review of Economic Conditions in the Middle East*. Italics added.

8. Ibid.

Chapter Three The Syndrome of Intervention

1. Quoted in Anna Louise Strong, *One Fifth of Mankind* (New York: Modern Age Books, 1938), p. 46.

2. Quoted in K. S. Karol, *China, the Other Communism* (New York: Hill & Wang, 1967), p. 66n.

3. Hugh Seton-Watson, *From Lenin to Malenkov* (New York: Praeger Publishers, Inc., 1954), p. 145.

4. Quoted in Strong, op. cit., p. 67.

5. Quoted in Karol, op. cit., p. 71.

6. Quoted in David Horowitz, ed., *Containment and Revolution* (Boston: Beacon Press, 1967), p. 186.

7. Quoted in Lloyd C. Gardner, *Economic Aspects of New Deal Diplomacy* (Madison, Wis.: University of Wisconsin Press, 1964), pp. 69-70.

8. Quoted in Strong, op. cit., p. 82.

9. Ibid.

10. Quoted in Karol, op. cit., pp. 117-18.

11. Quoted in Theodore H. White and Annalee Jacoby, *Thunder Out of China* (London: Victor Gollancz, 1946), p. 54.

12. Foster Hailey, *Half of One World* (New York: Macmillan, 1950), p. 51.

13. Quoted in Hans J. Morgenthau, *In Defense of the National Interest* (New York: Knopf, 1951), p. 257.

14. Quoted in John W. Spanier, *American Foreign Policy Since World War II* (New York: Praeger Publishers, Inc., 1960), p. 88.

15. Felix Greene, *Awakened China* (New York: Doubleday, 1962), p. 406.

Chapter Four The Background of Stalinism

1. Lewis L. Lorwin, *Labor and Internationalism* (New York: Macmillan, 1938), pp. 13-14.

2. International Confederation of Free Trade Unions, *The French Trade Union Movement, Past and Present* (no date), pp. 15ff.

3. Ibid., pp. 18-19.

4. Quoted in Lorwin, op. cit., p. 27.

5. Roy A. Medvedev, *Let History Judge* (New York: Knopf, 1971), p. 234.

6. Leon Trotsky, *The History of the Russian Revolution* (Ann Arbor, Mich.: University of Michigan Press, 1932), p. 10.

7. D. F. Fleming, *The Cold War and Its Origins, 1917-1950* (New York: Doubleday, 1961), p. 9.

8. Quoted in R. Palme Dutt, *World Politics, 1918-1936* (New York: International Publishers, 1936), pp. 45-46.

9. Lewis Broad, *Winston Churchill: A Biography* (Westport, Conn.: Greenwood, 1958), p. 183.

10. Fleming, op. cit., p. 16.

11. Quoted in Isaac Deutscher, *The Prophet Armed* (New York: Oxford, 1954), p. 290n.

12. Walter Duranty, *USSR: The Story of Soviet Russia* (Philadelphia: Lippincott, 1944), p. 44.

13. Quoted in Fleming, op. cit., p. 18.

14. Ibid., pp. 20-21.

15. Ibid., p. 23.

16. Duranty, op. cit., pp. 38-39.

17. George F. Kennan, *Russia and the West Under Lenin and Stalin* (Boston: Atlantic-Little, Brown, 1960), p. 179. Used by permission.

18. William Henry Chamberlin, *The Russian Revolution, 1917-1921* (New York: Grosset & Dunlap, Inc., 1935), II, 156.

19. Kennan, op. cit., p. 117.

20. Quoted in Deutscher, op. cit., p. 518.

21. Ibid., p. 517.

Chapter Five **The Causes of Stalinism**

1. *Handbook of Marxism* (New York: International Publishers, 1935), pp. 376, 379, 384.

2. Quoted in David Horowitz, *Empire and Revolution* (New York: Random House, 1969), p. 130.

3. Quoted in Manya Gordon, *Workers Before and After Lenin* (New York: E. P. Dutton & Co., 1941), p. 366.

4. Quoted in D. F. Fleming, *The Cold War and Its Origins, 1917-1950* (New York: Doubleday, 1961), pp. 43-44.

5. Ibid., p. 46.

6. Isaac Deutscher, *The Prophet Unarmed, Trotsky: 1921-1929* (New York: Oxford, 1959), p. 44.

7. George F. Kennan, *Russia and the West Under Lenin and Stalin* (Boston: Atlantic-Little, Brown, 1960), p. 181. Used by permission.

8. Gordon, op. cit., p. 137.

9. Quoted in Leon Trotsky, *The Revolution Betrayed* (New York: Pioneer Publishers, 1945), pp. 26-27.

10. See Boris Souvarine, *Stalin* (New York: Longmans, Green & Company, 1939), pp. 421-24. Also Trotsky, op. cit., pp. 25-33; Deutscher, op. cit., pp. 230-39; Sidney Lens, *A World in Revolution* (New York: Praeger Publishers, Inc., 1956), pp. 117-23.

11. Quoted in Souvarine, op. cit., pp. 389-90.

12. George Plekhanov, *The Role of the Individual in History* (New York: International Publishers, 1940), p. 50.

13. Quoted in Roy A. Medvedev, *Let History Judge* (New York: Knopf, 1971), p. 71.

14. Quoted in Souvarine, op. cit., p. 490.

15. See Walter Duranty, *USSR: The Story of Soviet Russia* (Philadelphia: Lippincott, 1944), p. 44. Also Trotsky, op. cit., p. 35; Souvarine, op. cit., p. 512; and Alexander Baykov, *The Development of the Soviet Economic System* (New York: Macmillan, 1948), p. 187.

16. Victor Serge, *From Lenin to Stalin* (New York: Pioneer Publishers, 1937), p. 63.

17. Quoted in Trotsky, op. cit., p. 33.

18. John Gunther, *Inside Europe Today* (New York: Harper & Bros., 1961), p. 510.

19. Serge, op. cit., p. 58.

20. Ibid., p. 61.

21. Ibid., p. 77.

22. Nikita Khrushchev, "The Crimes of the Stalin Era," *New Leader* (Special Supplement), July 16, 1956, p. 22.

23. Leon Trotsky, *My Life,* (New York: Grosset & Dunlap, Inc., 1930), p. 478; Souvarine, op. cit., p. 306.

24. Serge, op. cit., p. 41.

Chapter Six   **The Middle Years**

1. Quoted in William L. Shirer, *The Rise and Fall of the Third Reich* (New York: Simon and Schuster, 1960), p. 84.

2. Quoted in R. Palme Dutt, *World Politics 1918-1936* (New York: International Publishers, 1936), p. 261.

3. Quoted in David Horowitz, *Containment and Revolution* (Boston: Beacon Press, 1967), p. 69.

4. David Horowitz, *The Free World Colossus* (New York: Hill & Wang, 1965), p. 61n.

5. James Byrnes, *Speaking Frankly* (New York: Harper & Bros., 1947), p. 203.

6. Horowitz, *The Free World Colossus,* pp. 259-60.

7. Ibid., pp. 250-51.

8. Quoted in William Henry Chamberlin, *Russian Review,* vol. 9, no. 2, p. 84 (italics added).

9. Quoted in Adam B. Ulam, *Expansion and Coexistence: The History of Soviet Foreign Policy 1917-67* (New York: Praeger Publishers, Inc., 1968), p. 448.

10. Howard K. Smith, *The State of Europe* (New York: Knopf, 1949), pp. 99-100.

11. Quoted in Horowitz, *The Free World Colossus,* p. 85.

12. Ibid., p. 51n.

13. For a more complete, though unfriendly, recitation of this chapter in Soviet-East Europe relationships, see Zbigniew K. Brzezinski, *The Soviet Bloc, Unity and Conflict* (New York: Praeger Publishers, Inc, 1963), pp. 104-37.

14. Quoted in Brzezinski, op. cit., p. 284n., from J. Wszelaki, *Communist Economic Strategy: The Role of East Central Europe* (Washington, 1959), pp. 68-77.

15. Vladimir Katkoff, *Soviet Economy 1940-1965* (Baltimore: Dangary Publishing Co., 1961), pp. 140, 154.

16. Hugh Seton-Watson, *From Lenin to Malenkov* (New York: Praeger Publishers, Inc., 1954), p. 248.

17. Brzezinski, op. cit., pp. 94-97.

18. Ibid., pp. 133-34. Used by permission.

19. Samuel Pisar, *Coexistence and Commerce* (New York: McGraw-Hill, 1970), pp. 125-26.

20. Ibid., pp. 126-27.

21. Ibid., p. 14.

22. Ibid., p. 19.

23. Ibid., pp. 27, 502.

24. Katkoff, op. cit., p. 533; Brzezinski, op. cit., p. 480.

25. Dean Acheson, *Present at the Creation: My Years in the State Department* (New York: Norton & Co., 1969), p. 229.

26. Ibid., pp. 230-31.

27. Quoted in John W. Spanier, *American Foreign Policy Since World War II* (New York: Praeger Publishers, Inc., 1960), p. 35.

28. Quoted in David Horowitz, ed., *Corporations and the Cold War* (New York: Monthly Review Press, 1969), p. 164.

29. D. F. Fleming, *The Cold War and Its Origins, 1917-1950* (New York: Doubleday, 1961), p. 1060.

30. John Fischer, *Master Plan U.S.A.* (New York: Harper & Bros., 1951), p. 84.

Chapter Seven   **Socialism with a Human Face**

1. Roy A. Medvedev, *Let History Judge* (New York: Knopf, 1971), p. 166.

2. Nikita Khrushchev, "The Crimes of the Stalin Era," *New Leader* (Special Supplement), July 16, 1956), pp. 4, 22.

3. See Vladimir Dedijer, *Tito* (New York: Simon & Schuster, 1953), p. 345.

4. For more details see my book *The Counterfeit Revolution* (Boston: Beacon Press, 1952), pp. 75ff.

5. Dedijer, op. cit., p. 350.

6. Ibid., p. 371.

7. *The Progressive,* Dec. 1968, p. 34.

8. Denis Healey, *New Leader,* Dec. 31, 1960, p. 3.

9. *Guardian,* Jan. 24, 1973, p. 16.

10. *Current History,* May 1973, p. 204.

11. These figures come from Vladimir Katkoff, *Soviet Economy, 1940-1965* (Baltimore: Dangary Publishing Co., 1961), p. 462, and Harry Schwartz, *The Soviet Economy Since Stalin* (Philadelphia: Lippincott, 1965), p. 192.

12. Schwartz, op. cit., pp. 214-15.

13. Isaac Deutscher, *The Unfinished Revolution* (New York: Oxford University Press, 1967), p. 49.

14. Schwartz, op. cit., pp. 58-59.

15. Zbigniew W. Brzezinski, *The Soviet Bloc, Unity and Conflict* (New York: Praeger Publishers, Inc., 1963), p. 245n. Used by permission.

16. Ibid., p. 213.

17. Samuel Pisar, *Coexistence and Commerce* (New York: McGraw-Hill, 1970), pp. 26-27 (italics added); *Business Week,* Oct. 31, 1964.

18. Interview by author, Aug. 1968.

19. *The New York Times,* Mar. 7, 1967.

Chapter Eight   **Postponing a Debacle**

1. *Newsweek,* Jan. 21, 1971.
2. See Paul M. Sweezy, *The Theory of Capitalist Development* (New York: Monthly Review Press, 1942), pp. 136-37.
3. Victor Perlo, *The Unstable Economy: Booms and Recessions in the United States Since 1945* (New York: International Publishers, 1973), p. 9.
4. William J. Blake, *An American Looks at Karl Marx* (Cordon Company, 1939), p. 346.
5. The Lescure quotation is from his 1907 book, published in France, *General or Periodical Industrial Crises;* the Cassel quotation is from his *Theoretical Social Economies,* 4th ed. (Leipzig: 1927), p. 476.
6. Karl Marx, *Capital,* vol. 1 (Charles H. Kerr, 1906), p. 127.
7. Karl Marx, *A History of Economic Theories, from the Physiocrats to Adam Smith* (Langland Press, 1952), p. 25.
8. Karl Marx, *Theories of Surplus Value,* vol. 2, pt. 2 (Stuttgart: 1921), p. 301.
9. Quoted in John Strachey, *The Nature of Capitalist Crisis* (New York: Covici-Friede, 1935), p. 15.
10. Robert L. Heilbroner, *The Economic Problem* (Englewood Cliffs, N.J.: Prentice-Hall, 1972), p. 418.
11. Perlo, op. cit., p. 14.
12. Quoted in William E. Leuchtenburg, *Franklin D. Roosevelt and the New Deal* (New York: Harper & Row [Harper Torchbook]. 1965), p. 96.
13. Leonard P. Ayres, *The Economics of Recovery* (New York: Macmillan, 1934), p. 5.
14. Robert L. Heilbroner, *The Worldly Philosophers* (New York: Simon and Schuster, 1953), p. 264.
15. Ibid., pp. 257-64.
16. Ibid., p. 265.
17. Paul Samuelson, *Economics,* 3d ed. (New York: McGraw-Hill Book Company, 1955), pp. 320-21.
18. *Monthly Labor Review,* vol. 90, no. 9, p. 9.

Chapter Nine   **Doors Without Exits**

1. Both the Schilpp and Dewey quotations are from Robert Ginsberg, ed., *The Critique of War* (Chicago: Henry Regnery Co., 1969), p. 152.
2. Robert L. Heilbroner, *The Economic Problem* (Englewood Cliffs, N.J.: Prentice-Hall, 1972), p. 614n.
3. Gaylord Freeman, Mimeographed speech, First National Bank of Chicago, Mar. 7, 1973, p. 10.
4. Ibid., pp. 10, 12.
5. Ginsberg, op. cit., p. 153.
6. Quoted in Scott Nearing and Joseph Freeman, *Dollar Diplomacy* (New York: Monthly Review Press, 1966), pp. 243, 247.
7. Quoted in R. W. Van Alstyne, *The Rising American Empire* (New York: Oxford University Press, 1960), p. 201.
8. Thomas A. Bailey, *A Diplomatic History of the American People* (New York: Appleton-Century-Crofts, 1945), p. 700.
9. Lloyd C. Gardner, *Economic Aspects of New Deal Diplomacy* (Madison, Wis.: University of Wisconsin Press, 1964), p. 21.

10. Ibid., p. 29.

11. William Appleman Williams, *The Contours of American History* (New York: World Publishing Co., 1961), pp. 454-55.

12. For more on Germany see Franz Borkenau, *The New German Empire* (New York: Viking Press, 1939), pp. 16ff., and Gustav Stolper, *German Economy 1870-1940* (New York: Reynal & Hitchcock, 1940), pp. 254ff.; also *Annals of the American Academy,* vol. 198, p. 6.

13. W. G. Beasley, *The Modern History of Japan* (New York: Macmillan, 1957), p. 259.

14. Robert Leckie, *The Wars of America* (New York: Harper & Row, 1968), II, 143.

15. *Annals of the American Academy,* vol. 198, p. 59.

16. David Horowitz, ed. *Corporations and Cold War* (New York: Monthly Review Press, 1969), p. 156.

17. James McMillan and Bernard Harris, *The American Take-over of Britain* (New York: Hart Publishing Co., 1968), p. 32.

18. William Appleman Williams, *The Tragedy of American Diplomacy* (New York: World Publishing Co., 1959), p. 148.

19. Gardner, op. cit., pp. 282-83.

20. McMillan and Harris, op. cit., p. 32.

21. Basil Davidson, "Cashing In on Old Imperialisms," *The Nation,* Sept. 13, 1952, p. 209.

22. *Columbia Journal of World Business,* vol. 1. (Fall 1965), p. 23.

23. Amaury De Riencourt, *The American Empire* (New York: Dial Press, 1968), p. 283. Copyright © 1968 by Amaury de Riencourt. Used by permission of Dial Press.

24. Quoted in *Economic Notes, Labor Research Association,* New York, Jan. 1971, p. 6.

25. Quoted in Horowitz, *Corporations and Cold War,* p. 164.

26. Quoted in David Horowitz, *The Free World Colossus* (New York: Hill & Wang, 1965), p. 85.

27. Gar Alperovitz, *Atomic Diplomacy: Hiroshima and Potsdam* (London: Secker & Warburg, 1965), p. 242.

28. I. F. Stone, *The Truman Era* (New York: Monthly Review Press, 1953), p. 75 (italics added).

29. For further details see my article in the *National Catholic Reporter,* Apr. 4. 1969.

30. War/Peace Report. Nov.-Dec. 1972.

31. Freeman, op. cit., p. 43.

32. EPICA, Nov. 1972. Mimeograph, pp. 4-5.

33. Senate Committee on Foreign Relations Hearings on Nonproliferation Treaty, Feb. 18, 20, 1969, p. 509 (italics added).

34. Victor Perlo, *The Unstable Economy: Booms and Recessions in the United States Since 1945* (New York: International Publishers, 1973), p. 70.

35. Ibid., pp. 183-84.

36. Freeman, op. cit., p. 7 .

37. Quoted in Donald H. Meadows et al., *The Limits of Growth* (New York: New American Library, 1972) p. 21.

38. Ibid., pp. 49-50.

39. Ibid., p. 60.

40. Quoted by TRB, *New Republic,* Dec. 6, 1972.

41. Meadows et al., op. cit., p. 62.

42. Robert L. Heilbroner, "Growth and Survival," *Foreign Affairs,* Oct. 1972, pp. 140ff.

43. TRB, *New Republic,* op. cit.

44. Garrett De Bell, ed., *The Environmental Handbook* (New York: Ballantine Books, 1970), pp. 201-2.

45. Summary of Analysis of Hearings, June 22-26, 1959, Joint Committee on Atomic Energy, U.S. Congress, "Biological Effects of Nuclear War."

46. *New Leader,* Aug. 20, 1962, letter from Doug Ireland.

47. *The New York Times,* Jan. 14, 1961.

48. *Parade,* Apr. 26, 1970.

49. Jack Newfield and Jeff Greenfield, *A Populist Manifesto: The Making of a New Majority* (New York: Praeger Publishers, Inc., 1972), pp. 6, 35.

Chapter Ten Revolution in Stages

1. George Plekhanov, *The Materialist Conception of History* (New York: International Publishers, 1940), p. 16.

2. *Handbook of Marxism* (New York: International Publishers, 1935), pp. 371-72.

3. Quoted in T. B. Bottomore, *Classes in Modern Society* (London: George Allen and Unwin, 1965), pp. 24-25.

4. *Handbook of Marxism,* pp. 725-27.

5. Ibid., p. 730.

6. V. I. Lenin, *Selected Works,* vol. 5: *The Collapse of the Second International, Summer of 1915* (Moscow: International Publishers, n.d.), p. 174.

7. Herbert Croly, *The Promise of American Life* (New York: Macmillan, 1909), p. 1.

8. Norman Pollack, ed., *The Populist Mind* (Indianapolis: Bobbs-Merrill, 1967), pp. 60ff. Reprinted from *National Economist* (Washington, D.C.), July 9, 1892, and in all of the leading Populist newspapers in the weeks following the convention. The People's Party Paper (Atlanta) often ran the entire document as late as 1893 and 1894.

9. Silviu Brucan, *The Dissolution of Power* (New York: Knopf, 1971), pp. vii-ix (italics added).

Index

DATE DUE

HIGHSMITH #45230

Printed
in USA